Bully

An Empowering Companion
to the Acclaimed Film

An Action Plan for Teachers and
Parents to Combat the Bullying Crisis

Edited by Lee Hirsch and Cynthia Lowen
with Dina Santorelli

Printed in the United States of America.

Cataloging-in-Publication data for this book is
available from the Library of Congress.

ISBN: 978-1-60286-184-8 (print)
ISBN: 978-1-60286-185-5 (e-book)

Published by Weinstein Books
A member of the Perseus Books Group
www.weinsteinbooks.com

Weinstein Books are available at special discounts for bulk purchases in
the U.S. by corporations, institutions and other organizations. For more
information, please contact the Special Markets Department at the Perseus
Books Group, 2300 Chestnut Street, Suite 200, Philadelphia, PA 19103, call
(800) 810-4145, ext. 5000, or e-mail special.markets@perseusbooks.com.

First edition

10 9 8 7 6 5 4 3 2 1

Contents

Kelby, 16

Ja'Meya, 14

PART 5

David and Tina Long

PROLOGUE

Everything Starts with One

The documentary *Bully* began in the spring of 2009, with the conviction that NOW is the time for this film. It started with the voices of kids and parents, of teachers and administrators, of those who had been bullied decades ago and those who were targeted that day, coming into the light to talk about their experiences. Although bullying is not a new phenomenon, it is one that has been long shrouded in silence, shame, embarrassment, and helplessness. However, as the voices began to multiply, as more and more kids and adults courageously came forward to tell their stories and to speak to their commitment to change, so did the sense that *Bully* could catalyze a movement among youth, families, educators, and communities to turn the tide on bullying.

After three long years from production to the big screen, meeting kids, parents, and educators across the United States and documenting the many challenges and the hard-won triumphs, *Bully* arrived in theaters nationwide on April 13, 2012, with a PG-13 rating from the Motion Picture Association of America. The film's premiere in fifty-five cities across the U.S. was the culmination of hard work not only by the filmmakers, but by dozens of organizations and individuals partnering with the documentary to help promote its message and to make it accessible to those who need to see it most—our nation's young people.

A passion project for director Lee Hirsch and producer Cynthia Lowen, *Bully* became the little film that could, unifying a growing movement and rallying cry by shining a spotlight on a very big problem that for too long has gone unresolved—and unnoticed. By focusing on the specific struggles of five families, *Bully* provided a glimpse into the life of the bullied and how bullying is a problem that has become embedded in our schools. With its disturbing images of physical and emotional abuse, the film exposed the disconnects and communication breakdowns often found between parents and children, and families and schools, and tapped into a shift in the collective consciousness that says, "No longer should bullying be an individual or a private matter, or a rite of passage; instead, it is a social issue that concerns all of us, not just those who suffer in silence."

Bully is dedicated to the thirteen million children who will be bullied in the United States this year, as well as the generations of children who came before them, and to their families, whose cries for help have fallen upon deaf ears. With research showing that only 4 to 13 percent of middle- and high-school students indicate that they would report an incident of bullying to a teacher, administrator, or another school staff member, it is hoped that the film will encourage more students to speak out and trust that their stories will be both heard and taken seriously. It is also hoped that this film will inspire school systems across the nation to confront the bullying of students head-on with a whole-school approach that involves administrators, teachers, and counselors rather than with the well-intentioned but ineffective assurances, sympathetic looks, or shrugged shoulders of the past and that our nation's legislators will stand firm in their resolve to ensure that all students enjoy educational opportunities without discrimination or harassment.

THE BATTLE OF THE BULLIED

Bullying is the most common form of violence experienced by young people in the nation. Every day, more than 160,000 students skip school because they are fearful of being bullied. According to the Federal Bureau of Investigation (FBI), the third most common location nationwide for a hate crime to occur is on a school or college campus—the FBI's *Hate Crime Statistics, 2009* report states that 11.4 percent of hate crimes occur at schools or colleges, and 18.5 percent of those bullied were targeted because of their perceived sexual orientation. Additionally, in a survey commissioned by the Kaiser Family Foundation, more eight- to fifteen-year-olds picked teasing and bullying as "big problems" than those who picked drugs or alcohol, racism, AIDS, or pressure to have sex, and more African Americans saw bullying as a big problem for people their age than those who identified racism as one. Bullying is now considered a serious threat to students' ability to fully enjoy the educational opportunities and benefits of their schools.

Bullying is defined as an act of repeated physical or emotional victimization of a person by another person or a group. Although it's difficult to assign a number to describe the incidence of bullying, according to the National Center for Learning Disabilities, the collected statistics prove rather frightening:

- 10 percent of children report having been the victims of severe bullying at least once during the school year;
- 75 percent report being bullied at least once during the past ten months;
- 25 to 50 percent report being bullied at some point during their school years;
- 40 to 75 percent of bullying incidents in school take place during class breaks, in the lunchroom, bathroom, or hallways;
- 30 percent of children who suffer from food allergies report being bullied at school (sometimes by verbal taunting but more often, by having the allergen thrown or waved at them);
- 30 percent of children who report having been bullied said they sometimes brought weapons to school;
- 57 percent of the time when a peer intervenes in a bullying situation, the bullying stops within ten seconds; and

■ the average bullying episode lasts only thirty-seven seconds, and school personnel are reported to notice or intervene in only one in twenty-five incidents (in contrast to another report where teachers said they intervened 71 percent of the time and students reported teachers taking action only 25 percent of the time).

There are many reasons—or, perhaps, no real reason at all—why bullying occurs. According to antibullying speaker and expert Dr. Joel Haber, as much as 95 percent of all bullying is perpetrated by those looking to protect or increase their status within a group. Bullies maintain what Haber calls their "imbalance of power" by zeroing in on the things that make others different. It may be that bullied children are overweight or tall or that they wear different clothes or speak with an accent. While the list really can include almost anything, the following are some of the groups at risk for being bulled:

■ children stereotyped by cultural biases, including ethnicity and religious factors;
■ children labeled with a sexual identity (lesbian, gay, bisexual, and transgender youth);
■ children who contradict gender stereotypes;
■ children with social-skills deficits or special-education labels;
■ loners, those who do not have support of their peers; and
■ gifted children.

According to a study published in *Gifted Child Quarterly* in 2006 that examined 432 eighth graders in eleven states who were identified by their schools as gifted, more than two-thirds said they had been bullied at school and nearly one-third harbored violent thoughts as a result.

Bullying comes in many forms. Typically, most people envision bullying as a physical abuse of power: kicking, pushing, shoving, hitting, spitting, taking or breaking someone's personal belongings, knocking one's books down, shoving a child into a locker, or steal-ing someone's lunch money or food. However, there are other forms that are just as damaging. These include verbal bullying, which is more psychological in its intent and includes hurtful teasing, taunting, verbal threats, prejudicial remarks, and making fun of one's cultural heritage, and relational bullying, which is meant to damage another person's relationships through social isolation—gossiping, rumors, talking behind someone's back, eye-rolling or silence when a target walks in the room, or behavior meant to exclude someone from a clique.

The advancement of technology and its prevalent use among our nation's youth has produced what the American Academy of Pediatrics calls "the most common online risk for all teens": cyber-bullying. Cyberbullying is the deliberate use of digital media—social-networking sites, texting—to inflict harm or to communicate false, embarrassing, or hostile information to or about another person. Private e-mails forwarded without consent. Threatening texts. Verbal attacks on Twitter. Embarrassing photos posted on Facebook without permission. Video hate lists on YouTube. Cyber-bullying can happen anytime, anywhere—on the soccer field or

WHAT DO BULLIES LOOK LIKE?

According to bully expert Dr. Joel Haber, it is a misconception that bullies are troubled youths who are chronically insecure or lack self-esteem. Bullies may be popular, smart, confident, and socially adept. However, Haber says, most bullies tend to share several of the follow-ing characteristics:

- They lack empathy or self-control and need skill building and mentoring.
- They experience conduct problems.
- They feel the drive to be popular.
- They exhibit delinquency and intolerance for others.
- They experience violent contexts at home and/or in their community.

in the family living room—and often does. According to the Pew Research Center, a whopping 88 percent of social media-using teens say they have seen someone be mean or cruel to another person on a social-networking site. (Twelve percent of these say they witness this kind of behavior "frequently.") Further, about one-third of all teenagers who use the internet say they have been targets of a range of annoying and potentially menacing online activities.

Whether on- or off-line, the impact of bullying is devastating. Children who have been bullied suffer from physical, emotional, and social scars that can last a lifetime. Research indicates that bullying can lead to or worsen feelings of isolation, rejection, exclusion, low self-esteem, poor academic achievement, depression and anxiety, and can contribute to suicidal behavior. Additionally, an Associated Press 2009 survey showed that 60 percent of young people who have been bullied report destructive behavior such as smoking cigarettes, drinking alcohol, using illegal drugs, or shoplifting (compared to 48 percent of those not bullied). Additionally, bullied children might feel the urge to retaliate, sometimes through extremely violent measures—in twelve of fifteen school shooting cases in the 1990s, the shooters had a history of being bullied.

CATALYST FOR CHANGE

Bullying is by no means a new problem. For years, governments, schools, and courts have wrestled with how to deal with the issue, but as emerging technologies unite us in ways like never before, there is a growing activism, powered by dissatisfied students, parents, educators, and legislators who are banding together, collectively, as one unified voice. After years of being swept under the rug as a natural part of growing up, bullying is finally being recognized as an epidemic and is getting the attention it deserves.

The overwhelming success of *Bully* is a testament to the tenacity of the filmmakers and the bravery of Alex, Kelby, Ja'Meya, Kirk and Laura Smalley, and David and Tina Long and also to the tremendous power in all those who stand up, speak out, and make

THE STATISTICS

- A 2009 study from the Cyberbullying Research Center found that bullied students are three times more likely to drop out of school and one and a half to two times more likely to have attempted suicide.
- The Gay Lesbian Straight Education Network (GLSEN)'s 2009 School Climate Survey found that 61.1 percent of LGBT students felt unsafe at school because of their sexual orientation, 39.9 percent felt unsafe because of their gender expression, and nearly a third missed class at least once in the last month and missed at least one day of school.
- In a Web-based survey of about 1,500 twelve- to seventeen-year-olds, 90 percent reported that they do not tell adults about cyber-bullying incidents. The most common reason, cited by 50 percent of respondents at equal rates across age and gender, was the belief that they "need to learn to deal with it" themselves.

a difference. The film charges every one of us to become change makers, to be upstanders rather than bystanders, and to create a safe, supportive, and engaging school climate in which all of our nation's students can live and grow.

Together, we can become the generation that makes bullying history. It's time to become part of the solution. This book has been written to show you how.

PART 1

The Film

The Making of *Bully*

It has been said that everyone has a bullying story, an experience that despite a lifetime of success and happiness continues to haunt them. It was Lee Hirsch's bullying story that kept him from making *Bully* for many years. "I was too scared to start developing the idea in earnest because it would mean confronting my own demons and revisiting a painful period of my life," said Hirsch, who was bullied throughout middle school and much of his Long Island, New York, childhood.

Still, there was no denying the impact of those early bully experiences on Hirsch's life, how they helped to shape his worldview as well as his direction as a filmmaker. From the beginning of his career, Hirsch had always been attracted to subjects of struggle and redemption, as depicted in his debut film, *Amandla! A Revolution in Four Part Harmony*, which chronicled the history of the South African anti-apartheid movement through a celebration of its musical heroes. The film was released to acclaim, winning the Audience and Freedom of Expression Awards at the Sundance Film Festival in 2002, as well as one of the five Emmy awards it was nominated for, among many other honors. Hirsch also became an established director of music videos, his most recent being a narrative shot on location in Zanzibar for John Legend's song "Show Me," which was nominated for a 2008 NAACP Image award. He is also the recipient of the Best Video of the Year award from the National Television and Video Association of South Africa for his work with Bongo Maffin, a South African kwaito music group. By spring 2009, Hirsch was finally ready to take on the challenge of a bullying documentary, an idea that gained velocity when, that April, he learned about two eleven-year-old boys—Carl Joseph Walker-Hoover of Massachusetts and Jaheem Herrera of Georgia— who took their own lives: deaths linked to trauma from chronic bullying. He knew a film was needed that really hit home, one that would explore different facets of bullying and show how universal a problem it is, crossing boundaries of race, class, and geography. This documentary needed to be both a chronicle and an intimate portrait, an honest and gutsy film that didn't shy away from the real-life torment experienced by bullied children. Hirsch wanted to help heal a nation while, at the same time, reach out to those who needed an "empathy push," as he calls it, to get involved and take action.

Parents Speak Out

"My daughter is sixteen, and we live in a small town in the Bible belt. My daughter has been bullied for a couple of years now due to her sexual orientation. There have been fistfights with boys, horrible nasty notes, name calling, and on April 9, 2009, while walking back to school from lunch, she was purposely hit by a van, which, not to my surprise, held six boys from her school. Her dad and I have been to the school many times. Our fight is not only with the students, but the faculty who believe they are above any recourse for their actions. We are at the point of legal defense for our daughter, but don't really know where to start. It is a constant day-to-day battle for our daughter's spirit, and I fear we are losing her. She has been to counseling and is already on anti-depressants, but refuses to "LET THEM WIN" by leaving this school. All children deserve to be treated equally and humanely, and that is not happening at this school."

—*written by Kelby's mother, Londa Johnson,
on Ellen DeGeneres' blog*

Hirsch joined forces with Cynthia Lowen, an award-winning writer whose producing credits include the two-part documentary *Going Home* about teenage incarceration and recidivism. It turned out Lowen was just as passionate as Hirsch about the subject of bullying. Although she was teased at times for how she looked during her school days, she described herself as one of those kids who sailed under the radar and tried to go unnoticed for much of the time growing up so that she could avoid being the target of bullying. "I was someone who saw bullying taking place around me, but didn't have the tools or confidence to stand up to it," said Lowen, who serves as *Bully* producer and writer. "Looking back now, there are definitely kids I wish I had reached out to when I was in middle and high school, who were the ones who were always alone or made fun of, and I wish I had had the tools then to stand up for them when I saw them being bullied."

Not wanting to wait for a grant to come through, or a financier, the pair started research for the film—originally titled *The Bully Project* but later shortened simply to *Bully*. They were working from home and with their savings. They began consulting nationally recognized experts in the field of bullying prevention, including Jorge Srabstein of The Children's National Medical Center; Marlene Snyder, the director of development in the United States for the Olweus Bullying Prevention Program, a whole-school program that has been proven to prevent or reduce bullying throughout a school setting; Captain Stephanie Bryn, a Public Health Service officer overseeing the government's "Stop Bullying Now!" campaign; Dr. Jackson Katz, cofounder of the Mentors In Violence Prevention (MVP) program; and Kevin Jennings, the former Assistant Deputy Secretary of Education under President Barack Obama, among others. They watched YouTube videos, tracked news around the country and on websites such as Oprah.com and Facebook, and read blog posts, including the blog of Ellen DeGeneres of *The Ellen Show*, which put them in touch with an openly gay student named Kelby who had been ostracized by her community because of her sexuality. "Kids and families were desperate to find a way to voice their experiences of bullying, harassment, and loss," Hirsch said. "There were thousands of postings, filled with frustration and anger."

They read and watched news report after news report about the growing number of bullying incidents across the country, including the story of a young teenager named Ja'Meya in Yazoo County, Mississippi, who one day decided to take matters into her own hands and bring her mother's gun onto her school bus to scare off her bully. There were lengthy conversations with dozens of parents, including the Longs of Chatsworth, Georgia, and the Smalleys of Perkins, Oklahoma, who suffered the ultimate loss, whose children had been victims of bullying and subsequently died by suicide. In the end, Hirsch and Lowen filmed with some twenty to thirty families—shooting three hundred hours of film in all—who had been coping with bullying for years, had received no support from their school administrators, and felt they had nowhere to turn. "One thing all of these stories shared was a sense of frustration and helplessness, a desperate desire for their voice to be heard, and a call for change," said Lowen.

FINDING THE RIGHT SCHOOL

In order to accurately portray the realities of bullying, the filmmakers would need to be on the front lines, which meant that Hirsch and Lowen needed to embed themselves within the student population of a school—ground zero for bullying—preferably for an entire academic year. It was a tall order, and perhaps it is not surprising that many school districts were highly unreceptive.

In their preproduction research, the filmmakers came across the Workplace Bullying Institute in Bellingham, Washington, an organization run by Gary and Ruth Namie that was dedicated to the eradication of workplace bullying. The Institute had recently published the first study on the incidence of workplace bullying, which was funded by the Waitt Institute for Violence Prevention (WIVP), based in Sioux City, Iowa. It was there that the filmmakers met Cindy Waitt, the executive director of WIVP. (Waitt would eventually become an executive producer of *Bully*.) Since WIVP had invested deeply in the Sioux City School District with an anti-bullying curriculum, mentoring programs, and gender violence prevention work for many years, Waitt was able to introduce Hirsch and Lowen to Sioux City Superintendent Dr. Paul Gausman. "It was a great miracle that we connected with the Waitt Institute for Violence Prevention," Hirsch said. "It was a perfect storm of having a strong and meaningful introduction to the school district, coupled with a relatively new and progressive superintendent."

Celebs Speak Out

"I was bullied. . . . Most people in their lifetime have been bullied at some point. I think that it's about time that people start making a change. A lot of the time, principals let it go, or teachers let it go, or other students just let it go, but I think this movie's really powerful and can help change a lot of lives."

—Justin Bieber

In July 2009, the filmmakers presented their idea for *Bully* to the Sioux City Community School Board, requesting permission to film throughout the district for the 2009–2010 school year. The board felt it was an important project and agreed to be partners in the process. "This was a huge leap of faith and represented a brave commitment to their ongoing bullying prevention programs," Hirsch said. "The board was willing to take a tough look at their own community through the camera's lens."

Sioux City officials gave the filmmakers access to a number of schools in the district; Hirsch and Lowen filmed at three—West High School, Hunt Elementary School, and East Middle School— but it was at the middle school where they found the bullying to be most intense, and this is the school that is seen in *Bully*. "A lot of this has to do with maturity," Lowen said. "In middle school, kids are learning to recognize and use their power, their relationships are becoming more complicated, they are getting online, they are vying for popularity, their peers' acceptance is becoming increasingly more important, and their brains and bodies are changing. All of these factors, and many more, make bullying pervasive in the middle-school years."

Additionally, what the filmmakers discovered was that while

THE STORY OF WEST HIGH

Cynthia Lowen

In Sioux City, we were fortunate to film not only at East Middle School where we followed Alex through his seventh grade year, but also at West High School, on the other side of town. West High was a school that was facing many challenges ten years ago in terms of school climate and culture: lots of fights, absenteeism, low student achievement, and a reputation for being the community's toughest school.

One day, there was a brawl following a basketball game—trophy cases were smashed, police officers were called in and were injured, and it was broadcast all over the nightly news as yet another black eye on West High's reputation. However, this time, the students responded differently. Instead of letting the incident go by, it was a catalyst for change: The students held their own press conference to challenge the community's perception of them and to let Sioux City know that this was not who they were, this was not the image they wanted to project, and that they intended to take back their school's culture.

Under the leadership of a great principal, effective administrators, and engaged faculty, all of whom were also committed to change, these student leaders worked with educators and succeeded in radically changing the culture of their school. Over several years, the kids and faculty implemented various peer mentorship programs such as Mentors for Violence Prevention (MVP), a gender violence, bullying, and school violence prevention program using role-playing

West High School was already a decade into bullying prevention programs, and had a great climate and very established peer mentor programs and leadership, East Middle was in its first year of this work. "There are many studies that show long-term bullying prevention and climate change takes years of consistent effort, both in school, in the community, and at home, and East Middle was at the beginning of that journey," Lowen said, adding that the school was just beginning to implement a bullying prevention program called Second Step, as well as mentorship programs, and to allow students to explore and construct effective responses to harassment, abuse, or violence before, during, or after the fact. Upperclassmen developed close relationships with underclassmen and talked to them about bullying, dating violence, and conflict. Peers were also trained in responding to and resolving conflicts and bullying situations and were given the tools to recognize these behaviors. The faculty also made responding to bullying a priority, devoting the time it takes to effectively handle the many kinds of bullying situations that come up in a day, and to seriously address even those behaviors that might seem minor, like name calling, before they escalated.

Over the year we filmed at West High, we witnessed an environment in which the most popular kids were not "mean girl" types or ruthless jocks, but kids who were kind, well liked, and had status because they cared about the kids around them and who wanted to pass down the values that had made high school a great experience for them to the incoming freshmen.

After a year filming *Bully* and wondering if it really was possible to create school climates where bullying was not tolerated by either the kids or the staff, we witnessed—at this very typical public American high school, in a diverse community, struggling with budget cuts, big class sizes, and all the other problems schools are faced with today—that it *is* possible. It's also notable that as bullying and violence receded at West High they also saw the highest jumps in academic achievement of any of the district's schools.

getting buy-in from all members of the school faculty. "In a way," she added, "what we found at East Middle emphasized what Superintendent Gausman knew to be true when he courageously gave us permission to film throughout the district—that there were buildings in the district with great culture and climate (where kids felt safe and supported in the school community, where differences and diversity were honored, where cliques did not rule the day, where kids were empowered to stick up for each other and felt the lines of communication with teachers and administrators were open, where staff and administrators made preventing bullying a priority, and where effective action was taken to resolve bullying situations before they escalated) and also places in the district where there was still work to be done."

Hirsch and Lowen had permission to shoot film just about anywhere in the district—on school buses, in school yards and hallways, and inside the principal's office in order to capture the full scope of the problem. (All of the families of children who appear and speak in *Bully* signed releases to participate in the film, including the families of the children who exhibit bullying behaviors.) However, Hirsch knew that in order to truly serve as "flies on a wall," he and Lowen would need the acceptance of the East Middle School student body and asked to be introduced at the first assembly of the year, where he and Lowen talked about what they were doing and why.

With the full support of the administration, teachers, and students, filming for *Bully* began in August 2009 and continued throughout the school year. Hirsch and Lowen were very careful to protect the children they were following from any negative attention or increased bullying by virtue of having the camera crews follow them around. They filmed with lots of kids, in lots of classes, at lots of different kinds of school events—bake sales, fire drills, wrestling matches—so it wasn't apparent that they were focusing on any one child. Initially, the appearance of the cameras created something of a spectacle among the student population, but that quickly faded as the days, and then weeks and months, wore on and the students lived the daily drama of a middle-school environment. Over time, the project got support from several organizations, including Waitt Institute for Violence Prevention, Einhorn Family Charitable Trust, The BeCause Foundation, Cinereach, The Fledgling Fund, and Sundance, among others, but throughout production, the team remained very small. With the exception of a handful of days when filming needed to be done in several places at one time—such as the first day of school when a sound recordist or a second cinematographer and director were hired—it was just

Hirsch and Lowen. Hirsch, the film's director, served as cinematographer, while Lowen handled sound. And on shoots where Lowen was unavailable, Hirsch did both.

"WE FELL IN LOVE WITH ALEX"

The filmmakers met Alex Libby before the school year began, following his seventh-grade orientation. He was sitting outside on a bench, ostracized by—"or worse, invisible to," said Lowen—his classmates, waiting to be picked up from school. "We saw in Alex a young man full of promise and creativity," Hirsch said. "On his good days, he would laugh, sing, and come up with poems. Alex was someone we saw as having this incredible spirit. We really just fell in love with him and his family, who really let us into their lives. Alex was utterly unaware of the camera. That also matters when you are making a film. You really want to be with someone who is comfortable."

In fact, all of the students portrayed in *Bully* welcomed the filmmakers into their lives with a remarkable openness and honesty. Hirsch said that bullied children often suffer in silence because they think no one will believe them or can help them, so when adults finally do take notice, these children speak from the heart. "They want the world to know 'this is what I go through and you guys don't listen to me, but it's really bad, it's really, really hard, and I carry this around every day on my own,'" Hirsch said. "That is reflected in the ways in which kids write about bullying, they blog about it, think about it, Facebook about it.... All of those things are reflective of the kind of battling in silence that is part of the landscape."

The filmmakers soon discovered that kids had been bullying Alex for several years, and they continued to do so, even within plain sight of the camera. Hirsch shot on a Canon 5d Mark II, which resembles a still photographic camera, and perhaps many children were not aware that he was shooting video. Even so, Hirsch indicated, "We believe that the bullying was also much worse when the camera was not present."

On and off camera, the school bus was where Alex seemed to endure the most mistreatment—he is choked, slapped, pushed, taunted, and more. "It was incredibly difficult not to go and rip those kids off Alex," Hirsch said. "Had the violence increased, I'm sure there was a point at which I would have had to, and would have absolutely stopped it. But the reality is that Alex wanted people to know what happens to him. All of the kids who were in this film wanted people to know what they go through." Although documentary filmmakers try not to make themselves part of the story, Hirsch said that the bullying behavior ultimately became so alarming that he and Lowen made the decision to bring evidence of what was happening to the school, to Alex's parents, and to the Sioux City police department. "This absolutely put us into the story and is acknowledged in the film," Hirsch said. (Some disturbing instances of verbal abuse only became apparent to the filmmakers months later in the editing room, as they were not always monitoring audio as they shot.)

Lowen noted that the failure of some of the educators at Alex's school is not because they are not trying, or do not care about kids, but that they may simply be overwhelmed with test scores, oversized classrooms, and all the other challenges facing educators today or that they may not know how to protect a child who is the perennial target, year after year, when their first attempts to intervene have failed. "These failures are a result of not being equipped to effectively handle bullying and of not having the kind of leadership in their school that enables them to know they will be supported if they make bullying prevention a priority," Lowen said.

For example, during filming at East Middle School, there was a day when some money had been stolen out of a locker. "This was taken very seriously by the faculty and administrators—police were called, everyone was on alert—as a result of which, there was no question among students that stealing was a very serious offense in this environment," Lowen said. "However, when it came to bullying, the attitude was very different. As we saw in the film, kids routinely bullied Alex on the bus without fear of there being any repercussions. The bus driver did not intervene, Alex's parents struggled to get protection for Alex, and within the 'norms' of that particular school, bullying seemed to have far fewer consequences than stealing five dollars did." The fact that Alex had been assaulted, threatened, and otherwise abused was not addressed or taken seriously, and that sent a message to other students at the school that this behavior was "normal," Lowen noted. "I'm sure many of us who see *Bully* can see some of our own mistakes in the mistakes of the administrators in the film and can learn from them in how we respond to bullying in our own schools and communities," she said.

Celebs Speak Out

"When I was in middle school, I was bullied so badly. Girls started an 'I Hate Demi' petition and sent me mean texts. There were girls who stood outside my house and yelled things from across the street! It was the 'popular' girls who did it—they had all the power and wanted to make sure no one took it away. It got so bad, I kind of went into a depression. The only friend I had was Selena [Gomez], who always stood up for me. But being bullied scarred me for life. That's why I got involved with Love Our Children USA. I don't want anyone to suffer like I did."
—*Demi Lovato to* Seventeen

Since the filming, Hirsch and Lowen have maintained very close connections with the Sioux City community and the school district, which Hirsch calls "partners in the growing Bully Project movement." They have also kept in touch with all of the families and experts they met along the way, who continue to be great champions of the documentary and very active in advocating for bullied youth. Having been brought back to such a crucial and difficult time in her own life over the year of filming *Bully*, Lowen said she was awed by current educators who "truly get it," but mostly by today's generation of kids. "They really are taking ownership of this issue and are leading us all in creating schools and communities where bullying is not accepted," she said.

"We made *Bully* with the conviction that audiences, especially young people, can be moved off the sidelines and empowered to stand up for those around them," Lowen added. "We also made this film with the conviction that those children will become the next generation's leaders, and CEOs and educators and innovators, and will show us new possibilities, not only in how we treat the people around us, but in how we lead as citizens of the world."

PART 2

Alex, 12

Alex's Story

"I feel good when I'm in this house and when I'm with my family. Maya, my sister, she is annoying, but that's normal for a sister. Then there's Ethan, he's my six-year-old brother. He got all *As* in preschool through kindergarten. I'm proud of him for that. Then there's Jada, she talks a lot. Then there's Logan, my two-year-old brother, then my mama and my dad. And then there's me."

Alex Libby, a sweet-natured twelve-year-old boy from Sioux City, Iowa, was just about to start middle school and wanted nothing more than to fit in, and he spent the summer trying not to think about what might happen when he returned to school. Alex has Asperger's Syndrome, an autism spectrum disorder that often affects one's social interactions. For years, he has been punched, choked, sat on, had things stolen from him, and called names.

Although he assured his worried parents that the kids who taunt and hit him are only "messing with him," bullying has trailed Alex throughout his life like a shadow. As his seventh-grade year unfolds, the physical and emotional abuse escalates—the slurs, curses, and threats often occurring before he even boards the school bus, which is a hotbed for some of the cruelest bullying against him.

Bully's Lee Hirsch and Cynthia Lowen met Alex before the start of the 2009–2010 school year, right after his seventh-grade orientation. He had been sitting outside East Middle School on a bench waiting for his parents to pick him up. While the other kids gathered in groups, loudly chattering about what they did over the summer and which teachers they had for which period, Alex was distinctly alone, shoulders slumped around him, looking both determined to fly under the radar and acutely in need of a friend. For Alex and his family, *Bully* was a chance for Alex to talk about what he had been experiencing because it was very hard for him to talk about it or even admit it was taking place. It was also a chance for his parents to understand what was happening to him because in Alex's silence, they often didn't know what was going on at school, or causing him to seem depressed, withdrawn, and upset. They had become deeply troubled by the school district's inability to keep him safe.

In the end, despite the support and love of his family, who he knows loves him, Alex felt powerless, hopeless, and very alone. "I feel kind of nervous going back to school 'cause. . . . I like learning, but I have trouble making friends," Alex said as the summer before seventh grade came to a close. "People think that I'm different, I'm not normal. Most kids don't want to be around me. I feel like I belong somewhere else."

Bullying and Children with Autism Spectrum Disorders

Connie Anderson, Ph.D.

Connie Anderson, Ph.D., has a son on the autism spectrum and is the Community Scientific Liaison for the Interactive Autism Network (IAN), an innovative online project of the Kennedy Krieger Institute that is supported by Autism Speaks, the Simons Foundation, and the National Institute of Mental Health. It brings together tens of thousands of people affected by autism spectrum disorders (ASD) and hundreds of researchers in a search for answers. For more information, visit http://www.ianproject.org

The Kennedy Krieger Institute in Baltimore, MD, is internationally recognized for improving the lives of children and adolescents with disorders and injuries of the brain, spinal cord, and musculoskeletal system. Kennedy Krieger provides a wide range of services for children with developmental concerns mild to severe and is home to a team of investigators who are contributing to the understanding of how disorders develop while pioneering new interventions and earlier diagnosis. For more information, visit http://www.kennedykrieger.org

Just as the film *Bully* was bringing the bullying crisis to the world's attention, the Interactive Autism Network (IAN) launched a survey asking parents of children with autism spectrum disorders (ASDs) about their child's bullying experiences. The survey found children with ASDs are more than three times more likely to be bullied than their siblings who do not have an ASD. What makes these children so vulnerable?

WHAT IS "ASD"?

People talk about autism all the time, but there are many who don't have a true grasp of what it *is*. That is understandable because ASDs are complex, involving all kinds of different issues.

Individuals with an ASD may have restricted and repetitive behaviors (like hand flapping or lining up toys), sensory issues (like sensitivity to sounds, light, or textures), obsessive interests (like an all-consuming fascination with *Star Wars* or trains), and a tendency to inflexibility and meltdowns. They may also suffer from a number of co-occurring conditions, such as attention deficit hyperactivity disorder (ADHD) or anxiety. At its core, however, autism is a *social disability*. People with ASDs have impaired "social software." No matter what their IQ, from intellectually disabled to genius, they have a very tough time reading and responding to the social world.

What is being socially disabled like? Imagine being set down in the middle of a foreign country where you don't know what is polite or rude, what is cool or gross, who has high or low status, and what remarks are socially appropriate or completely unacceptable. Now imagine your brain isn't wired to know that you need to *watch* the people around you to figure this out. You wouldn't be able to "do as the Romans do" because you wouldn't get that all that social stuff is important, if you noticed it at all. You'd be lost, stressed, and overwhelmed. You'd make a million unintentional social mistakes and misinterpret the intentions of other people. Those around you might view you as very odd. If you seemed smart because of your big vocabulary and vast knowledge of some topic like history or science, people would assume you were being intentionally rude or unreasonable when you made social blunders. Why? Because it really confuses people when someone who seems intelligent doesn't know things about the social world most kindergarteners know. Unusual brain wiring and social blindness are, after all, invisible.

There's something else you should know about people "on the autism spectrum." They can be incredibly engaging, innocent, and sweet. Part of this is because they are rarely jockeying for social position. They are not trying to be the "alpha," and they don't care much about externals. They can seem quirky to "neurotypicals" (that is, people with so-called normal brain wiring), but they are extremely genuine. Sadly, due to their differences, they are often alone.

Maybe that is what makes them such tempting targets for bullies.

BULLYING: FAMILIES OF CHILDREN WITH ASD DEMAND ANSWERS

The Interactive Autism Network (IAN) is the world's largest online autism research project. Located at the Kennedy Krieger Institute in Baltimore, Maryland, we collect information from thousands of families of children on the autism spectrum—that is, children with autism, Asperger's disorder, and pervasive developmental disorder–not otherwise specified (PDD–NOS). (To register visit http://www.ianresearch.org)

Part of our philosophy is to give back to the families taking part in our research, and one way we do that is by focusing on topics they have told us are a top priority. That is why we decided to develop a national survey on bullying. Thanks to some earlier, small studies, we knew that children with ASD might be bullied more frequently than other children. Through phone calls, e-mails, and our online discussion forum, we knew families were extremely concerned about how often this was happening and the devastating impact on children with ASD.

IAN'S BULLYING SURVEY RESULTS: A BULL'S-EYE ON THEIR BACKS

Nearly 1,200 families took the IAN Bullying and School Experiences of Children with ASD Survey. When we sent out notices about the survey, we asked families to take the survey whether or not their child had been bullied. That way, we would be able to compare children with ASDs who were and were not being bullied. We also asked about the children's siblings and their bullying experiences. This gave us a way to compare children with an ASD to children who do not have an ASD.

We found that 63 percent of children with ASD had been bullied at some point in their lives. Just in the past month, 39 percent had been bullied. Only 12 percent of unaffected siblings had been bullied over the same time period, which means the rate of bullying for the children with ASD was more than three times higher. Because these numbers are based on parent-report, the actual rate is probably higher still. Just like other children, children with ASD may not tell adults when they are bullied. In the case of those who are intellectually disabled and/or nonverbal, they may not be able to do so.

We were interested in what types of bullying the children had experienced and any factors that were associated with it. We found that the types of bullying most often reported by parents choosing from a "check all that apply"–type list were "being teased, picked on, or made fun of" (73 percent); "being ignored or left out of things on purpose" (51 percent); and "being called bad names" (47 percent). Nearly 30 percent of children who had been bullied had been pushed, shoved, hit, slapped, or kicked.

Bullying occurred at every grade level, although the worst time of all appeared to be from fifth to eighth grade. Between 42 percent and 49 percent of children with ASD in those grades had been bullied in the past month. School setting was another important factor. The percentage of children with ASD currently bullied in regular public schools was 43 percent while it was 28 percent for regular private schools, 30 percent for special education public schools, and 18 percent for special education private schools. (Basically, in more protected spaces, with less contact with unaffected peers, children were bullied less.)

Some typical behaviors and traits of children with ASD put them at particularly high risk. These included:

- Clumsiness
- Poor hygiene
  (This is part of not caring about "externals.")
- Rigid rule keeping
  (This is part of an inflexible adherence to routine and rules; peers often dislike it when a child with ASD tries to enforce adults' rules.)
- Continuing to talk about a favorite topic even when others are bored or annoyed
  (This is an almost classic autistic behavior, where the person with ASD delightedly goes on and on about astronomy or dinosaurs with no sense that the other person is beginning to roll their eyes, fidget, and give increasingly desperate social signals to indicate they have had enough.)
- Frequent meltdowns
- Inflexibility or rigidity

Children with ASD and an additional condition like ADHD, depression, or anxiety were all more likely to be bullied than children with ASD who did not have these co-occurring conditions.

There were also large variations by type of ASD diagnosis. While 28 percent of children with autism had been bullied in the past month, 61 percent of children with Asperger's syndrome had suffered this fate. This may be because these children, who have normal-to-gifted intelligence, are most likely to be in public school settings and are also eager to engage with other children, even if they are not very good at it. Indeed, our research showed that aloof children were bullied far less than those who were trying very hard to interact socially.

A mother of a daughter with Asperger's spoke about this on National Public Radio (NPR).[1] She said her daughter didn't seem to get what was going on in the minds of the children who yelled "Police, police, take her back to the insane asylum" every time she walked by. "She wouldn't consider them off-limits to try to interact with because she just wanted friends," the mother said. Frustrated when she couldn't make her daughter understand she should avoid these children, she would plead, "Why are you going to hang out with kids who have been so cruel to you?"

In so many ways, children with ASD are walking around with a bull's-eye on their backs. Socially odd, with few friends, and little ability to understand the complex social order of any school, they are easy pickings for bullies.

THE ENIGMA OF "BULLY-VICTIMS"

Some of the children with ASD who had been bullied had also bullied others. Bullying researchers have noticed before that children with behavioral, emotional, or developmental issues may behave as both bully and victim. Unlike victims who are more passive, bully-victims insult their tormentors or otherwise try to fight back in a way that only makes the situation worse. They are often "disruptive and impulsive, with poor social and problem-solving skills."[2]

Considering the deficits in social understanding that children with ASD have, it may be that their "bullying" is different than that displayed by typical children who, according to research, generally use aggression to increase and maintain social status in the peer group. Some parents taking the IAN survey who reported their

---

1 Hamilton, J. (April 23, 2012). Children with autism are often targeted by bullies. National Public Radio. Retrieved from: http://www.npr.org/blogs/health/2012/04/23/151037898/children-with-autism-are-often-targeted-by-bullies

2 Berger, K. S. (2007). Update on bullying at school: Science forgotten? *Developmental Review, 27,* 90–126.

child had "bullied" noted that the motivation behind the behavior had nothing to do with becoming top dog:

- "My son doesn't realize he is bullying. He is trying to get other kids to pay attention to him so he does it by grabbing their ball away from them or getting 'in their face' when they say to stop."
- "He has very set rules of behavior that he expects all to follow. He doesn't see how his reaction to perceived slights or rule-breaking is sometimes bullying."
- "Our boy wants what he wants when he wants it. He may take an object from another child or scream when unhappy but any purposeful cruelty, he would never do."

Individuals with ASD usually do not have the social awareness to stay quiet or even lie when called for in social situations. Unfortunately, their complete honesty was viewed as bullying in some cases. (Imagine a very honest child saying, "You're really fat," or "I don't like you and I don't want to sit by you.")

One key issue was the aggressive behaviors or meltdowns, which many children with ASD have, and which are all too easy to induce. Parents were asked if another child, who knows what bothers or upsets the child with ASD, had ever used that knowledge to trigger a meltdown or aggressive outburst on purpose. Fifty-two percent of parents said "yes."

In some cases, bullies got the child to fall apart emotionally. "Often kids try to upset her because they find it funny when she gets upset and cries. She is overly emotional, and they seem to get a kick out of this," one mother shared. In some cases, bullies provoked much more aggressive meltdowns, with immediate consequences for the child originally bullied. Said one parent, "I'm so glad you asked about other children knowing how to press buttons. That has happened with my son with ASD.... Being in a class of gifted children has costs and benefits—kids are more intuitive, which means they can excuse a lot of unusual behavior, but it also means they know exactly how to elicit behaviors when they feel like it. It's never okay for my son to hit, but what happens is kids pick at him until he pops, and oftentimes his target is the teacher! His stress builds up as the kids mess with him, then, if the teacher reprimands him, he loses control, scratching, pulling clothing and hair, and trying to bite the teacher."

BULLYING AND CHILDREN WITH ASD: AN URGENT PROBLEM

Bullying is extremely common in the lives of children with ASD and occurs at a much higher rate for them than it does for their typically developing siblings. It is crucial that educators, providers, advocates, and families be aware of this and be prepared to intervene. Children with ASD are already vulnerable in multiple ways. To have to face teasing, taunts, ostracism, or other forms of spite may make a child who is already struggling to cope completely unable to function. If a child is anxious, or dealing with issues of self-control, or unable to focus *before* there is any bullying, imagine how impossible those issues must become when bullying is added to the mix.

Cruelest of all, bullying may further impair the ability of a child with ASD, who is already socially disabled, to engage with the social world. "The bully made life a complete hell for my son," said one mother who withdrew her child with ASD from school. "He came home from school crying every day and begging to never have to go back."

When many are advocating for "inclusion" (that is, educating children with ASDs alongside their typical peers), this is a major problem. A child will clearly not benefit from inclusion if bullying is permitted to occur.

PROTECTING CHILDREN ON THE AUTISM SPECTRUM

IAN's research findings illustrate that children with ASD are especially at risk of being bullied. It should therefore no longer be possible for schools and other programs serving these children to behave as if each case of bullying were an isolated incident.

At the level of policy, advocates can now fight to improve the lot of children with ASD in whatever setting they are educated, especially inclusive settings. Institutions should be on the alert, working toward prevention, and with a plan to follow the instant a child with ASD is bullied. The potential damage that can occur to a child's self-esteem, ability to connect with others, and academic achievement is crystal clear. So is the fact that progress achieved through treatments, like occupational therapy or social-skills training (most of which are delivered at school), can be undermined.

In the short term, a parent supporting a child who is being bullied in a school may want to write a letter documenting not only what bullying has occurred and its consequences but also that children with ASD need extra protection from bullying. Such a letter should go to the principal, to the people in charge of special education at the school and at the district level, and to the superintendent of schools.

Another strategy is to call an Individualized Education Program (IEP) meeting to discuss the child's struggles because bullying is impacting his or her ability to achieve the goals outlined in the IEP document. In the United States, an IEP is the official and legal document negotiated between parents, teachers, school administrators, and others that sets down the educational plan for a special-needs student. According to the United States Department of Education, the IEP is the major mechanism for ensuring a child receives a free appropriate public education (FAPE) as required under the Individuals with Disabilities Education Act (IDEA).

In brief, IEPs are legal documents that are taken very seriously. Bringing up bullying in an IEP meeting lends the topic much more weight. It has another advantage, as well. Generally, there will be a number of school staff present, with varying degrees of authority. Instead of discussing the bullying with one administrator or teacher, who may or may not take the matter seriously, the issue is raised in a more formal setting and with multiple witnesses. It may even be possible to address the bullying, or to document that it has been a problem, in the IEP itself. The matter is far more likely to be given the consideration it deserves when this is the case.

OUR HOPE: MAKING A DIFFERENCE

The IAN Research team is so pleased that the results of our research on bullying and children with ASDs became available at the same time The Bully Project and the *Bully* film brought to light the dire consequences of bullying for all children. What families were telling us about the bullying experiences of their children with ASD is now revealed as part of a widespread bullying crisis that affects children on the autism spectrum at extremely high rates, threatening to undo all the good that parents, teachers, therapists, and all those who care are trying to do to support these children. There is now solid evidence that these children need special protection and real hope that they will receive it.

The Truth About Bullying and LD

Sheldon H. Horowitz, Ed.D., National Center for Learning Disabilities

Dr. Sheldon H. Horowitz is the director of LD resources and essential information at the National Center for Learning Disabilities (NCLD). Prior to his work at NCLD, he directed hospital-based evaluation and treatment programs in psychiatry and developmental pediatrics and has teaching experience at primary, secondary, and college levels. His professional interests include neurobiology of learning, educational assessment, fetal alcohol effects in children, language-based learning disabilities, disorders of hyperactivity and attention, and learning disabilities in adolescents and adults. Dr. Horowitz is a regular presenter at professional meetings, and is frequently cited in the popular press on topics including parenting children with special needs, LD and attention deficit hyperactivity disorder, LD evaluation, and LD throughout the lifespan.

Are children with LD at special risk for being harassed, bullied, or intimidated? Consider the following:

- A second grader with dyslexia whose difficulties with decoding unfamiliar words results in giggling and name-calling whenever he is called upon to read aloud or write on the board in class (with this taunting more often than not carrying over into other settings, such as the cafeteria and school yard, and leaving an indelible impression about this child that will mark him as different for years to come)
- A fifth grader with LD and ADHD who, despite her enthusiasm, creativity, and deep knowledge of the subject matter, is always the last to be chosen by peers for group projects because of her disorganized approach to work and her need for initial modeling and structure when working on assignments
- A ninth grader with LD and ADHD who is told not to climb on the new gym equipment but is egged on by his peers until he succumbs and breaks the rules, resulting in punishment and further victimization by his peers
- An eleventh grader with LD who struggles with rapid reading and short-term memory and comprehension deficits whose guidance counselor is discouraging him from setting his sights on enrollment in a competitive college physics and robotics program (when math and science are areas in which he excels academically)

Some might agree that these are examples of bullying behavior, and others might say that they describe how individuals with LD often suffer from the "soft bigotry of low expectations." The reality is that all students are vulnerable to the negative impact of bullying, and students with dyslexia and specific learning disabilities, ADHD and other disorders that impact learning and behavior are indeed at special risk. They are often vulnerable by virtue of their having low self-esteem triggered by low achievement. They might see themselves as outsiders in their peer groups and often have trouble making and keeping friends because their need for special types of intervention, accommodations, and support are misunderstood.

What can parents and other concerned adults do to diffuse the powerful negative impact of bullying?

Don't wait for bullying to present as a problem. Assume it is happening, assume that students are at risk, that teachers and other school personnel are either unaware or incapable of dealing with this problem alone, and that it's just a matter of time before someone close to you is affected by bullying. Parents need to know that their comments and complaints about bullying (to children, other parents, and school personnel) are taken seriously, and they should not hold back sharing information in fear of retribution or ostracism.

Punishing the bully is not the answer. Pointing a finger at the perpetrator doing the bullying may seem like a feel-good answer to the problem, but it is only the tip of the iceberg and will likely not change the person's behavior. The underlying problem has much more to do with how each person in school, at home, and in the community appreciates diversity. Whether a person has big ears or long legs, whether they have light skin or dark features, whether they are athletic or klutzy, outgoing or reserved, or whether they are accelerated learners or have special learning needs, the ways that we talk about these differences and the underlying value we place upon these individuals need to be clear: Everyone is deserving of respect. Period. No exceptions.

Provide support for everyone involved. No single approach to preventing or stopping bullying is recommended for all situations, but a number of options have been found to be effective. They include:

■ Implementing school-wide antibullying awareness programs that include all members of the school community, setting clear expectations and acknowledging and rewarding positive behaviors and acceptance of diversity in ways that are visible and recognized

- Offering social-skills training and other such interventions for students who are likely to be perpetrators or victims of bullying
- Creating safe and confidential ways for students to report bullying
- Conducting parent awareness and training programs that link to school policies and practices regarding reporting bullying and resolving conflicts in ways that minimize stigma to the children involved
- Improving vigilance by school faculty and student leaders (especially in often unsupervised areas) so that bullying behavior is recognized and stopped

What can parents do? The best advice is to follow your heart and stop bullying from claiming your child as its next victim. But there's more parents must do. They need to be the firm, unwavering voice that says "no" to bullying wherever it happens and holds all responsible adults accountable for their actions (or inaction) to ensure that children are safe, appreciated, and valued members of the community.

PART 3

Kelby, 16

Kelby's Story

"You know what my philosophy about rain is?" asked Kelby Johnson. "You know when people can't hold it anymore, they cry? The world is taking so much in, it can't hold anymore. That's why it rains. Because it's letting go."

After Kelby came out as a lesbian, teachers and administrators turned a blind eye when she was beat up by boys in between classes and run down by a carful of classmates, puncturing the windshield with her head. Though her parents had offered to move to another town, Kelby returned to school filled with determination to stand up to her tormentors—and graduate with honors. As much as she is buoyed by a small group of friends, her determination was challenged throughout the year by students and adults alike.

It was through *The Ellen Show* that the *Bully* filmmakers first met Kelby. Her mother, Londa, had written into Ellen DeGeneres's blog about the terrible bullying Kelby had been enduring, how members of her school and community turned on her. "You can always count on something happening when you're walking down the hall at school, in the classroom, after school when I'm walking home, when I'm walking through the parking lot in the morning to school," Kelby said. "I wasn't welcomed at church. I'm not welcomed in a lot of people's homes. I know [my friends] get called gay just for hanging out with me."

When Hirsch and Lowen reached out to Kelby's family, the Johnsons had felt ostracized by their community. Yet, Kelby was determined to stay in Tuttle, Oklahoma, and pave the way for the next young person to come out. Being part of the film was a chance for her to find community in others who had been bullied and to take her stand beyond Tuttle, to youth across the United States. Kelby is now transgender and today identifies as male.

Bullying Has Legs
...and Teeth

Dr. Robyn Silverman

Dr. Robyn Silverman is a well known parenting resource and child and teen development specialist who appears regularly as an expert on many national TV programs such as The Today Show, Good Morning America, *and* Anderson Cooper 360°. *Known for her positive solutions to challenging problems, she speaks worldwide to diverse audiences, from company leaders and corporate women's groups to youth workers, teachers, students, government officials, and parents. Her topics range from bullying, body image, and character development to leadership and mentoring.*

An award-winning writer and success coach, she has been the content consultant for seventeen books for middle-school students. Dr. Robyn has also provided thousands of helpful parenting/educator tips to popular magazines, newspapers, and online sites and writes a character education/leadership curriculum called Powerful Words *for top level after-school programs worldwide. Her most recent book,* Good Girls Don't Get Fat: How Weight Obsession Is Messing Up Our Girls and How We Can Help Them Thrive Despite It, *is based on her passion to help all girls and young women reach their potential and highlight their strengths rather than their perceived deficits.*

For me, it happened in the fifth grade.

The girl who bullied me wore red high-top sneakers. Her dark brown ponytail would swoosh back and forth as she walked down the hall.

I know.... Not exactly the school-yard ruffian or even the beautiful-mean-girl type pictured in the movies. It's almost embarrassing to admit that she was shorter than me since I was so scared of her. Scared of what she would say. Scared of the power she had over me. Scared of the power she had over my classmates.

Her impact on my life was apocalyptic. Not just my fifth-grade year. Not just my elementary-school days. My *life*. I say this not to be dramatic, but to dispel the "they'll get over it" attitude that some adults employ when writing off the impact of bullying. Sure, there are little things that I've forgotten over the years that my bully did to me, but the bigger things? Those stuck. Like the days when she was able to corral my entire fifth-grade class to sit on top of the hill by the school—that is, the entire fifth-grade class, but me. Or the time when she orchestrated a "sing off" timed perfectly for when the teacher was out of the room and I walked in. At first, there was a hush. Then, an explosion of voices as each student pointed at me in time with an old David Lee Roth tune popular that year: "I ain't got nobodyyyyyyyyyyyyyyyyy! Nobody, cares for me! Nobody!"

And you know what? That's exactly how I felt. Even now, I feel it in my gut as I write down the words—that horrible, lonely, nauseating feeling of being excluded by my peers. Even though my story pales in comparison to some of the ones we follow in *Bully*, it's mine. It's visceral. It's deep-rooted. It's ever-present. And every so often, even though I'm now a professional, a mother, and, yes, a successful, grounded adult, the memory sometimes comes back to me and coats me with an elusive sense of doubt.

Bullying doesn't just have legs—it has teeth. The memories hold on tightly even as we leave our school days behind.

THE PROBLEM IS OBVIOUS, OR IS IT?

Watching *Bully*, we feel overwhelmed and unsure of how to tackle such a large-scale problem. Bullying. What to do? Breaking down the concerns one by one makes it possible to address them.

1 **Adults can't stop what they don't see.** On the bus, in the hallways, or just outside the school doors lies opportunity after opportunity for children to bully and to be victimized. Why? Because they are left on their own to police themselves. Some may argue that children must be able to behave with character or defend themselves even when adults are not present. However, this isn't happening for some students. To simply talk about what is supposed to happen as a solution to a problem that is actually happening is idiotic. Adults must be present in areas where children convene in and around the schools.

2 **Adults can't fix what they don't know how to fix.** Clearly, solutions are complex and can't be generalized from one student to the next. Eliminating or reducing bullying is not a one-size-fits-all exercise. Still, we can hear the frustration of the administrator at the Sioux City, Iowa, school that Alex Libby attends. She whispers to herself in the hallway "How do I fix this? How do I fix this?" as loudly as her non-committal promise to Alex's exasperated parents: "We will take care of this." How can she take care of what she doesn't know how to fix? Continued education on the part of educators and administrators is necessary in areas where they quite obviously are deficient in knowledge and skill.

3 **Rules can't just be articulated without enforcement.** I was brought in as an expert on Fox News when the stringent, controversial bullying laws were put into effect in New Jersey on September 1, 2011. During the segment, a veteran teacher held the opinion that teachers already announce the rules of conduct at the beginning of the year—as if to say

that should be enough. Perhaps in a perfect world it would be enough. However, that is not reality. Asserting the rules isn't the same as enforcing the rules. Consequences must be immediate and commensurate with the offense. That's the only way children take what adults say seriously. Otherwise, it's just bureaucratic chatter.

4 **Stating what *is* doesn't make it right.** We heard iterations of this throughout the documentary:

- "Buses are notoriously bad places for lots of kids."
- "Kids will be kids, boys will be boys…they're just cruel at that age."
- "Every school has some problems with bullying."

Yeah, and? Stating the obvious doesn't give us permission to turn a blind eye and throw up our hands. Children have a legal right to learn in an environment in which they feel safe. If we know the issues, it's time to address them rather than ignore them.

5 **Effectiveness can't be assumed.** When Alex was asked if he trusts the school officials to take care of his bullying problem, he very clearly says he had reported that a child "sat on my head" and nothing was done. The school official balks at his accusation and tells him that she did indeed talk to the boy and fixed the problem. Her evidence? "He didn't do that again, did he?" Of course, the boy terrorized Alex in different ways. You definitely got the feeling that school officials wanted so badly to hear that things were fine that they didn't investigate whether or not they were resolved. Ignorance may be bliss, but it's not effective in counteracting bullying. The school official never followed up with Alex to see how effective her discussion was or to assure Alex that his words did not fall on deaf ears.

6 **Teachers can be part of the problem.** We are very fortunate to have many capable, caring teachers in the lives of our children. However, that doesn't mean they are all competent

and kind. Sometimes there is a lack of skill to cope with a bullying problem, and other times the teachers perpetrate similar aggression that is typically pegged to the kids themselves. We learn about the problem from Kelby Johnson, a sixteen-year-old who came out as gay while living in the heart of "Bible Belt Oklahoma" and now identifies with a transgender label. In *Bully*, Kelby reports, "One teacher was calling roll…and she was, like, 'Boys,' and then said 'Girls,' and then she stopped and said 'Kelby.' There were a lot of snide remarks from teachers. None of them had my back. They joined in with the kids, a really unsupportive school system."

7 **Adults who are trying to help can inadvertently make things worse.** Many young people don't feel that they have at least three adults in their lives to whom they can turn in a time of need or challenge. They often feel that adults make things worse for them by trying to quickly Band-Aid the problem or by giving them unproductive advice.

We are left to wonder how Alex will fare on the bus after several of his fellow riders are questioned and warned about their behavior toward him. Given past ineffectual warnings to his bullies, will going "half in" really help Alex in the long run? We can't help but cringe when Alex's father tells him that he has to fight back and not be a doormat. As Alex so desperately wants to fit in and believe that his bullies are just "messing around," how can such advice help? It may very well be the action his father would have taken, and it is obvious that it is the advice his father would like his son to employ. But these points are moot because it's Alex, not his father,

"My parents had been to the school multiple, multiple times, and we had done just about everything we could, and no one was there to support us. No one really had anything to say. So where do you go when the teachers don't help?"

—*Kelby Johnson*, Bully

who must get on that bus. It's vital that we ask ourselves what the answer is for the bullied child—an answer that will keep him or her safe while being practical and successful.

YES, BUT WHAT'S THE ANSWER?

An intricate problem has no quick-button answer.

It's understandable that we want to focus on the here and now. With so many children suffering, we yearn to take away the immediate pain. And we need to address the present problems. We need to help these kids. The Alexes. The Kelbys. All of the kids who were represented by *Bully*. But there is more to it. We need to begin earlier—before the problems start.

My mantra has always been to see young people as assets to be developed, not deficits to be managed. In this case, it means that we must focus on how we can promote positive development in young people in their early years rather than waiting to fix the bullying issues once they arise later.

I'm not talking about risk and prevention—a practice that, in my opinion, assumes our children are prone to fail without intervention. My assumption is of resourcefulness and inherent success—that is, when these kids are afforded the chance to acquire the necessary tools. Workable skills. Healthy opportunities to grow. Self-worth, empathy, and determination to achieve.

Studies tell us that children are more likely to thrive, even against the odds, when we help them to connect, sharpen their character, and strengthen their confidence. Young people are more likely to succeed when we help them to gain competence and expertise in areas in which they are passionate. And when we recognize their unique contribution to our families, our communities, and this world, they begin to see themselves as wanted and useful. I had the pleasure of interviewing three young people who have been able to thrive in middle and high school: Amber, a teen who is openly gay; Kacie, a young person who went through high school as a size 22; and Kyle Maynard, an inspirational speaker, author, and athlete who was born with legs that stop at his knees and arms just up to his elbows. Each one provided some insight into what made them successful during their teen years. Their tips seemed to fall into three main categories: (1) friendship opportunities, (2) adult connections, and (3) setting goals that are followed through to mastery. So let's jump in.

DIVERSIFY YOUR CHILD'S FRIENDSHIP CIRCLES

When our children are only exposed to a small group of people, they can pull friends from a limited circle. If they are feeling left out, picked on, or targeted in any way, there is little they can do to escape other than either join in or remain aloof.

Remember when the moviemakers stopped production of the film to reveal to Alex's parents that he was being threatened, abused, and tormented on the bus by other kids? His mother sits down and questions him about why he would allow these boys to treat him that way since, she offers, they clearly aren't his friends. Alex's answer reveals the narrow scope of friendships in his life at that moment. "If they're not my friends, then what friends do I have?"

When I was presenting to an audience of parents at a school in New York City, one parent voiced, "But everyone knows each other on the local teams and in the area activities." I have no doubt that was true. So I said to her, "Go a few blocks down. A whole new world can open up for your child if you just travel a little ways down the road." What we are seeking are places in which our children feel accepted, don't have to try so hard, don't need to explain themselves, and feel surrounded by people who understand them and like them. If your teen is feeling particularly marginalized or cast out, finding a group that serves other teens like him or her can be a great comfort and resource.

The teenage girl, Amber, whom I interviewed always knew she was gay. She is part of two organizations outside of school that afford her many other friends who have a great deal in common with her. One resource is SunServe, a nonprofit social-service agency serving the Lesbian, Gay, Bisexual, Transgender, and Questioning (LGBTQ) community in South Florida and the other is Drag It Out, a performance group that challenges gender stereotypes through community acceptance, entertainment, volunteerism, and mentoring. While Amber was often called names in high school, she told me, "Those people didn't really matter. I always knew that my friends from SunServe and Drag It Out had my back. They are my best friends."

A martial-arts school or gymnastics facility a few towns over. A community theater outside of your immediate community. Churches, temples, clubs, meet-ups, special events, sports teams, and nonprofit organizations. It may not be a matter of making a long drive or spending a lot of money. There are so many ways to branch out, and it truly can make a difference.

BE ONE OF THE THREE

We're all so busy. Teachers and parents are some of the most over-loaded people, and somehow we always want to pile more on.

Parents, in particular, want to do it all. But it's important to know that sometimes it's okay to take a backseat. Kacie, a girl who always felt a lot bigger than her friends as a size 22, could have been the object of bullying in high school. And while some people teased her quietly from time to time, it was of little consequence because, in addition to great friends, she had a wonderful support system that consisted of her mother, her mother's friend Jen, and her youth counselor George, who were always there when she needed to vent, get advice, or get help. I could tell you stories in which Kacie was feeling left out and how she asked Jen for advice instead of her mother, how Kacie's mom reeled in her ego for the sake of her daughter. But the more important message is that while her mother always remained available, checked in, and followed up, she stood out of the way those times Kacie needed an unemotional perspective.

Our children's teachers can also provide that perspective, and thankfully, there are plenty of amazing teachers and administrators who are there for them. These adults take time out of their days and make themselves available in their free time. These are the teachers our children remember because they make a real difference in their lives. "My English teacher was my favorite teacher," Amber told me one afternoon on the phone. "I went to her whenever I needed to talk to someone, when people were calling me names like 'dyke' or 'butch' or 'lesbian.' There were times when I felt like nobody accepted me, and I would spend every day at lunch in her room talking to her. I remember one day I felt so alone. I didn't feel like I had anyone to turn to but her. I just knew I had to go to school because she was there to listen. I just had to get to school. I knew I always had her."

When Amber told me this, I couldn't help but think of the statistic from The Bully Project that tells us that three million kids will be absent from class because they feel unsafe in school. And here is this one teen rushing to school because that is where she found an adult who helped her feel secure and heard. We need more of that.

Celebs Speak Out

"Because I was an actor, when I was in school there was a little bullying going on. Not physical bullying, but people making fun of what I do…I just had to tell myself I can't let this get to me. This is what I love to do. And I'm going to continue to do it."

—*Taylor Lautner to* Rolling Stone

In *Bully*, it seemed that many of the teachers were either out of touch, unaware of the problem, ill equipped to cope with the issues properly, or quick to offer advice or commands without really listening to the concerns of the affected children and families. Remember when one school administrator attempted to resolve the conflict between a bully and his victim, Cole, with a simple handshake? "You are just like him," she accuses when Cole refuses to stretch out his hand. And when Cole reveals the way his bully has tortured him over the years, she naively says, "He apologized." She was so wishful to smooth things over that her ears were closed, and you can feel her reaching for a bridge: "I think you could be really good friends at some time." She isn't being the person this teen needs her to be. School should be a safe haven, not a battleground.

ENCOURAGE GOAL SETTING, STICK-TO-IT-IVENESS, AND MASTERY

Becoming great at something—especially an activity that you are passionate about—can help build self-esteem in young people. It gives children something productive to focus on, strive toward, and attain. They learn to gain worth from what they can do and who they are rather than who they know and how their peers behave around them.

Watching *Bully*, I was struck by the lack of extracurricular activities, hobbies, and constructive (yet passion-filled) learning time featured in the lives of some of the young people highlighted. I wondered how Alex would have fared if he had something constructive and creative in which he could focus his energy and feelings. Sometimes connecting to one's passion can help one to connect with others as well.

For Kelby, who was a star on his basketball and softball teams, consistent verbal abuse due to his declared sexuality caused him to give up on his passions as well as a likely scholarship. By doing so, he leaves behind a piece of himself as well as a productive, rewarding part of his life that makes him who he is. When asked about this great loss, he told one reporter: "That was hard letting go of the sports. I'm going to have to get back out there, but I picked my battles. I was trying to stay away from it as much as I could, so I had to let go." I hope he gets back out there.

Aside from the friendships and adult connections they are afforded, when children are involved in team sports, activity clubs, dramatic or fine arts, and individual sports like martial arts, gymnastics, or dance, they gain opportunities to set goals, gain a feeling of accomplishment, and master skills. Striving and developing an

WHAT'S IN *YOUR* CHILD'S SUITCASE?

Every child carts around a suitcase full of past experiences, talents, and voices of people whom they've met along the way. Good or bad, that baggage comes with them. It is our job, as the adults in our children's lives, to help them sort through that baggage and uncover their assets.

For some, the strengths are easily spotted. They are gifted students. Outstanding athletes. Prolific writers. For others, those strengths are buried under a pile of dirty laundry. It's easy to see these children for their deficits. But that's what everyone else does. We must be the ones who dig through the baggage and uncover their strengths.

What are Alex's strengths? Or Kelby's? It will take a special person to help them uncover those assets so that they can see them for themselves.

For Kyle Maynard, it would have been easy to simply see him for his disability. But that's not what his parents did. Or his teachers. Or coaches. They saw him for his strengths and made sure to point it out enough times so that Kyle saw it also. As he told me, "My parents never focused on my disability. In fact, I didn't even know what my disability was called until I became an adult. They didn't focus on what was wrong—they focused on what was right. So that's the way I looked at myself, too."

expertise can give young people a feeling of purpose and passion in their lives, but it takes perseverance, inner strength, and the support of those around them to create a nurturing environment where it's okay to be one's self. Kelby didn't have that, but those who do can achieve great things far beyond their expectations.

Like Kyle Maynard. Despite his extensive physical limitations, he joined the wrestling team in high school with the support of his parents. And although he lost every match in the first year and a half, "my Dad wouldn't let me quit," he told me. "I would cry, kick, and scream. I'd beg to quit. I'd bawl my eyes out and he still made me continue. He even told me that he lost every match his first year to keep me going." Kyle's father's encouragement wasn't shown just through words. He was the one who drilled the skills with his son for hours and days and weeks and months until his son figured out how to make the skills work for his body. With that kind of perseverance and family commitment, who could be surprised that Kyle became a state champion wrestler? Or that he would later become the first man to crawl up Mount Kilimanjaro?

Mastery shows others your talents. It tells them "I am strong" and "there is much more to me than you first thought." But, more importantly, it shows *you* your talents and allows you to define yourself by your strengths rather than give permission to others to define you by any perceived deficits. "Masters" often discover that they have an ability to succeed even when the odds don't seem to be stacked in their favor, and these are the lessons they take with them and can apply to every other facet of their lives.

ACCOUNTABILITY

At the end of the day, it comes down to accountability. It's apparent that some school officials want to pass the buck to parents while many parents are looking to the schools, their towns or cities, and other parents to help solve the problem. The truth is that community movement doesn't happen without the cooperation of all its members. And cooperation means that everyone takes on a little accountability to ensure that a safe and fair learning environment is an enforced right for every child.

When I conduct presentations on very large, heated topics such as bullying, I find that either people feel completely overwhelmed and powerless to act or that they feel they must implement every single suggestion I offer in order to make a difference. The answer, however, lies more in tackling the problem realistically. I often ask my audiences the following questions:

- What are you going to do? Pick one, two, or three things that you can implement now. Every small effort can make one small difference in the lives of our young people.
- By when are you going to do it? "Someday" is not a time frame. "Later" isn't either. Pick a day. Monday? Next

Friday? The start of next semester? Make the commitment
so you make the time.

- Who will be your accountability partner? In other words,
  who will keep you on task? When we confide in someone
  else, it keeps us honest and motivated.

- How will you inform your accountability partner that the
  task is done or the goal has been completed? In this day
  and age, there are many methods. Text. Phone. Instant
  Message. E-mail. Twitter. Facebook. Face-to-face.

Ultimately, whatever action you choose to help at least one child
steer clear of, cope with, or overcome bullying, will be felt. Individually, we may not have all the answers, but collectively we can
work toward one solution. The answer to bullying starts here. It
starts now. And it starts with us.

Free to Be...
Not Anymore.

Marlo Thomas

As part of her commitment to combat bullying, Marlo
Thomas and the Free to Be Foundation joined with the
Ad Council, the U.S. Department of Education, AOL,
Facebook, The Bully Project, and the Waitt Family
Foundation to start a new campaign in 2012 to help educate
parents about bullying. You can learn more about the
campaign by visiting http://MarloThomas.com

Exactly how many dead teenagers, driven to end their own lives, is it going to take for adults to stand up and say, *What the hell is going on?* There was a time when the words "Free to Be" embodied a hope that whatever a kid was, was good enough. But "freedom" doesn't describe the world of this generation. Or of their parents. One of those parents contacted me on my Facebook page.

"Hi, Marlo," wrote Kevin Jacobsen of New York. "Our son Kameron was bullied relentlessly and died by suicide on January 18th. He was fourteen. In lieu of flowers, we asked for donations to go to St. Jude Children's Research Hospital, my mom's favorite for decades. I know you're busy, but just wondering if you could take a look at our son. We have nothing else to lose."

Kevin then posted the link to a website he'd built to honor his son, called KindnessAboveMalice.org. I logged on, but could barely look at the child's face. He was beautiful.

Thirty-seven years—and two generations of children—after the creation of *Free to Be...You and Me*, I can't help but remember the lovely words lyricist Bruce Hart wrote that anchored the opening anthem:

"Every boy in this land grows to be his own man,
In this land, every girl grows to be her own woman."

Kameron will never grow to be his own man.

For all the walls we thought we'd broken down with "Free to Be"—and all the stereotypes we thought we'd shattered—children today are not free to be anything they want to be, nor anything they are, and they are dying for it. And there is no beautiful lyric that can fix that.

According to current statistics, one out of every four teenagers across America is bullied in their neighborhoods and schools; 160,000 students stay home from school every day because of their fear of being bullied; and each month, nearly 300,000 students are physically attacked inside their secondary schools.

Online, things are even worse: 43 percent of kids are cyberbullied, while 53 percent admit to having said something mean and hurtful to another child online.

Then came that tragic September—2010—when over a period of just three weeks, nine gay or questioning youths—all male, average age fifteen—were "bullied to death" and died by suicide when they were no longer able to endure.

Like many people, much of what I knew about bullying is what I read in the headlines: fifteen-year-old Irish immigrant Phoebe Prince of Massachusetts hanged herself in the stairwell of her family apartment, after yet another day of relentless bullying. The harassment continued on her Facebook memorial page. And in May 2012, fourteen-year-old Ambriel Bowen of York, Pennsylvania, died by suicide at home when the daily terrorizing by bullies— which included two black eyes and a broken nose—became too overwhelming to bear.

Reading the horrid accounts of bullied kids is devastating. But hearing the voice of a bereaved father brings tears to your eyes.

I called Kevin Jacobsen after I read his Facebook post, and my heart broke as he recounted his son's tragic story.

"Bullying is not the same old issue it used to be," Kevin said softly. "With cell phones and social networking, it's turned into an around-the-clock problem that our kids cannot escape from. And the other thing that's different is that the bullies can be anony- mous. Without that face-to-face encounter, it's impossible to stop them."

When I hung up with Kevin, I reread his post, and seeing his mention of St. Jude made me think about how different those chil- dren are there. I've seen them express compassion, not cruelty, to each other. I've seen four- and five-year-old boys and girls offering hugs and giving comfort to two- and three-year-olds, telling them that they understand the pain they're going through and that they will be all right.

So the idea that healthy children should die, not from an errant cancer cell, but because of the abject malice of another child, is something we need to take on. And stop.

Kevin Jennings, the former assistant deputy secretary at the Department of Education, told me that most parents of bullied children have no idea about the anguish their sons and daughters are enduring because the kids aren't talking. They're ashamed to admit it because they think it's a sign of weakness, and they want to handle it themselves.

Leaders Speak Out

"Victims of bullying often feel an enormous amount of shame and self-doubt, and somehow feel they have brought this upon themselves. That means that young people who are willing to talk to an adult about the issue must be truly desperate. So my first warning to a parent or teacher is if a kid's willing to talk to you about it, then the problem is probably ten times worse... There are provisions in law, such as the Unsafe School Choice Option, that guarantee your right, as a parent, to have your child attend a safe public school. And there are organizations that will, if necessary, litigate on your behalf, including the U.S. Office of Civil Rights. You should avail yourself of every resource, because it could make a difference between whether your child lives or dies. Forget whether they graduate from high school and go to college—it can make the difference in whether or not they get to be an adult. I know that fighting the system is sometimes hard. I know that sometimes it seems like you can't win. But the law is on your side. Do not quit until your child is in a safe place."

—*Kevin Jennings, the former assistant deputy secretary at the Department of Education*

But if more parents would get into the game, Jennings said, we might be able to turn things around. He told me that a majority of parents haven't been trained to look for signs of bullying in their child's life. But they need to. And they can start by asking themselves a few questions:

- Does your child not want to ride the school bus anymore?
- Does your child often wake in the morning complaining about stomachaches and asking to stay home from school?

- Are your child's friends not coming around so much any more?
- Has your child stopped receiving invitations to parties?

Most important, said Jennings, is if you suspect that your child is being bullied, you must become proactive and try to get that child to talk.

And I think we *all* have to start to talk.

If there's one thing I've learned over the years about tackling problems, it's that the first thing you need to do is spark the conversation. So let's start talking about bullying. With our neighbors. With our friends and family. With fellow parents at PTA meetings. And with each other. It's time to take bullying down. We don't have the time—or any more kids' lives—to waste.

Or adults' lives, either: On January 7, 2012—just nine months after he first contacted me on my Facebook page—Kevin Jacobsen took his own life. The one-year anniversary of his son's suicide was only days away, and apparently the pain was too much for him to bear.

I can't begin to say that I have insight into this second act of sadness. I only knew that I was hit by an unrelenting wave of shock and grief. I continue to pray for Kevin's wife, Wanda, and her family to find strength.

Kevin inspired those around him. He inspired me. When he spoke to a crowded room at the U.S. Department of Education at a bullying conference in late 2011, he roused them to a standing ovation. He hid his pain behind actions. His notes to me about antibullying legislation were carefully considered. He served as a bridge to other families. He decided that no family should suffer as his had.

My resolve strengthened after Kevin's death. I just cannot stand by and see other families destroyed. We must defeat this issue. Parents, teachers, grandparents—and, most of all, kids—need to band together to stop this epidemic in our schools and on our playgrounds. No child should ever be made to feel such desperation.

No parent should have to lose a child. No wife should lose a husband and son.

Our children deserve better. Our families deserve better. It has been nearly four decades since the debut of the Free to Be message. But I'm hopeful that all of us can realize that place that Bruce Hart imagined, where:

> "Every boy in this land grows to be his own man,
>   In this land, every girl grows to be her own woman."

A land where the children are free...from bullying.

PART 4

Ja'Meya, 14

Ja'Meya's Story

Looking around Ja'Meya's bedroom, her mother says, "This is her comfort zone, to herself. She was a basketball player. These are her trophies, her awards. Got her names on 'em and everything. She was an honor student. Yeah, she is an honor student. She said when she finished school, she want to go to the navy... Because she didn't want to see me work so hard. She wanted to help me out."

New to her school, Ja'Meya had wanted to get away from the "drama" at her old school, but despite being an athlete and a top student, she was picked on every morning and afternoon of her hour-long bus ride through Mississippi. "It all started back when school first began, and there was a lot of kids on the bus saying things about me," she explained. "I tried my best to tell an adult, but it got worse." Ja'Meya finally had enough. One morning while on the bus, she took out the gun she found in her mother's closet. Although no one was harmed, Ja'Meya was arrested and charged with forty-five felony accounts, enough to send her to prison for a hundred years.

While researching *Bully*, Lee Hirsch and Cynthia Lowen came across the news story about a young man who had wrestled a gun away from a teenage girl—a story that was making headlines on news programs across America. However, they were acutely aware that no one was asking why this young woman had brought a gun on the bus in the first place. And when they met Ja'Meya, she hadn't had the chance to tell people what had been happening to her on that bus.

Yet, Ja'Meya and her mother wanted people to know what had pushed her to take such extreme actions that fateful morning.

And as they waited for the criminal justice system to determine Ja'Meya's fate, her family struggled to understand how she could have become so desperate, while Ja'Meya, in custody, tried to come to terms with the consequences of her actions and with being away from the home she missed terribly.

A Little "I'm Sorry"
Goes a Long Way

Amy McCready

*Parenting expert Amy McCready is the founder of Positive
Parenting Solutions and the author of* If I Have to Tell
You One More Time . . . The Revolutionary Program That
Gets Your Kids to Listen Without Nagging, Reminding
or Yelling *(Tarcher/Penguin, 2011). She is a champion of
positive parenting techniques for happier families and
well-behaved kids.*

Amy reaches a worldwide audience with her Positive
Parenting Solutions Online *course, live webinars, and
media appearances. She is a frequent guest on* The Today
Show *and has also appeared on* Rachael Ray, *CNN,* Fox &
Friends, *MSNBC, and elsewhere.*

Amy's Pay It Forward Parenting *program supports
military families by providing complimentary online
parenting training to any military family who wants to
participate.*

*She is a sought-after keynote speaker, writer, parenting
coach, and corporate spokesperson. In her most important
role, she plays mom to two teenage boys. Amy has been
married to her husband and business partner, Dave, for
over twenty years and lives in Raleigh, North Carolina.*

"I'm sorry."

Whew. There's the apology. Now we can all just be friends, right?

Looking back on the particularly heart-wrenching hallway apology scene in *Bully*, we know that's not the case. We all silently cheered when Cole declined to accept the falsely apologetic handshake of the boy who'd bullied him every day in the school yard. And then we anguished as the assistant principal compared Cole to the bully. "You're the same as him!" she insisted over and over as he refused the hollow handshake. Why could a young boy see through it when a grown woman could not? More importantly, why is there no such thing nowadays as a meaningful apology?

Most of us first learned the words "I'm sorry" to smooth over the fact that we recently gave our brother's favorite teddy bear a bath in the toilet, or another similar offense. As far back as that tender age, however, "I'm sorry" can mean so many things. Often, it can be translated, "I'm just saying this so I'm not in trouble anymore." Or, it might be a sarcastic, "We both know I'm really not sorry," a glaring, "Dorkface, why did you tell on me?" or even a threatening, "I'll get you for this later!"

Fast-forward a decade, and put your child in a middle school filled with peer pressure, emotions, and uncertainty. When an apology is tossed out by a thirteen-year-old who harasses as a daily ritual, "I'm sorry" means anything but "My actions were really out of line, and they will never be repeated." Yes, even bullies know how to say, "I'm sorry." But they've never learned how to attach any meaning to it.

This leads us to a central characteristic among bullies: They aren't accustomed to taking responsibility for their actions. And when we allow these kids to continue with their meaningless apologies, we enable that trend to persist. Instead, we need to follow a path that takes a step back, draws connections between kids' actions and emotions, holds them accountable, and helps both people in the conflict reach resolution. And a *meaningful* apology is just the tool we need to do so.

Let's take a minute to look at all the facets of an apology. A true apology is an amazing tool that enables both parties to resolve a conflict and leave it on peaceful terms. It fosters accountability and responsibility, ensuring no wrong toward another person goes unchecked. It helps the offending child gain emotional maturity by tuning into her own feelings and those of the other person. The perpetrator gains the experience necessary to make a different decision next time, learning from her mistakes. She'll develop long-term abilities to empathize and problem-solve. And by intentionally making amends, she'll create an emotional connection that will render similar altercations less likely in the future. Any one of these outcomes is much more powerful than a forced "I'm sorry."

Parents and administrators alike can teach kids the art of a true apology by applying a formula designed for ages four through the teens. Start early, and you can give children the lifetime gift of positive conflict resolution and empathy—but even late beginners will benefit greatly from this training and experience revolutionary changes in both thinking and behavior. The five steps outlined in the next section will lead you through the process, including the words to say and actions to take to facilitate learning.

In short, there's much more to a heartfelt "I'm sorry" than just the words—and much to be gained by a bully of any age. But to really help the bullying child grow, we first need to understand a few basic facts about him.

WHAT EVERY KID NEEDS, AND WILL DO ANYTHING TO GET

Two of the fundamental emotional needs of all children, according to the work of world-renowned philosopher and psychiatrist Alfred Adler, MD, and the principles of Positive Discipline, are a sense of belonging and a sense of significance. Belonging refers to feeling emotionally connected and part of a group, whether that's family, a peer group, or the community. Significance is feeling like a capable, contributing member of a group—a family, a peer group, a classroom—and also feeling personally empowered, independent, and in control.

Both of these needs are hardwired from birth and in high demand every day on a subconscious level. If kids can't meet these needs in positive ways, they will resort to negative means. We see the battle for autonomy and significance, for example, in an infant who struggles while we try to restrain her, a toddler who throws tantrums, a third grader who talks back, or a teenager who battles us at every turn. And if a child continually lacks a strong sense of significance through positive and productive means, she may resort to bullying as an attempt to use her internal need for power to control and influence others. Being the terror of the playground or the locker room gains the child a shadow of the significance and attention she's been craving.

It's important to recognize that these needs are natural and healthy as kids move toward independence, and all misbehavior can be traced back to a deficit in either belonging or significance. Rudolph Dreikurs, MD, author of the classic *Children: The Challenge*, says, "A misbehaving child is a discouraged child." So, when Blake "decorates" the class whiteboard with language that's a little too creative during English class, or Hannah develops the ability to

---

NO BULLIES HERE

Maintain a bully-free zone in your family, classroom, and group by employing the Crucial C's to meet kids' basic needs:

Connected Help each child feel like she belongs, fits in, and is secure.

Capable Give them opportunities to take responsibility and demonstrate competence.

Count Ensure every child feels significant and impactful.

Courage Foster the ability to handle difficult situations and overcome fear.

Bettner & Lew, 1990

make other kids cry just by looking at them, it's likely they aren't feeling a strong sense of belonging and significance, nor do they know how to achieve them in positive ways. As a result, they resort to negative means to get the attention and power they crave. What's more, bullying characteristics begin in the formative years and might be practiced throughout childhood (and adulthood). It's not only the twelve-and-older crowd we need to concern ourselves with, because to leave a five-year-old's needs unmet is to set the stage for a future bully. Only by addressing the underlying cause can we expect to correct the misbehavior permanently.

Fostering a sense of belonging and significance in our kids doesn't have to be a complicated endeavor. It begins with giving them a sufficient dose of positive attention and emotional connection on a daily basis by simply taking ten minutes once or twice a day to be fully present and to get into a child's world. (This is explained in more detail in Step Two below.) You can also foster his hardwired need for autonomy and control by letting him make meaningful contributions around the house and loosening the reins a bit to give him more age-appropriate control over his own world. Encourage him to help decide anything from which flavor of yogurt to buy this week, to how to spend a day of a family vacation, and ask his opinion about challenges your family faces— such as how to get everyone through the bathroom in time for school every morning. Inviting your child into decision-making opportunities when appropriate and soliciting his input for solving problems will bolster his sense of significance as well as prepare him for the real world. This is a case where a little can go a long way toward preventing future bullying episodes and fostering positive relationships inside the family and out.

When children are receiving the positive attention and positive power they need, you can work on holding them accountable for their actions, developing empathy, and familiarizing them with effective conflict-resolution skills. And while it's never too late to take action, the best prevention for bullying is to begin educating

early and continue the practice throughout childhood and adolescence. The five steps below will guide you as you help your kids
put the meaning back into an apology—and learn from it along
the way.

STEP 1: NO SHAME, NO PUNISHMENT

You can hear the fight a block away as you hurry toward the bus
stop to meet your nine-year-old son, Andrew. When you get closer,
you're surprised to see that the other side of the altercation is his
best friend, Jacob. Or, former best friend, by the sounds of things.

"Geek wad!" Andrew voices for the whole neighborhood to hear
because, as you later find out, Jacob wouldn't let him borrow his
new spy binoculars for the weekend. "Hamster breath!"

Then, you watch in horror as Andrew swings his fist at Jacob,
landing a punch right on his arm.

"What is WRONG with you!?" you start, screaming yourself
into a sore throat and then dragging Andrew home to his room
while you debate whether to take away the TV and video games for
the week or just ground him for the rest of the school year. You're
steaming mad and your son was clearly in the wrong, but is punishment really the right answer?

Punishment vs. Discipline

There is a reason that punishment is often the response of choice
to situations like this. Logic tells us that if his negative behavior
receives a negative response, Andrew won't repeat his misdeeds.
After all, what's wrong with a little hurt or humiliation, since he
did the same thing to someone else? But whether that punishment comes as being grounded for a week or in the embarrassment
of standing in the corner in front of his classmates, it only puts
Andrew in a mode of self-defense—feeling humiliated, hurt, and
powerless. Rather than looking inside himself and learning from
his misbehavior, he will instead find ways to blame others for his
pain. He'll focus his energy on avoiding future punishment, or

worse, getting revenge. We miss the opportunity to help him learn, and we virtually guarantee that he'll repeat the behavior.

Instead, we should start by understanding that for most adults, the words "punishment" and "discipline" are interchangeable. But in reality, their meanings—and outcomes—are far from the same. While punishment centers on negative attention and incorporates physical or emotional hurt or humiliation, discipline can be a very positive experience.

Rooted in the Latin word *discipulus*—a student, one who is learning—discipline is a much more fitting way to approach our troublemaker. Parents and teachers alike can make good use of each small squabble or larger conflict by treating it as an opportunity for education. By using discipline, instead of punishment, with Andrew we ensure he won't repeat his bad behavior—because he's been allowed to learn from it, and not because he went a week without playing his favorite video game.

Take Action: Cooling the Conflict

Punishment isn't the answer. But you're still eager to put this whole situation behind you, as fast as possible, whatever it takes, and coax the boys to be friends again. You find yourself seeking the instant gratification of resolving the conflict *right now*.

Unfortunately, it's that same need for immediate resolution that will likely leave Jacob feeling forced to accept a hollow apology from Andrew and the two youngsters on shaky ground. Be the adult, and resist the urge to bring about a hurried solution. Everyone will learn more and feel better if you can use these strategies to settle the scene before seeking to solve the greater conflict:

Use a calm voice to approach the situation, regardless of how you feel on the inside. Emotions are likely running high, and by speaking calmly, you will not only keep yourself calm and collected, but everyone else as well.

Put the "sorry" on standby and revisit it after using the next two steps to thoroughly talk through the conflict. While adults might feel better knowing apologies have been given, they will have more meaning—and our children will appreciate them more—when the offending child understands the effects of his misbehavior.

Lose the lecture about the misdeed. Reminding your child that "you know better than that!" and that you "didn't raise him that way" won't help you—or him—understand why he did what he did. Instead, steer the conversation toward questions that will help your child explain his actions and emotions, as detailed in the next step.

Separate the squabblers so that they feel safe and secure as you address the root of the problem. It'll give everyone a chance to cool down and consider their actions, too.

STEP 2: CONNECT THE DOTS: FEELINGS TO ACTIONS

You've all taken a deep breath (or two, or twenty). You've settled the situation. Now, it's time to get to the heart of the matter. Why, exactly, did Andrew feel the need to lash out at Jacob? Take note: your job is not to play judge and jury, but rather to help Andrew understand what feelings motivated him to call names and land punches. You'll then need to make sure Andrew understands that we all get upset, frustrated, angry, sad, jealous—you name it—but that it's not okay to hurt others, whether with words or actions, no matter how we feel.

Here's what to do: Start by asking Andrew, "What were you *feeling* when you hit your friend?" Then listen to his response so you know where he's coming from. Using a calm voice, validate his feelings—we all feel angry, jealous, and frustrated at times. Help him realize that while his feelings were understandable, he can, and should, act respectfully toward others no matter how he feels. Being angry, for instance, is not an excuse for harming another person physically or emotionally. This process will help Andrew learn to take responsibility for his own actions.

LABELING KIDS IN CONFLICT

We now know why children fight: Kids of all ages will resort to negative means, if necessary, to gain attention and a sense of significance. But do we see how we often play into that strategy by labeling the roles of those involved?

Let's look again at Andrew and Jacob. We almost instinctually label Andrew the "aggressor" of the situation and Jacob the "victim." Our conscience insists we rescue the victim and punish the bully, to ensure that Jacob is soothed of his sore arm and hurt feelings, and that Andrew doesn't get away with his misbehavior.

This line of thought, however, only serves to reinforce those roles by providing an ample payoff for each child: attention. We overwhelm Jacob with comfort, implying that he's gained our favor and almost encouraging his victim mentality. Andrew, meanwhile, earns his own fill of negative attention and learns that by playing the powerful perpetrator, he gains the sense of significance and power he's seeking. While it's important to make sure Jacob's okay, there's no reason to go overboard with our gushing. As for Andrew, avoid labeling him as the troublemaker and instead use the five-step apology process to stick to the facts.

Losing these labels helps us keep Jacob and Andrew on equal ground while addressing any misbehavior on either party's part. By understanding—and removing—this label payoff, we take a big step toward eliminating these hidden benefits of a conflict.

What's more, as Andrew grows older, he'll gain more and more understanding of his emotions and how to keep them from negatively influencing his actions. With this sense of self-control, he'll be less likely to resort to the desperate measures of physical violence, name-calling, and disrespect when confronted with conflicts in the future. Andrew becomes one less bully in his future tenth-grade classroom.

Even kids who are already considered bullies can benefit greatly from discussing emotions. Chances are, they never have—and learning to recognize their feelings will empower them to make better choices.

For instance, consider sixteen-year-old Erin. No one noticed her—until she performed the stunt that got her in with the "cool" crowd. The terrible misdeed involved shy and awkward Rachel and a school dance, but the details aren't important. Now, she's made bullying her trademark and never misses an opportunity. After Erin was caught in the act of texting locker-room pictures of a prior best friend to her entire homeroom, her parents resist the urge to ground her through graduation and finally sit her down for the talk they've never had with her before.

"What were you feeling when you decided to take those photos and text them?"

Erin defiantly resists sharing any meaningful information. And resists, and resists—but after her parents lead the way by talking about some tricky situations they'd gotten themselves into in high school, she opens up. "Mad, I was really mad!" she relates. "She told everyone I have a crush on Mr. Eldridge in Math. And I don't, he's my stupid teacher and he stinks. But they all believed it, so now they're calling me Mrs. Eldridge, and it sucks."

Erin's parents take more opportunities in the future to talk to Erin about her emotions. As Erin begins to see that they care, she also begins to think more about how her feelings influence her behavior—for better or worse. With some practice, she starts to feel more in control of herself and more respectful of herself and others, too.

While feelings may seem obvious to you, we all could use a reminder—so don't skip this step. Be sure to reinforce the fact that feelings are okay. Actions that hurt others aren't. Once you've discussed your child's feelings, you can move on to Step Three to talk about the offended party's feelings.

Take Action: Engage in One-On-One Time

There comes a point in *Bully* when the filmmakers become so concerned for Alex's welfare that they share footage of him being bullied with his parents. It's a poignant moment when their concern moves them to reflect on their own response to their son. This moving scene illustrates the importance of fostering open and honest communication with our kids, and that it's not always easy, even for well-meaning parents.

The solution starts with spending one-on-one time with your child daily to emotionally connect: Set aside just ten minutes, twice a day, and have fun together. Let your child choose something you can do, just the two of you, with no phones or other distractions allowed. Whether it's an impromptu tea party with your five-year-old or checking out the trending videos on YouTube with your teen, you are taking the most important step toward increasing your emotional connection with your child and creating a comfortable environment for her to open up in. Not only are you strengthening communication, but your proactive positive attention also increases your child's feeling of belonging and significance and reduces negative attention-seeking and power-seeking behaviors—like bullying.

STEP 3: CONNECT THE DOTS: ACTIONS TO EFFECT

After you've discussed Andrew's feelings, it's time to turn his attention to Jacob's. Pose the question, "When you *felt angry and hit Jacob*, how do you think he felt?" Make sure to give it a thorough talk-through so that he'll learn how his actions affect others, and he'll begin to develop a sense of empathy.

If the conversation stalls out with an "I don't know," simply ask, "If someone bigger and more powerful than you did the same thing to you, how would you feel?" This might enable your child to better relate to the child he hurt. You can also share experiences of your own in which someone did something hurtful to you, including how you felt afterward.

Take Action: Managing Emotions

When it comes to developing empathy, it takes lots of practice to make "permanent," especially considering the fact that many adults aren't exactly experts. Help your child practice empathy by regularly talking about others' emotions. To a four-year-old, this might mean bringing feelings into everyday play with action figures or stuffed animals: "Buzz Lightyear sure looks excited to celebrate his birthday! How do you think he'd feel if his best friend Woody doesn't show up at his party?" or, "Mr. Bear seems lonely—maybe Katie Kitty could invite him to play on the slide!" Alternatively, you could discuss feelings presented in TV shows and real-life situations with your older kids or teens: "How would you feel if you were new at school and no one sat with you in the lunchroom?" or, "How do you think Jason feels when he's never invited to parties?"

To further bolster your child's ability to empathize, encourage the kind actions you see every day. Tell her, "You sure put a smile on your sister's face when you gave her a ride to school!" or, "Your letter will be such a happy surprise for Grandma!" Comments like these will provide a dose of positive attention and help her see that she can affect others for good.

Labeling feelings, however, is only part of the solution. It's also important to take time to train your kids how to manage their emotions, respond well to arguments and frustrations, and respect their peers in daily interactions. As such, your discussions about feelings should not be limited to conflicts. Regularly take other opportunities to talk through a variety of emotions to help your kids gain a deeper understanding of their own moods and how to manage them with positive actions. Remember, even positive emotions can get us into trouble—from cutting in line because we're so excited to feed the giraffe at the zoo to discussing a funny incident too boisterously in a restaurant.

Kids who are used to talking about emotions in low-pressure situations will be more likely to recognize and manage their feelings in a positive way when the heat is on. What's more, they're also more likely to show empathy for their peers facing tough situations and leadership in resolving conflicts.

STEP 4: ACTIVELY MAKING AMENDS

Now that Andrew understands the undercurrent of emotion surrounding the incident, he gets the opportunity to make amends.

Whether he's grateful for the chance to make up, or still grumbling, ask, "What can you do to *make it right* with Jacob?" He might need suggestions, so help him brainstorm after you've given him a chance to think up some ideas on his own.

Think beyond a traditional apology—a simple act of kindness like a hand-drawn picture, a note, or help fixing a broken toy might do a better job of helping smooth relations between both parties. Whatever Andrew decides on, make sure it's meaningful for him and for Jacob. Making it right will help your child learn to be accountable for his actions, which will go a long way toward helping him consider his behavior in the future. Kids who are used to making amends will be less likely to bully others in the first place.

Take Action: Methods for Making Amends

Misdeed	Make Amends
Harmed a sibling's toy	Help fix it; use allowance money to replace it.
Called a friend names	Write a note, poem, or story about what's great about the friend.
Physically harmed another child	Offer a cool Hello Kitty bandage (whether there's blood or not) or dinosaur cold pack. Or, play board games together while the hurt child is resting a sore arm/leg.
Had trouble sharing	Take turns with the coveted toy; let your friend play with one of your super-duper, most special toys; tell her she'll get to "go first" the next two times when taking turns.
Ruined sibling's homework	Offer to help redo it; complete a chore for sibling while she redoes it.
Took something from another child	Return item and share another; draw a picture; give something special to the child that belongs to you.
Started a rumor about a friend	Write a letter explaining how the rumor hurt the friend and why that friend is important to you; tell the truth to anyone the rumor reached.
Was mean to a pet	Give the pet some quality time—take dog for a walk or give the hamster's cage a thorough cleaning.
Blamed a classmate for something she did	Come clean to the teacher; offer to help the classmate clean out her locker or help with an upcoming school project.

STEP 5: LEARNING FROM MISTAKES

Thanks to your wise counsel, Andrew and Jacob are friends again. But you're not quite done yet: you'd miss an excellent learning opportunity if you don't help your child practice making better decisions in the future. After all, you certainly don't want Andrew tormenting Jacob again tomorrow.

In order to arm your child with strategies for peaceful relations in any difficult situation, you'll need to deliberately train good behavior, respect, coping strategies, and conflict-resolution skills. Here's how.

Take Action: Training

First, be sure your kids know that badgering, teasing, shaming, disrespecting, and picking on others are unacceptable—and put a stop to these activities whenever you see them coming from your kids. Make sure they don't catch you "in the wrong" either—end any tendencies you might have to bully others with teasing or sarcastic comments as well. Even what seems to parents as "just having a little fun" can look threatening to a child.

Be deliberate about training on conflict resolution, as well as how to avoid being a victim of bullying. Pick a time when you and your child can calmly talk through the following techniques (Grab Mr. Bear to role-play for young children.):

Rewind and replay. In Andrew's case, you can start by asking, "Next time you feel angry or powerless, what could you do instead?" Then, hold a mini brainstorming session to come up with some workable solutions, including practicing the words to say. You can apply this to a variety of situations, whether real or hypothetical, to help your child navigate the tricky world of peer relations.

Walking away. The easiest way to avoid a bully is to stay out of his path. Practice walking confidently and calmly around the bully and out of the way. For a child engaged in a conflict that's spiraling out of control, this might mean saying, "We'll talk about this more later," and seeking out a quiet place to cool down.

Using "I feel..." statements. A difficult situation or conflict can often benefit from a little understanding. Equip your kids with the ability to use "I feel" statements to describe what they're thinking and then to invite their peers to do the same. In so doing, they'll learn to own their feelings and take responsibility for them—a skill that many adults struggle with (for instance, when we spout an accusatory, "You always..." or, "You never..."). In a disagreement about whose turn it is to use the car this Friday night, for instance, your teen could say, "I feel upset because I have plans and I need the car." Her brother could reply, "I'm angry because I see you using the car all the time without checking with me first." This gives kids an easy way to start a conversation rather than a fistfight. Younger kids arguing about a really cool Lego tower that got knocked down could say, "I feel sad because I was really excited about my tower," or, "I feel mad because you wouldn't let me play, too." While you can't expect this type of maturity to come naturally, you can help your kids develop it with guidance and plenty of patience. With practice, your kids will address conflict with healthy communication rather than a shouting match.

Persistently seeking help. Although in most cases it's important for kids to learn to work out their problems on their own, *Bully* showed us that in cases where safety is in question (both emotional and physical), adults are needed. However, *Bully* also brought up the fact that many adults ignore the problem, feel powerless themselves, or question the seriousness of the situation—and render themselves ineffective. You can train your kids to overcome this at school by playing the part of the tuned-out teacher (again, with Mr. Bear's help if necessary) and coaching your kids to stick it out until they get the attention and help they need.

You can read more about several of these strategies, and learn others, at http://www.kidpower.org/resources/articles/prevent-bullying.html

With these techniques, you'll be empowering your kids to put a stop to their own tendencies toward bullying, giving them tools to respond to other bullies, and preparing them for real-life success.

FAMILY AND CLASS MEETINGS

Getting kids on board with positive conflict-resolution techniques can be a challenge, whether in your family of five or classroom of twenty-five. Jump-start the process by holding regular meetings. Family Meetings and Class Meetings are an excellent tool to facilitate communication, foster a sense of belonging within the group, allow opportunities for kids to make meaningful contributions, and provide a forum for training and problem solving. Here are a few ideas to get you started:

- Assign and rotate official tasks, even if some are made up (meeting leader, keep-on-tasker, timekeeper, note taker, snack maker, snack server, joke teller, etc.).
- The first item on the agenda should be "Compliments and Appreciations," in which everyone says something nice about everyone else (in a family), or the person sitting next to them (in a school classroom).
- Introduce new training topics each week, such as the ones listed above, focusing on one step at a time. Practice the new skills by role-playing.
- Use the Family or Class Meeting as a forum for problem solving. Kids will learn that disagreements can be solved respectfully.
- Keep it short and make it fun! Serve a snack and find a fun activity to wrap up your meeting.

Hold Family and Class Meetings weekly to foster a strong sense of belonging and significance, as well as to create regular training and problem-solving opportunities on issues like bullying and other important topics.

For more information on implementing Class Meetings: Positive Discipline in the Classroom, *by Jane Nelsen, Lynn Lott, and H. Stephen Glenn (Three Rivers Press, 3rd edition, 2000).*

Only practice makes permanent, but soon enough you'll begin to hear playground stories about peaceful resolutions rather than tyranny.

The five steps for a meaningful apology will help you empower your kids as they face high-pressure situations. They'll become accustomed to taking responsibility for their actions; they'll tune in to others' feelings (and their own); and they'll learn peaceful ways to resolve conflict and respectably coexist with their peers. Your kids will be able to deliver a genuine apology and make amends when they've wronged another person. All of this will help keep their own bullying tendencies to a minimum.

If you begin employing these steps and strategies with a young child, you'll be less likely to raise a bully. And even if you start with a teenager—a teenager who might already be known as a bully—you'll see results with persistence and patience. You, and your children, can help turn the tide in school hallways, lunchrooms, playing fields, and beyond. The most important thing is to start now—don't miss a learning opportunity, and don't let bullying behavior go unchecked.

This chapter, like *Bully*, ends with a challenge. Try the five steps in your home this week. Write them on notes and stick them to your mirror or your dashboard to help keep them fresh in your mind. Then, next time you need to step in to an incident your kids can't work out themselves, take them through the process. Even if it seems strange at first, once you start seeing results, you'll be hooked—and so will your children. The more kids are held accountable for their actions, and the more they learn to consider the feelings of others and peacefully resolve conflicts, the less bullying we'll see. Tyler Long's father is right. Ending bullying starts with one: one person, one action—and one meaningful apology.

Girl Talk

Inspiring and Helping Middle-School Girls Through *The Drama Years*

Haley Kilpatrick

Haley Kilpatrick is the founder and executive director of Girl Talk, a national nonprofit organization through which high-school girls mentor middle-school girls, and the author of The Drama Years. *Her difficult middle-school experience inspired her to be a part of the solution and to start Girl Talk in 2002 at the age of fifteen. Today it is an organization that now reaches 40,000 middle-school girls in forty-three states and eight countries and aspires to reach many more.*

Haley knows from both personal experience and ten years in the trenches with today's preteens that the issues these girls face are both challenging and universal. It is this knowledge that inspired Haley to give girls a voice in her book, The Drama Years: Real Girls Talk about Surviving Middle School—Bullies, Brands, Body Image and More, *which serves as a guidebook to help weather these challenging years. The Drama Years is published by Free Press and was released in April 2012.*

Haley has been named one of Glamour *magazine's* "20 Young Women Changing the World Now," *the* Huffington Post's *"Greatest Woman of the Day," and* People *magazine's*

"All-Star Among Us," among many other honors. She has been featured on NBC's The Today Show, *NBC Nightly News,* CNN, HLN, *and* USA TODAY.

Haley enjoys traveling, speaking, volunteering, and inspiring others to discover their passions through community service. She lives in Atlanta, Georgia.

It's definitely not easy to be a middle-school girl today. In the few short years between grade school and high school, girls go through an incredible number of changes, making these the most formative years of their lives.

Throughout elementary school, I loved life! I did well in school, loved to dance, got along with everyone in my class, and spent most of my time with my childhood best friend, Maryashley. Everything changed during sixth grade, when Maryashley's family moved away. I started Girl Talk because sixth, seventh, and eighth grades were all one big rollercoaster. Each day felt like a game of Jenga, and it was exhausting trying to predict when someone would push that final block that would make my world come crashing down.

It wasn't until summer of eighth grade that I met Christie, who was in high school, through my school dance team. Since she was four years older (and captain of our dance team), she was automatically cooler. I respected her and listened to her more than anyone else. When I finally opened up about my fear of being made fun of by my peers, she told me she could relate. She shared that she'd had a really hard time in middle school, too, but she'd gotten through it, and she was certain that I would, too. "Forget about them," she'd say. "Let's go to the mall." I remember thinking to myself: If she thinks I'm cool enough to hang out with, I can't be *that* bad. Christie, who I thought of as an adopted older sister, inspired me to keep going with my head held high. She will never truly know the impact she had on my life at such a critical time.

It was not until my younger sister started middle school that I decided to do something to help make middle school easier for girls. It was my sophomore year of high school, and I wanted to be a part of the solution. I could see my sister was about to go through three tough years, too. While I knew I couldn't save her and her friends from the pain I experienced, I knew I had to tell them they were not alone, just like Christie did for me. *It doesn't have to be this way*, I thought. Just because so many girls are used to being teased, or left out, or aren't sure where to go for help or who to turn to—that doesn't make it okay. Then it hit me: What if I could be a part of the solution now? Maybe I could create a way for other middle-school girls to have the same experience that I did with Christie? A way for middle-school girls to share their experiences openly and honestly, without worrying about being judged? And what if high-school girls led the group? They'd share *their* experiences: what worked for them, what didn't, and what they'd learned. They'd be there for the middle-school girls, to inspire and guide them. And by sharing in this safe space, the middle schoolers would learn to rely on and trust each other, rather than turn on each other. I drafted details for this new idea, named it Girl Talk, and lobbied my school administration for approval. After my incredibly supportive principal signed on, it started soon after. Girl Talk was born.

In the first few meetings, middle-school girls asked me to share what middle school was like for me. Memories came flooding back, some more painful than others. I shared that school became a really dark place after Maryashley moved away. I tried to get closer to some of the girls I'd known since elementary school, girls who had quickly formed our grade's popular group. They made it clear that they did not like me, and I struggled to understand why. I'd head toward an open spot in the lunchroom only to see a girl place her purse down on the empty chair, letting me know that I wasn't welcome at that table. Friday night football games were the worst! After the game, it was heartbreaking to see "my friends" pile into a Suburban for a not-so-discreet sleepover. What was wrong with me? I told the girls how on Mondays, I'd hear about birthday parties over the weekend that I wasn't invited to. Yet, sometimes they'd be nice to me, and I'd think we were friends. The constant back and forth was overwhelming and exhausting. School quickly became a place I dreaded. My grades began to drop because I couldn't focus in class. I was never sure when I was going to be given that look, or I would worry about what was going to happen in the cafeteria, or why the girls around me were passing notes. As I shared, they listened. Together we sat in a circle with a few girls nodding, some raising their hands to share what they were going through, and others quietly sat there with tears rolling down their cheeks. It was a first for all of us—the first time I felt loved and accepted in my old middle school, and for them, it was the first time they truly felt like they were not alone.

At the next meeting, I shared that the roller coaster continued. It was full of the highest of highs (like actually getting invited to a party!) and the lowest of lows (my mom finding out I ate lunch in the restroom all of eighth grade). It was during seventh grade when the bullying got a lot worse. Everyone started to use e-mail and instant messenger, and there was one day I knew I would never forget. I learned just how much words *did* hurt. What made it even worse—they could be spoken, written, and now typed. I told them about the first time I had been hurt online, in hopes that middle-school girls would learn the importance of thinking before they say or do such hurtful things.

I was at home on our family computer, while my parents were out running errands. I signed on to instant messenger and saw that my friend Josh, who was a year ahead of me and felt like an older brother-type I could confide in, was on, too. "How's it going?" he asked. "You looked sad in the hallway yesterday."

"I've had a rough week," I typed. "I just feel like no one likes me here." The popular girls had been seriously harsh lately; I gave him the details of their latest Haley takedown attempts. "I don't know if I want to come back here next year," I typed. I'd hoped he'd say, "Aw, don't let them get you down, you know you're awesome," or something like that, like he normally did.

Instead, he wrote back: "Well, Haley, you *are* really snobby."

What? I was shocked at Josh's response. Stay calm, I told myself. He must be telling you the truth for your own good. "Really?" I wrote back.

"Yeah, people think you're fake," he responded. Suddenly, he sent a flurry of IMs: "You think you're too good for everyone." *Send.* "You should probably go to a different school." *Send.* "In general, you're just an annoying bitch." *Send.*

Each time a message popped up on my screen, I felt my stomach lurch. Tears sprung to my eyes. *This* is what everyone thinks of me?!

I couldn't take it: "Thanks for telling me, Josh," I typed, and then signed off. I was in shock.

Actually, Josh hadn't written that at all. I found out later that he'd been swimming in his pool—not sitting at his computer—the whole time. So who was pretending to be Josh? Three of the popular girls who taunted me almost every day—the very same girls I was confiding to him about. They happened to be at Josh's house and decided to bait me anonymously. It was devastating. And girls go through this kind of cyberbullying every day. That meeting, we took a pledge to T.H.I.N.K. before we speak, write, or type. T.H.I.N.K. was an acronym to remind us to ask ourselves, is what we are saying True, Helpful, Important, Necessary, and Kind. The girls made posters and hung them around the school to inspire everyone to do the same. It was in that meeting that I truly understood how much high-school girls could help make middle school a more inspiring time in girls' lives. These girls felt empowered to make a difference and desperately wanted to band together to ditch the drama.

Today, Girl Talk's foundation is the same as it was ten years ago. High-school girls lead middle-school girls in weekly discussion groups about everything from body image to self-respect; from how to deal with mean girls and bullying to the importance of being kind; from guys and dating to getting along with your parents. Our organization offers the program for free, trains the leaders, and provides themed curricula for each meeting. The middle-school girls get instant adopted big sisters and a safe place to talk openly. The high-school girls become real-life role models, and are expected to act accordingly. And we emphasize volunteering and service throughout each chapter's community, so every girl involved comes away with greater compassion and perspective on the world around her.

It's a simple idea, but it works. Most of the girls involved—83 percent—become Girl Talk leaders when they get to high school. And we've found that if girls feel more cared for emotionally, they'll improve in the classroom (as I instinctively knew in sixth grade when *my* grades dropped, thanks to my social situation): We found a 14 percent improvement in Girl Talk participants' math grades and a 24 percent improvement in language arts since they started the program. And of course we've seen positive effects that can't be measured; our Girl Talk girls and leaders report feeling more confident, kinder to others, and more sure of themselves.

After ten years of running Girl Talk and traveling around the country speaking to groups of middle-school girls, I can't tell you how many times a parent, teacher, coach, or counselor has asked for Girl Talk's help. Parents, especially, constantly come to us, saying, "We don't know what to do or say about situation X, Y, or Z—how can we help our girl get through this?"

That's why I wrote *The Drama Years* (Free Press, 2012). I wanted to share what we've learned and to shed some light on these key years. After three years of research and more than two thousand hours of interviews, we share the information you need to help the middle-school girl in your life grow up healthy, happy, and whole. It's an accessible and comprehensive guide to the issues middle-school girls face, filled with the voices of girls themselves. I'd like to share a modified excerpt from the introduction in *The Drama Years* that sheds light on what girls are going through.

This information couldn't be more vital. Research has shown that the period between sixth and eighth grades is one of the most critical times in a young person's development: The decisions girls make during these years, and the paths they start to walk down, directly affect and inform who they will become. These are also the years in which peers replace parents and other adults as major influencers. This means that it's crucial for parents and other adults who work with middle-school girls to understand the situations that will inevitably arise in girls' lives, and to hear, direct from the source, how girls want the adults around them to handle these changes.

It is no secret that girls today are facing many issues. We've learned the main challenges are around self-awareness (finding out who she is); stress; name brands, materialism, and competition; body image and body awareness; dealing with friendships, including mean girls, frenemies, and bullying; guys and relationships; dealing with parents and boundaries; and serious topics like family drama, depression, and self-harm.

There's the social minefield: Their list of friends is changing on a daily basis. Groups form and turn on each other; classmates whisper about who's saying what to whom; childhood friends tell trusted secrets; and just deciding where to sit in the lunchroom can be a daily struggle. Then there's the biological wave of changes—all the growth spurts, new curves and new hormones—and suddenly, there are more grown-up things to worry about: dealing with their first real crush or relationship; negotiating how they feel about their bodies and their appearance. And there's the personality crisis: they want to be themselves (although, who is that, anyway?), but they desperately need to fit in with their friends and classmates. All the while, they're constantly bombarded by contradictory and utterly confusing messages from society and the media. And it happens so quickly. To parents and girls, it often feels like the transition from elementary school to middle school is much more than a three-month summer break; it might as well be years. Because suddenly, everything changes, and as part of the natural growing-up process, parents aren't around as much as they were in elementary school. For a middle-school girl, it can feel groundless: your body is changing, you're not as cute anymore, and your teachers aren't so empathetic. All of a sudden, you're expected to grow up—and fast.

Today, girls face even more challenges. More than ever, they feel they must be "perfect"—in school, in sports, in other after-school activities, at home. And because of this increasing pressure, more and more girls report feeling severely stressed out, negatively affecting both their emotional and physical health. All while their drive for perfection has dovetailed with our culture's increasing emphasis on looks, resulting in the pressure to meet the unreasonable standard of beauty and thinness to be pretty, to stay in their friends' good graces and to get boys' attention.

But the biggest shift in the world of middle-school girls is undeniably technological. Girls in sixth through eighth grade today live in a different world than any previous generation of girls. They are digital natives who have grown up in the new world of cell phones, video chat, instant messaging, texting, and Facebook. It's now effortless to anonymously bully someone else over IM, to create a fake social-networking account to use against someone, to harass another person through a text message. After all, girls shared that it is easier to say hurtful things when it is not face-to-face. All of this can be utterly exhausting!

While it is easier to talk about all of these problems, I feel it is most important to talk about what we can do to help. We have learned that the dynamic of the parent/daughter relationship changes at middle school and adults can feel helpless, and I want to assure you that this is normal. One minute she's laughing and hugging you and the next she's rolling her eyes and asking you to pick her up around the corner so her friends don't see you.

Middle-school girls are truly in the middle; they have one foot in the kid world and one foot in the adult world. They still need you as parents, but they also need you to give them space to start growing up.

We spent thousands of hours interviewing girls, and they repeatedly told us they crave your support. I know most experts would say communication is most important, and while I agree that it is beyond important, I want to tell parents that the key thing you can give your daughter is your presence, being there both physically and emotionally. Show her that you are one of the few things that are *not* changing in her life.

We learned that there are several signs that your child is suffering from either social pressure or an unhealthy self-image. Girls shared with us that when they are struggling, they are more likely to give short responses, they are easily frustrated, they have a negative attitude, and they are more likely to withdraw socially. Girls shared they want you to have the tough conversations with them to open the line of communication with you. Talk about boys and dating, bullying, underage drinking, and many other topics (yes, even if it is awkward!). That way when they are faced with these pressures, they know they can come to you.

Remember this is the time when girls are beginning to develop into adults. They are going to make mistakes. Know it is not a parent's job to prevent their children from ever feeling disappointment or pain. Aside from bullying, you do not want to step into your daughter's drama because you send a message that you are going to "save" her or that you believe she can't handle it on her own. If you can visualize your daughter walking on a tightrope, you should be at the bottom cheering her on; if she falls into the net you want to encourage her to get back up and try again, but you can't walk that tightrope for her. The falling down and the getting back up help your daughter to grow. Girls say they still need you as adults, but they also need their space to grow.

We have learned that the three main pressures girls feel today are around bullying—physical, emotional, and cyberbullying; body image and how others perceive them; and brand consciousness, who has what and how that affects their lives. We know bullying is an epidemic. It is all of the things an adult experienced, except today it doesn't end when students leave school. Digital drama is hard to escape, and it is 24/7. Girls are bullying each other through texts, pictures, Facebook, Twitter, and many other means. Girls being bullied can't seem to catch a break. As for girls who watch reality television, it is no wonder they accept more drama in their lives and have a skewed definition of friendship. These girls have grown up watching women be paid to tear each other down. That kind of television doesn't make it easier to raise kind, confident girls. A recent MTV/AP poll found that 56 percent of people ages fourteen to twenty-four have experienced some form of digital abuse. We know a girl's body image is so wrapped up in her self-esteem. We've learned that tween girls don't understand self-esteem; they define it as how others see them instead of how they see themselves. Adults need to model good behavior whether you think they are watching you or not—I promise you they are. These are also the years where girls simply want to blend in, and they are going to materialistic extremes to not be the subject of ridicule. As backward as it may seem, we learned having the "it" things merely prevents the spotlight from being on her. In short, her materialistic desires are more about blending in than standing out.

There are three things you can incorporate into their lives that don't require too much time or a lot of money to help with the three main challenges they face (and many others, too). They help keep her mind off the drama and also serve as a source of confidence and validation. Each of these is invaluable, but when they're used in tandem, they can be transformative. How do I know this? I'm not an adolescent psychologist, and I can't point to a heap of academic studies as evidence. What I do know is that these three things worked in my own life and in the lives of so many girls I've grown to know over the past ten years. These things are an anchor activity, a helping hand, and an adopted older sister.

An Anchor Activity This could be a sport, a musical instrument, theater, art classes, babysitting, a school club, environmental activism, etc. As long as it's something she actively enjoys, that she can throw herself into; that keeps her engaged; that takes place outside of school, so she can be free from the social pressures of school; and that seems to fulfill her creatively, intellectually, socially—some kind of stimulation.

A Helping Hand A chance to be a part of something larger than herself, to connect to a larger world, to instill gratitude for what she has, and allow her to see the reality of others' lives. This could be a weekly or monthly volunteer commitment, but the emotional gains that volunteering offers are so much deeper if it's a regular priority in her life—not just a one-time Saturday afternoon activity.

An Adopted Older Sister A positive role model your middle-school girl can look up to. Someone who's just been in your girl's shoes and can both relate to her, so she doesn't feel as alone, and can advise her on how to handle whatever she's going through. When each of these is a part of her life, she has an outlet to keep her mind off the ups and downs of middle school; she has an opportunity to be of service, to give her perspective about what's really drama and what's not; and she has someone to decipher and decode her experiences, to let her know that she's not alone.

I've dedicated my life to being a part of the solution. I remember my middle-school experience all too well, and I see firsthand, every day, how tough today's middle-school world can be. Guiding you—parents, teachers, school counselors, and other mentors of middle-school girls—through these tricky waters is what my life is all about. I am committed to creating ways to help middle-school girls deal with these issues and to grow into confident, kind, and humble women who will model this behavior to their children and beyond. Together we can take a stand and help build awareness about the long-term effects of all kinds of bullying. It is my hope that we will all continue to shed light on this epidemic and that bullying will become an unacceptable behavior in our schools, homes, and workplaces. For more information about Girl Talk or *The Drama Years*, please visit http://www.desiretoinspire.org

PART 5

David and Tina Long

David and Tina Long's Story

"From the day Tyler was born, I was probably the proudest dad in the world," said David Long. "Because he was the firstborn. He was the first son. He always had that laugh about him, I don't know, it was infectious, it caught you."

After years of relentless bullying, on October 17, 2009, Tyler Long died by suicide. David, a retired military service member, and his wife, Tina, a registered nurse, mourned the loss of their son, whom they tried to protect. Like Alex, Tyler had Asperger's Syndrome, and the Longs took to task the school system that failed him so miserably. Tyler's death sparked heated debate in the community—playing out in public forums throughout Chatsworth, Georgia, which was being forced to face its bullying demons.

"Tyler wasn't the most athletic," David said. "When he was in PE, he was always the last one to be [chosen]. Nobody would be on his team, because they said he was a geek and a fag and they didn't want to play with him. And it took a toll on him early in middle school. To where he, he cried, and then it got to the point where he didn't cry anymore. And that's when it became difficult to truly understand what he was going through."

Lee Hirsch and Cynthia Lowen met the Longs a few weeks after Tyler had taken his own life. David and Tina were holding a town-hall meeting to discuss bullying in their community, and the filmmakers were stunned by the Longs' commitment to engage kids, parents, community leaders, and educators on how to make a difference in Murray County's schools. Unfortunately, the school district declined to participate in the meeting, but the Longs were undeterred, and Hirsch and Lowen continued to follow their fight to ensure that no other child would have to endure the torment that Tyler suffered.

Bullying's Special Problem

James Wendorf

James H. Wendorf is executive director of the National Center for Learning Disabilities (NCLD), which seeks to ensure success for all individuals with learning disabilities in school, at work, and in life. He directs NCLD's efforts to connect parents with resources, guidance, and support; deliver evidence-based tools, resources, and professional development to educators; and develop policies and engage advocates to strengthen educational rights and opportunities.

For the past two decades, Mr. Wendorf has worked in the not-for-profit sector to build national and international partnerships supporting learning and literacy programs. Prior to joining NCLD in 1999, Mr. Wendorf served as vice president and chief operating officer of Reading Is Fundamental, Inc., the nation's largest nonprofit children's literacy organization, based in Washington, DC.

Mr. Wendorf currently serves on the advisory board of the National Center on Educational Outcomes (University of Minnesota), the National Association for the Education of African American Children with Learning Disabilities, the Education Policy and Leadership Center (Southern Methodist University) and previously with a variety of civic and education organizations. He recently served as vice chair of the congressionally authorized Advisory Commission on Accessible Instructional Materials in Postsecondary Education for Students with Disabilities.

Bullying is a very important issue for me and all of us at the National Center for Learning Disabilities (NCLD). What I know is this: Bullying is occurring in epidemic proportions across the country, but for students with learning disabilities and other disabilities, bullying is a pandemic. It occurs every day, with 60 percent of students with special needs being bullied as compared with 25 percent of all students—and there are some studies that put this percentage even higher.

For many of us, bullying hits home. While I never experienced it, my older daughter did. Throughout sixth grade she was hounded by other girls, and then they managed to enlist a student teacher in their quest to isolate and bully her. The classroom teacher and principal paid lip service but did nothing. The school year ended and it was over. But not forgotten.

Given how pervasive the problem is and how serious the consequences of bullying are, it is imperative that organizations—not just individuals—find a way to take action. We need to work together to act, to prevent bullying before it starts, and to address it when it occurs. This is what led to my decision for NCLD to partner with the remarkable documentary film *Bully* and to become a lead supporter of this important cause.

Thanks to a generous grant, NCLD has been able to provide financial support to The Bully Project, and we have become involved in substantial ways. We've worked with The Bully Project to promote the film, sending hundreds of people to opening weekend in New York and Los Angeles. We are supporting the Safe Schools Improvement Act, which for the first time establishes a federal definition of bullying and protects all students nationwide, including students with disabilities and other recognized protected classes such as religion and national origin. We are leading a special-needs task force that consists of NCLD, Autism Speaks, PACER'S National Bullying Prevention Center, and AbilityPath, which is working hard to stop the bullying of young people with disabilities. Working together, this task force has created a toolkit for parents, educators, and students to deal with the bullying of this special population. In just the first four weeks since its release, more than fourteen thousand people have accessed these helpful resources.

I am proud that NCLD has been able to step up in this way, working with Lee Hirsch and his team. And we've learned a lot from doing so. I've been overwhelmed by the intensity of people's responses to both the film and the issue of bullying. People are passionate about this. This is a film and an issue that people want to and *need* to talk about in order to understand, experience, and take action.

The effects of bullying stay with people for a long time. I've seen the hundreds of stories we've received from all over the country. One woman recalls, "I am twenty-seven years old and I can still remember the abuse and the words from my so-called friends." She is not the only one. A mother notes, "My daughter is twenty years old and I consider it a miracle she is alive today. She has a severe learning disability . . . In public school she was bullied, isolated and alone. . . . To this day I do not know how she or my family survived. I can only say that the scars are there and have not healed."

There are many stories like this on our website, http://www. LD.org. But what I've learned is that as much as people still feel the pain of being bullied in their past, they want to take action to stop it from affecting their children's future. To support these efforts, NCLD has set up discussions with expert panelists and audiences who share information, support each other, and identify ways to take action, individually and together. We've connected with nearly seven hundred independent schools, public schools, learning clinics, and parent groups around the country and have spoken with many people about how they're trying to combat bullying. Some schools have taken whole grades of students to the theater to see

Bully. Others have created special days in their school with activities and classes for students to discuss these important issues in a safe environment.

But what seems to be a constant is that everyone who sees this film wants to share it with others. I was in attendance at a screening of *Bully* we organized in Chicago at a conference of the Learning Disabilities Association of America. After viewing the film, one conference member stated, "I applaud you for this movie and I give you my heart and soul, and I will tell you that I will notify every employer, every school board around. I also run an ADHD and LD clinic; I teach about bullying in my office. You have my word that I will work hard for this." It is clear to me—people want to get involved.

One of the unspoken themes of *Bully* is the impact bullying has on children with special needs. Students with disabilities are disproportionately affected, and so I believe it is our duty to take disproportionate action to stop bullying. Together we can create a bully-free world.

Teaching to End Bullying

Michael Mulgrew, president, United Federation of Teachers

Michael Mulgrew became the fifth president of the United Federation of Teachers (UFT) in August 2009 and was elected to a full term by the UFT membership in April 2010.

As UFT president, Michael has advanced the union's commitment to transforming education in New York City and to elevating the role of parents and the community in governing our schools. Building strong alliances and creating opportunities for collaboration with parent, civic, and community groups has become a hallmark of Michael's presidency. A staunch advocate for equality in education and fairness for all working families, Michael led advocacy campaigns for educational equity, for transparency and oversight in school governance as well as for jobs and city services. His persuasive negotiation skills have helped avert teacher layoffs and bolster resources targeted to struggling schools. In addition to his UFT responsibilities, Michael is a vice president of the American Federation of Teachers (AFT) and an executive board member of the New York State United Teachers (NYSUT). Michael also sits on the boards of the Council for Unity, City University of New York (CUNY)'s Joseph S. Murphy Center for Labor, Community & Policy Studies, and New Visions for Public

Schools. He has received numerous labor, education, and public service honors including the 2011 NAACP Benjamin L. Hooks "Keeper of the Flame" award.

Michael began teaching as a substitute at South Richmond High School while volunteering on weekends at CUNY teaching creative writing to at-risk students. He then spent twelve years teaching at-risk students at Brooklyn's William E. Grady High School, where he also served as the school's chapter leader from 1999 to 2004.

Before being elected president of the UFT, he served as vice president for Career & Technical Education (CTE) high schools and later chief operating officer of the union, which represents 200,000 teachers, guidance counselors, paraprofessionals, and other personnel in New York City's public schools, along with nurses and home day care providers.

A Staten Island native, Michael attended CUNY's College of Staten Island and has degrees in English literature and special education.

I don't like bullies. Growing up, I was the third of four kids in my family, so maybe that has something to do with it.

When I began teaching at William Grady Career and Technical Education High School in Brooklyn, I discovered early on that bullies tend to target kids who are special-needs students. So I paired up the kids from my class—those who were identified as at risk of academic failure—with the special-needs students who were being picked on in the school. I would say to my students, "We're bringing this student into our class, and we're all going to work with him." I would literally go around the school and see which kids were being bullied and picked on—and then brought them into my class and created this kind of support for them.

I saw a lot of kids benefit from this buddy system. The kids who were struggling learned how to watch out for others. It really broke down barriers. The kids who are bullies, they don't see the other child as a real person; they see only their own anger and frustration. But once they get to know the other kid and see him or her as a person, they start to empathize.

In a short span of time, the guidance counselors and social workers began to work with our class. They knew that students who were transferred into the school could be potential targets of bullying, and my classes became known for being open and safe for all.

If you stand up to bullying and let kids know they can't do that, you will see it diminish. Here's what it comes down to: The child who is a bully is at risk, and the child being bullied is at risk, both oftentimes due to a lack of self-esteem. So how do we take these two and use them to help each other?

Now as president of the teachers' union in New York City, I have embraced the issue, and our union has launched a campaign to combat the problem. It's called the Be BRAVE Against Bullying campaign, and it provides educators with resources so they can be proactive in confronting and stopping bullying. It includes an after-school hotline for students to call Monday through Friday; posters and stickers for teachers to use so that students can identify visible allies in their school; and workshops for teachers and parents throughout the school year on the issue. For more information and to view some of the resources, go to http://www.uft.org/brave

The challenge now is to make sure that this campaign reaches every school in New York City. It comes down to changing the culture in school buildings and setting the tone. We need a combined effort of all stakeholders—parents, educators, administrators, and elected officials. Where we've worked together, it's been successful.

Bottom line: bullying hurts school communities. That's why as a union, we are putting time, energy, and resources into the issue and working with partners to make a positive difference.

Bully—A Catalyst for Changing Our Culture

Randi Weingarten, president, American Federation of Teachers

Randi Weingarten is president of the 1.5 million-member American Federation of Teachers, AFL-CIO, which represents teachers; paraprofessionals and school-related personnel; higher-education faculty and staff; nurses and other health-care professionals; local, state, and federal employees; and early-childhood educators. She was elected in July 2008, following eleven years of service as an AFT vice president. Weingarten served for twelve years as president of the United Federation of Teachers, representing approximately 200,000 nonsupervisory educators in the New York City public school system, as well as home child care providers and other workers in health, law, and education.

As AFT president, Weingarten has launched major efforts to place educational innovation high on the nation's agenda. She is known as a reform-minded leader who has demonstrated her commitment to improving schools, hospitals, and public institutions for children, families, and their communities. She has fought to make sure teachers and school support personnel are treated with respect and dignity, have a voice in the education of their students, and are given the support and resources they need to succeed in the classroom.

The AFT agenda fights against finger-pointing and calls for a continued investment in education. It also highlights the work that teachers, nurses, and public employees do every day to make a difference in the lives of others.

Weingarten holds degrees from Cornell University's School of Industrial and Labor Relations and the Cardozo School of Law.

Bullying in all its forms is reprehensible. Over the last few years, it has become clear that this harmful behavior is pervasive in America's schools. While bullying has always occurred in schools, today we have a deeper understanding of the lasting damage bullying inflicts on children and how it impacts the rest of their lives.

Every seven minutes, a child in the United States is bullied, according to the Justice Department. Every day in America, tens of thousands of kids stay home from school because they fear being bullied, according to the National Association of School Psychologists. As the stories in the documentary *Bully* show us, some of the kids who are bullied ultimately come to see suicide as the only way to escape those who torment them. It's up to us as adults to lead on this issue and to put a stop to bullying.

The movie *Bully* has significantly advanced efforts to raise our national awareness that bullying is not right. It graphically shows that kids harassing other kids can have tragic consequences, and it highlights the series of actions Americans must take to end bullying in our schools. We must empower those who have been bullied by listening to them and hearing their anguish, so they know they are not alone. We must find ways to educate the people who bully others, so that they can know the harm their behavior causes and understand it is wrong. We must intervene to protect kids who have been bullied—and any action we take must be designed so it does not wrong them again. If we can do those things and others, we will have moved a great distance toward our goal of changing the culture of our schools to make them places where bullying is not tolerated and students can feel safe and thrive without fear of taunts, shame, or humiliation.

One of the most powerful messages Lee Hirsch's film drives home is the impact of simply sharing our stories and speaking out. Our voice is our strongest tool to combat bullying. The real force of this documentary about the cruelty that kids sometimes inflict on one another is that these stories can become a catalyst that helps drive the emergence of a new culture that rejects bullying and demands a different set of behaviors.

People are moved when we tell our stories and share our common experiences. I will never forget the reaction after I spoke publicly many years ago about being a lesbian. Several young people—mainly eighteen- and nineteen-year-olds—came up to me afterward. They hugged me and held my wrists and said, "Thank you for telling your story." I was in my forties at the time, and I felt old in this crowd. But these teenagers were hungry to hear someone talk about what it means to be bullied, or to be frightened, or to be out. It gave them courage to be who they were. Sharing our stories and our experiences makes these kinds of issues real for people. It says it is okay to be different. That is an incredibly powerful statement for kids to hear. It may be just words. But as we know, and as *Bully* clearly illustrates, words can drag kids down or build them up.

This film did not originate the campaign against bullying in our schools. At the American Federation of Teachers, we started our own bullying prevention program at the beginning of 2011. We call it "See a Bully—Stop a Bully," and it aims to both increase awareness of the problem and offer educators, students, and parents the tools to respond and create safe and supportive schools. The AFT program has assembled an array of bullying prevention materials that are available at http://www.aft.org/bullying. We have raised awareness of the problem by distributing hundreds of thousands of our blue wristbands imprinted with the "See a Bully—Stop a Bully" slogan to teachers, staff, and students in schools across the nation. In addition to simply focusing attention on the bullying problem, the wristbands are a sign to children who are being bullied that they have friends they can turn to for help—they have people at school they can trust. Anyone can order the wristbands through a link at http://www.aft.org/bullying

The effort against bullying extends beyond the schoolhouse. The Safe Schools Improvement Act, which would require schools to have codes of conduct that prohibit bullying and harassment, is currently pending in Congress. The bill also provides for training that would help school staff respond to and prevent bullying. Since the release of the *Bully* documentary, the White House has endorsed this legislation. And laws addressing bullying are on the books in forty-nine of the fifty states and the District of Columbia. It is important to remember that despite all these laws, we cannot mandate that people treat one another properly or that children be nice. The laws help address the problem; it's up to us to respond and create loving and supportive communities.

What *Bully* brings to this fight is an energy that can reinvigorate all of our efforts. In an ideal world, we would focus the power of this film on increasing our understanding of the problem and what we need to do differently to solve it. Many of the tactics against bullying are simple, commonsense. We must be sure that all educators and school staff are adequately trained to recognize bullying and respond to it. That training should include administrators and all adults who come in contact with students. In our schools, the best approach to this problem—the one most likely to succeed in putting an end to bullying—is a holistic response that creates a learning environment where kids and adults, alike, can feel safe, secure, and respected.

The response to bullying cannot be left to individuals on their own. We must address it in our schools and across our communities. This is because bullying is so often a group offense, and those on the receiving end of this harmful behavior often feel alone, without allies. Everyone—the bullies and the bullied, their parents and siblings, their classmates and educators—must be part of the conversation. This is a problem that must be taken seriously by all. When kids take it seriously, those who are targeted will know they are not alone. When principals take it seriously, parents will see that and feel more confident about the safety of their children. When teachers and staff take it seriously, kids who are bullied will understand that they have adult allies who will support them in the classroom, in the hallway, in the cafeteria, on the playground, and on the school bus.

The overriding goal of our efforts must be to change the entire school and community culture that categorizes bullying as simply a rite of passage—that sees it as a natural part of the journey from childhood to adolescence to young adulthood. This view holds that bullying is just something kids have to get through and that getting through it somehow helps them develop and mature. In many schools, that culture is deeply embedded—but it has to stop, period. There is nothing natural about terrifying a child, or about one kid assaulting another simply for the sport of it, or about spreading vicious falsehoods about a teenager through the lunch line at school or across the digital channels of the Internet. We can no longer excuse bullying by saying that "boys will be boys" or "kids will be kids." We must create a different environment in our schools. They absolutely must be places where the safety of all children is the norm and where bullying is understood by all to be outside the boundaries of acceptable behavior.

Changing the culture and environment of our schools starts with the leadership in each building. Leadership is a resource that is not controlled by budgets—it does not depend on dollars. Of course there must be other resources, such as counselors, school nurses, social workers, and training. But leadership is absolutely essential. The principal and assistant principals set the tone in each school, which determines how teachers, paraprofessionals, and support staff see the bullying problem and how they understand their roles in intervening and responding to it. And the top administrators for the school district set the priorities and shape the system-wide environment and culture. Parents and the kids themselves are also necessary members of the partnership to end bullying; changing our attitudes about bullying will not happen without them.

In the *Bully* movie, considerable attention is devoted to the relationship between the school and the parents of kids who have been bullied. This is entirely appropriate. It is the parents of the bullied students who often find themselves pressing school leaders for an appropriate response. We must provide parents with the tools and resources they need to become effective advocates for their children. And the school community must listen to parents' concerns, take them seriously, and implement the interventions necessary to keep our kids safe.

The assistant principal at the Sioux City, Iowa, middle school that Alex attended has become one of the takeaway images of the film. I believe this assistant principal was trying to do the right thing—but over and over again, she failed. Why? It is because she did not know what the right thing was. Her understanding of bullying seemed trapped in the old culture, where bullying remains a rite of childhood passage. It is a culture that expects the target of physical assault and verbal taunts to shake hands with the bully and be "friends" with his or her tormenter. And it is a culture in which the adults who intervene too often bring about consequences that impose a penalty on the child who already has suffered at the hands of the bully. This kind of intervention can take many forms. It may be the forced reconciliation with the bully, or requiring the bullied child to change buses to avoid those who have harassed him, or moving the targeted student to a different classroom or a new school while the bullies are allowed to continue in their established routines. These are just a few of the "solutions" that require the child who has behaved properly to change or move or adapt. This approach simply is not fair, and without a doubt, the children who have been bullied see and understand and *feel* the injustice of it.

Alex's plight as the target of constant harassment on the ride to and from school every day reminded me of another story about bullying on the school bus. This is a story with a very different ending because at least one adult stood up to do the right thing.

When West Virginia fourth-grader Chancellor Coger had a bully problem, his school-bus driver, Lester Lemasters, came to the rescue. "My bus driver saved my life," Chancellor wrote in an essay nominating Lemasters for a Bus-Driver-of-the-Year award. The essay told of how a bigger kid punched Chancellor in the stomach every day when they got off the bus together at the same stop. His mother and school officials tried to stop the bullying, but nothing worked.

Then Lemasters stepped in with what the harassed youngster called "a brilliant plan." When he drove to the end of the street to turn around, he stopped there to let Chancellor off—before pulling down to the regular stop, where he dropped off the bully. By finding a way to keep the two boys separated once they left the bus, Lemasters solved the problem. In 2011, the bus driver was recognized with an AFT Everyday Hero award. What a contrast with what we see in *Bully* of Alex's experience on the school bus.

In the end, the kids being bullied and their parents want the same things from the school community. They want to know the safety of all children is a priority for school officials—and for all the adults at school. They want to feel listened to when they bring bullying concerns to the attention of principals and teachers. These are not easy conversations for either child or parent. Kids come to them scared and hoping for an ally against the bullying that they almost always have faced alone until then, that has defined them among their classmates in a way they do not want, and has undermined their own sense of identity and self-worth. What they need is for the grown-ups to respond and to act like adults. These kids need to feel that the leaders of their school take their problem seriously. They need to hear what the principals and the teachers are going to do to help them. And because they probably have been disappointed before, they need to see those adults follow through and take action. To make this possible, the adults at school—teachers, staff, and others—must be assured that they will not face discipline or retaliation when they intervene to stop bullying. This is crucial because as the movie *Bully* shows and experience confirms, there are still school systems where officials are not pre-pared to respond to bullying—and where some prefer to pretend the problem does not exist.

When parents come to school to talk about bullying, they often are angry, upset over the treatment of their child. And, like their kids, parents can come to the principal's office feeling apprehensive. Just like their kids, parents want the principal to show them that he or she cares. They want the principal to listen—really listen—and hear the concerns and fears they have for their child. If school officials brush parents' concerns aside as though they are of no consequence, this treatment will only feed the frustration parents already feel at having to come to school to get someone to notice that their child is being harassed.

Obviously, parents also want teachers and staff to hear and address their concerns. *Bully* probably has been something of a reality check for many classroom teachers. Some teachers who see the film find themselves wondering if they have missed bullying in their classrooms and hallways: Have kids suffered because they didn't notice? Is this behavior happening in their school? The fact that those questions are being asked and that educators are hav-ing ongoing conversations about the answers is another example of how the power of this documentary extends far beyond the individual stories it tells. It is generating important discussions within our schools and across our communities, discussions that are essential to establishing the new culture of caring and safety for all kids in our schools.

There is another issue involving teachers and staff that is not part of the stories in *Bully*, but it is something that anyone who speaks for teachers must acknowledge and address. Occasionally, not very often, allegations come to light that teachers themselves have bullied or harassed their own students. There can be no excuse or justification for such behavior. In the rare cases that allegations of this sort have been substantiated, the American Federation of Teachers has condemned such actions. Any incident of bullying is unacceptable. As a teachers union, the American Federation of

Teachers supports the highest standards of professional conduct, character, and accountability to ensure that the learning environment is safe and secure. Students must be able to trust their teachers and other school employees to refrain from any conduct that would violate those standards. Bullying by anyone, anywhere, under any circumstances is hurtful, and as we have learned on too many occasions over recent years, it can be deadly. Parents entrust their children to educators not just to teach them academic subjects, but also to help them know right from wrong. Taunting and humiliating students are wrong—no matter whether the source is a classmate or the teacher at the front of the classroom.

The American Federation of Teachers is deeply committed to ending the culture of bullying in our schools and communities. There never has been and never will be an acceptable reason to bully a child. All of us who firmly believe this owe a great debt to Lee Hirsch and his team for having the courage and commitment to make *Bully*. It is one of the most important movies in recent years. Audiences—including parents and their children, teachers and other educators, and school administrators and staff—should continue to see it for years to come. The lessons it teaches will not grow old.

PART 6

Kirk and
Laura Smalley

Kirk and Laura Smalley's Story

"We'd go and work on our clubhouse," said Trey, Ty Field-Smalley's best friend. "It's way back out in the woods and no one but me and Ty knows where it is. We would just entertain ourselves for about five hours, it would feel like thirty minutes. Just hanging out, having a good time. Ty was just the coolest kid I knew.

"Even when people would bully him, I'd get so angry, and I could have hurt those kids so badly that done something to him," Trey continued. "Like, they'll push him down, and say, 'Shut up, spaz,' or throw him into a locker, or shove him into one. And I'd just go to take off after them and he'd be, like, 'Trey, it isn't worth it, be better than them, it's all right,' and he'd walk off with a smile. And I don't know how he could do it. He was way stronger than I was."

But at age eleven, after being bullied repeatedly, Ty took his own life.

Lee Hirsch and Cynthia Lowen met Ty's parents, Kirk and Laura Smalley, in the spring of 2010, at the tail end of that long school year, just days after their son had passed away. In the midst of mourning such a profound loss, they were struck by the Smalleys' determination to transform this tragedy into change. Within just a few months, Stand for the Silent was launched by a group of upward bound students, aiming both to inspire young people to stand up for those who are bullied and to cherish their own self-worth. Today, through Stand for the Silent, Kirk and Laura have reached more than half a million.

"I'll fight bullying wherever it's found. Schools. Workplace," vowed Kirk Smaley. "I'm not going to quit until bullying does."

Bullying

U.S. Congressman Mike Honda

U.S. Congressman Mike Honda has represented the 15th Congressional District of Silicon Valley, California, in the U.S. House of Representatives for over a decade. Prior to being elected to Congress in 2001, where he serves as the founding Chair of the Congressional Anti-Bullying Caucus, his career as an educator for over thirty years included serving schools in El Salvador through the Peace Corps, being a science teacher, serving as a principal at two public schools, and conducting educational research at Stanford University.

Along with serving as a senior member of the powerful House Budget Committee and House Appropriations Committee, Representative Honda is the Chair Emeritus of the Congressional Asian Pacific American Caucus after having served as Chair for an unprecedented seven years. He coordinates with his colleagues in the Congressional Black Caucus and the Congressional Hispanic Caucus, known as the Tri-Caucus, to champion the causes of underrepresented communities by promoting social justice, racial tolerance, and civil rights. Congressman Honda is also the original author of the landmark Commission on Equity and Excellence in Education, now housed within the Department of Education.

Congressman Honda also serves as vice chair of the LGBT Equality Caucus; Immigration Taskforce Chair and Appropriations Taskforce Chair of the Congressional Asian

Pacific American Caucus; and vice chair of the Democratic National Committee, where his priority is to make sure that the DNC, state, and local Democratic parties/bodies are more reflective of America. Congressman Honda has dedicated his life to public service and has been lauded for his work on education, civil rights, immigration, transportation, technology, and Asian American and Pacific Islander issues.

My experience with bullying began with a presidential order.

At the height of World War II, on February 19, 1942, President Franklin D. Roosevelt signed Executive Order 9066, incarcerating over 120,000 Japanese Americans behind barbed wire, labeling us as "enemy aliens" just because of our heritage or how we looked. My family was hauled to Merced Assembly Center in California and then imprisoned behind barbed wire at the Amache internment camp in southeast Colorado.

I was less than a year old.

Over the next four years, my family and I were in and out of Amache, even as my father, Byron, answered his nation's call for servicemen who could read and write Japanese by serving with distinction in the U.S. Military Intelligence Service. He was recently awarded a posthumous Congressional Gold Medal for his service.

Sadly, the treacherous government action to intern Japanese Americans spread fear and intolerance far beyond the wire and towers of the camps. After the war, my family and I found ourselves in Heights Park, Chicago, and eventually returned to California where we were strawberry sharecroppers in San José's Blossom Valley. In my early years of public school, being called a "Jap" was a common thing, and I was often confronted and insulted because of my appearance. On too many occasions, the parents of my classmates encouraged the insults due to the racist tensions that continued to exist after the war.

Making my way through school while experiencing bullying

was difficult, to say the least. I struggled as a student. I was shy to speak up and lacked self-esteem. I struggled to understand why I felt this way and became internally oppressed, struggling to understand why I was targeted for being Japanese American. Over time, my father taught me a few powerful and liberating truths: Japanese Americans had been treated unjustly—bullied by their government—because of "war hysteria, racial prejudice, and a failure of political leadership" at the highest levels of government. He helped me to understand that our nation's founding principles meant that we all truly belonged in America, regardless of race, gender, ethnicity, ability, sexual orientation, political philosophy, or age.

My father's lessons changed my heart and mind and helped me to understand that power—whether used by governments or individuals—can be very dangerous when not used for good. This understanding of empowerment helped me to do better in school, to join the Peace Corps, to become a schoolteacher, to serve my community, to fight for the voices of the underserved and under-represented to be heard at the highest levels of American society. This journey, in 2001, brought me to the United States Congress.

In the seventy years since internment, our nation has made leaps and bounds in reparations for the internment and ostracizing of individuals of Japanese descent. Today, however, America is threatened by an epidemic where more than thirteen million children are teased, taunted, and physically assaulted by their peers each year—whether out of racism, xenophobia, homophobia, sexism, or just plain meanness. The fear and hurt that so many young people feel in America today is an urgent call to action. We must not fail. We need adult leadership, teaching of tolerance, and acceptance of differences to ensure our children don't fall prey to bullying. We must act to stop bullying in communities everywhere—both online and off-line.

The messages of Lee Hirsch's landmark documentary *Bully*—messages of inclusion overcoming intolerance, of understanding and preventing violence—have reinvigorated a crucial conversation among teachers and students, parents and administrators, advocates and thought leaders. We all have an immense responsibility to speak loudly and to act clearly to create, manage, and maintain school environments where our children can learn, grow, and thrive as individuals fully empowered to reach their highest potential.

As an educator of more than thirty years and a member of Congress who was bullied as a child, I am inspired to do my part. That's why I founded the Congressional Anti-Bullying Caucus. The caucus will provide a premier forum to develop legislative solutions to prevent bullying and help raise public awareness.

As Frederick Douglass said, "If there is no struggle, there is no progress," and we must struggle to combat the bullying epidemic on all scales. Changes in laws, the way we think, and ultimately our behaviors are difficult to create, yet that is the challenge ahead of us. We need new and innovative solutions to combat bullying, solutions that protect young people by empowering school leaders and responsible adults everywhere to create safe campus environments for each child.

We must better equip educators—not only teachers, but all professionals and adults who have a role in caring for our youths—with the funding and training they need to keep each child safe and secure. Bus drivers must be trained and empowered to safeguard the children in their care. School infirmaries must be properly staffed, and each medical staff member must be properly trained to identify and treat the emotional trauma of bullying—social anxiety, substance abuse, and a sudden drop in academic performance.

Administrators and teachers must be fully prepared to deal with bullying in their schools. These educators play key roles in managing the front lines of bullying by coping with situations of physical and emotional violence, addressing situations with students and their parents, and fostering an environment of tolerance and inclusivity in their classrooms and playgrounds. These educators must be equipped with the training and tools they need to break existing cycles of bullying and to prevent countless more before they even start. Parents and other adults also need to be leaders and set the right examples for all children.

Stopping bullying means real liberation for each child. It means activating the power and strength that is within each child. I know what it feels like to be left out, ignored, name-called, and made to feel unworthy of people's respect and attention.

I also know what it is like to embrace that moment of empowerment, to feel safe and secure, to feel ready and able to pursue your greatest hopes in life. I am ready to do my part to ensure that each and every young person in America has the opportunity to embrace such a moment.

Empowering Bystanders: Creating Cultures of Dignity

Rosalind Wiseman

An expert in parenting, bullying, and social dynamics, Rosalind Wiseman is also the author of renowned nonfiction title, Queen Bees and Wannabes. *In addition to pioneering the* Owning Up Curriculum *social justice program, Rosalind is a columnist for* Family Circle *through which she addresses child and teen issues. She has spoken widely at national bullying conferences, the most significant of which was the White House Summit on Bullying in 2011.*

BEING A BYSTANDER

It's not like any of us look forward to the opportunity of confronting a bully. Ironically, it can often be harder to confront a bully we're close to than someone we don't know or don't like. And no matter how you feel about the bully or the target, it can be easy to stay silent because you don't want the abuse directed at you.

But here are three inescapable facts:

- Almost all of us will be in a situation at some point of our lives where we see someone bully someone else.
- Bystanders often decide to get involved based on their feelings toward the bully and/or the target. If you like the bully then you are more likely to excuse the behavior. If you think the target is annoying, then you'll more easily believe the target was asking for it. But a bystander's decision to get involved should be based on the merits of the problem, not on their relationship to the people.
- In that moment, we will have three choices: 1. Reinforce the abuse of power by supporting the bully; 2. Stay neutral—which looks like you're either intimidated by the bully yourself or you support their actions; 3. Act in some way that confronts the bully's abuse of power.

In the face of seeing someone bullied, here are some common reactions:

- Deny it's going on.
- Distract yourself so it looks like you don't know what's going on. And if you don't know then you have no obligation to stop it.
- Remove yourself from the situation.
- Laugh to try to convince yourself that what's going on isn't serious.
- Join in the bullying, because it's safer to be on the side of the person with the most power.
- Ignore it in the hope that it will go away.

WHAT DO YOU DO IF YOU ARE A BYSTANDER?

Even if you aren't proud of how you handled the bullying when it occurred, it's important to recognize how hard it is to know what to do in the moment. But that fact doesn't mean it's too late now to speak out. Especially if you are friends with the bully, reaching out to them is actually the ultimate sign of your friendship.

SUPPORTING SOMEONE WHO'S BEEN BULLIED

Say, "I'm sorry that happened to you, do you want to tell me about it?"

Don't tell them what they should have done or what you would have done. Listen and help them think through how to address the problem effectively. And if they ask you to back them up the next time it happens, ask them what that looks like to them. If it means upholding their right to be treated with dignity and not getting revenge on the bully, then do it.

SUPPORTING SOMEONE WHO IS BEING THE BULLY

In your own words say something like, "*This is uncomfortable to talk about but yesterday when you sent that picture of Dave, you know that really embarrassed him. And I know I laughed and I know he can be annoying, but it's still wrong. If you do it again I'm not going to back you up.*"

Yes, the bully is going to push back, make you uncomfortable, try to get you on their side, but remember what happened and why you feel like the bully's actions were wrong.

WHY ARE BYSTANDERS SO RELUCTANT TO COME FORWARD?

Let's move away from the bystanders and focus on the adults. The prevailing explanation of why kids won't come forward is because there's a code of silence that forbids them. No one wants to be a snitch. While there's some truth in that—I think just as powerful a reason for kids' silence is that the adults haven't created an environment where kids think reporting will make the problem better instead of worse. Yet, the most common advice we give to bystanders is to tell an adult. Like it or not, the truth is **it's not good enough to tell kids to tell an adult**.

Telling an adult won't magically solve the problem. What far too many kids know and experience on a daily basis but we deny is that far too many adults are ill equipped to respond effectively and often only cause the child to give up on adults entirely. Furthermore, the very way a lot of adults treat young people—in a condescending or dominant (i.e., "bullying") manner—makes it impossible for children to have any confidence in our ability to be effective advocates.

While there are many effective counselors, even the suggestion to "talk to your counselor" may not be realistic. The child may have no idea who the counselor is—let alone a strong enough relationship with him to take this leap of faith. Recent budget cuts have led many school districts to cut back on their counselors or eliminate them completely. And it has always been the case that kids tend to form strong relationships with their teachers and coaches. It's these people who bystanders will more likely tell what's going on. Especially for a bystander that could easily think that since the bullying isn't technically happening to them, reporting to a counselor is too extreme.

That's why teachers need to know what to do. Instead of, "That person just needs to get a tougher skin," "It can't be that bad can it?" they need to respond with "I'm really sorry this is happening. Thanks for telling me. I know it can be hard to come forward about things like this, and I really respect the fact that you did. Let's think about what we can do about it."

Let's be clear: Beyond the peer pressure not to snitch and adolescent cynicism, adults matter. If our kids see us treat people with dignity, if we are outspoken about our respect for people who come forward, if we are honest with how scary reporting can be but assure them that we will be with them throughout the process, I guarantee our kids will find the courage to speak out.

PART 7

The Movie
That Became
a Movement

$\mathfrak{Sioux}$ $\mathfrak{City}$ $\mathfrak{Journal}$

OUR OPINION: WE MUST STOP BULLYING. IT STARTS HERE. AND IT STARTS NOW.

The Journal editorial board

April 22, 2012—Siouxland lost a young life to a senseless, shameful tragedy last week. By all accounts, Kenneth Weishuhn was a kind-hearted, fun-loving teenage boy, always looking to make others smile. But when the South O'Brien High School 14-year-old told friends he was gay, the harassment and bullying began. It didn't let up until he took his own life.

Sadly, Kenneth's story is far from unique. Boys and girls across Iowa and beyond are targeted every day. In this case sexual orientation appears to have played a role, but we have learned a bully needs no reason to strike. No sense can be made of these actions.

Now our community and region must face this stark reality: We are all to blame. We have not done enough. Not nearly enough.

This is not a failure of one group of kids, one school, one town, one county or one geographic area. Rather, it exposes a fundamental flaw in our society, one that has deep-seated roots. Until now, it has been too difficult, inconvenient—maybe even painful—to address. But we can't keep looking away.

In Kenneth's case, the warnings were everywhere. We saw it happen in other communities, now it has hit home. Undoubtedly, it wasn't the first life lost to bullying here, but we can strive to make it the last.

The documentary "Bully," which depicts the bullying of an East Middle School student, opened in Sioux City on Friday. We urge everyone to see it. At its core, it is a heart-breaking tale of how far we have yet to go. Despite its award-winning, proactive policies, we see there is still much work to be done in Sioux City schools.

Superintendent Paul Gausman is absolutely correct when he says "it takes all of us to solve the problem." But schools must be at the forefront of our battle against bullying.

Sioux City must continue to strengthen its resolve and its policies. Clearly, South O'Brien High School needs to alter its approach. We urge Superintendent Dan Moore to rethink his stance that "we have all the things in place to deal with it." It should be evident that is simply not the case.

South O'Brien isn't the only school that needs help. A Journal Des Moines bureau report last year demonstrated that too many schools don't take bullying seriously. According to that report, Iowa school districts, on average, reported less than 2 percent of their students had been bullied in any given year since the state passed its anti-bullying law in 2007. That statistic belies the actual depth of this problem, and in response the Iowa Department of Education will implement a more comprehensive anti-bullying and harassment policy in the 2012–13 school year.

But as Gausman and Nate Monson, director of Iowa Safe Schools, are quick to remind us, this is more than a school problem. If we want to eradicate bullying in our community, we can't rely on schools alone.

We need to support local agencies like the Waitt Institute for Violence Prevention and national efforts like the one described at stopbullying.gov. Bullying takes many forms, some of them—Internet, Facebook, cell phone—more subtle than others. Parents should monitor the cell phone and Internet usage of their children. All public and private institutions need to do more to demonstrate that bullying is simply unacceptable in our workplaces and in our homes. We need to educate ourselves and others.

Some in our community will say bullying is simply a part of life. If no one is physically hurt, they will say, what's the big deal? It's just boys being boys and girls being girls.

Those people are wrong, and they must be shouted down.

We must make it clear in our actions and our words that bullying will not be tolerated. Those of us in public life must be ever mindful of the words we choose, especially in the contentious political debates that have defined our modern times. More importantly, we must not be afraid to act.

How many times have each of us witnessed an act of bullying and said little or nothing? After all, it wasn't our responsibility. A teacher or an official of some kind should step in. If our kid wasn't involved, we figured, it's none of our business.

Try to imagine explaining that rationale to the mother of Kenneth Weishuhn.

It is the business of all of us. More specifically, it is our responsibility. Our mandate.

If we're honest with ourselves, we will acknowledge our community has yet to view bullying in quite this way. It's well past time to do so.

Stand up. Be heard. And don't back down. Together, we can put a stop to bullying.

FROM R TO PG-13: HOW *BULLY* SUPPORTERS TOOK ON THE MPAA

As is standard in the movie industry, every new film is assigned a rating (G, PG, PG-13, R, or NC-17) by the Motion Picture Association of America (MPAA) that indicates the degree of caution parents should exercise in weighing whether a movie is suitable for children. When it was first released, *Bully* was slapped with an R, which meant that children under seventeen—the film's intended viewers—were not allowed to see it unless accompanied by a parent or adult guardian.

In the view of the MPAA Ratings Board, an R-rated motion picture contains some adult material, meaning it may include adult themes, adult activity, hard language, intense or persistent violence, sexually oriented nudity, drug abuse, or other elements. In the case of *Bully*, there were merely six mentions of the F word—several of which occurred during a crucial scene in which Alex Libby is harassed on the school bus—that were the basis for the R rating. When the filmmakers, including The Weinstein Company (TWC), *Bully's* distributor, criticized the restrictive rating due to a few expletives, the MPAA agreed to lower the R to a teen-friendly PG-13 if the filmmakers simply removed the offending words.

That was not an option.

Director Lee Hirsch explained that altering the school bus scene with Alex would be a disservice to both the film and its audience. He argued that the F words at issue—words heard every day by millions of school-age children—were too important to the truth, integrity, and message of *Bully*. "I made the film for children to see," Hirsch said, "and with the intent to give an uncensored, real-life portrayal of what it's like to be a bullied child." He urged the MPAA, headed by former United States senator Chris Dodd, to reconsider its rating.

So began a contentious battle. While Joan Graves, chairperson of the MPAA Ratings Board, acknowledged in a public statement that the film was a vehicle for "important discussions," she said "the R rating is not a judgment on the value of any movie" and that the "voluntary ratings system enables parents to make an informed decision about what content they allow their children to see." In a last-ditch effort to sway the Ratings Board, in February 2012 TWC cochairman Harvey Weinstein and young Alex Libby himself made a final appeal to the MPAA to have *Bully*'s rating changed to PG-13. "It was unbelievable," Hirsch said. "When the doors opened and Harvey and Alex walked out, literally, Harvey was crying. He was so proud of Alex." Alex had made an eloquent statement, read from handwritten notes, saying the only way to make a real change was to allow children to see *Bully* on their own, not with their parents. Despite Alex's impassioned plea, the appeal was denied—by only one vote.

KATY BUTLER TO THE RESCUE

Katy Butler, a seventeen-year-old Michigan high-school student who had been bullied in middle school after revealing her sexual orientation, was following the ratings controversy closely and decided to take a stand. She started a petition on Change.org, a social-action platform, in order to bring more attention to the film and rally supporters to help urge the MPAA to lower *Bully*'s rating—her petition became one of the most popular campaigns in Change.org's history.

> ### Kids Speak Out
> "One of the things that really stood out to me was the lack of help the administration provided the bullied kids. That has inspired me to want to become a principal when I grow up."
> —*Abby Erickson*

Within only a matter of weeks, more than half a million people, including government leaders, public figures, and celebrities such as Johnny Depp, New Orleans Saints' quarterback Drew Brees, and Ellen DeGeneres—who featured Butler as well as families from the film on her daytime talk show—signed the petition, turning the protest into a national movement:

- New York Yankees manager Joe Girardi, along with players Derek Jeter, Alex Rodriguez, Mariano Rivera, and Curtis Granderson, shot a public-service announcement during spring training in Tampa, FL, about the effects bullying has on children and what people can do to make a change.
- Justin Bieber promoted the film on Twitter and featured his song "Born to Be Somebody" in a *Bully* television spot.
- Meryl Streep and her daughter Mamie Gummer cohosted a screening of the film in New York City with David Boies, one of the two attorneys responsible for overturning Proposition 8 in California, and his daughter, Mary Boies.
- Kelly Ripa and Anderson Cooper also hosted a screening in New York City that was presented by Bing, the search engine from Microsoft. Cooper also hosted a town-hall special on CNN to discuss bullying with Dr. Phil, Ripa, and Hirsch.
- Victoria Justice, Giuliana Rancic, and Joel McHale hosted the Los Angeles premiere.
- American designer Tommy Hilfiger designed an exclusive T-shirt inspired by the *Bully* movie poster that was sold in Tommy Hilfiger stores; a portion of proceeds benefited Facing History and Ourselves (http://www.facing.org/).
- Famed photographer David LaChapelle offered to donate his talents toward an advertising campaign.
- In Congress, Representative Mike Honda (D-CA) issued a bipartisan letter to the MPAA, supporting Katy Butler's petition and urging former Senator Dodd to overturn the ruling; more than thirty-five members of Congress signed the letter. Also, Senator Kirsten Gillibrand (D-NY) called for a PG-13 rating on Twitter and has told TWC that she intended to play an active role in the protest.

What's more, the film was gaining support from other ratings organizations. In its review for *Bully*, Common Sense Media, a group dedicated to improving the lives of kids and families by providing the trustworthy information, education, and independent voice they need to thrive in a world of media and technology, declared the film appropriate for children ages 13 and older—urging parents to know their children and that some content may not be right for some kids. "None of the swearing is gratuitous," the review stated. "Like it or not, it's a realistic portrayal of what every middle schooler and older hears every day." Additionally, movie classification boards across most of Canada were giving the film a PG rating; it received a G rating in Quebec. (Canadian movie ratings are set by individual provinces.)

Celebs Speak Out

"I watched this with my four college roommates. We get together every year. A child psychologist, a woman who's a lawyer, a columnist, and a businesswoman—we were all stunned. It brought me back to New Jersey in 1950. A long time ago. I was eight years old and up a tree. And my nemesis, this one bully, was hitting my legs with a stick until they bled. It was very *Lord of the Flies*...Seeing this, you realize it's been around, bullying. But I hope this film will give encouragement to the kids who are being bullied. My dad had a little statue on his desk of three little monkeys, a carved Chinese statuette—doing [See No Evil, Say No Evil, Hear No Evil]. I thought maybe this will encourage all those little monkeys to stand up and open their eyes and take the earbuds out of their ears and say something. Because a team is stronger than a bully."

—*Meryl Streep at the New York City screening for* Bully

With such tremendous support, the filmmakers then took a courageous step—they announced that they would move forward and release *Bully* unrated, which would give theaters the chance to use their discretion when admitting children to the theater and hopefully enable more of the film's intended audience to view it.

Katy Butler speaks to a reporter for Los Angeles TV station KTLA. Butler's petition eventually was signed by more than half a million people.

Normally, releasing a movie without a rating carries a high risk of compromised distribution, but *Bully* got a boost from American Multi-Cinema Theaters (AMC), the second biggest theater chain in the United States. AMC agreed to allow minors in to see the film even if they're unaccompanied by an adult, as long as they are carrying a note of permission from a parent or guardian. Gerry Lopez, AMC's chief executive officer, even spoke out against the R rating, saying that the chain wanted to invite patrons to engage in "the dialogue its relevant message will inevitably provoke."

Still, the filmmakers and the MPAA continued to negotiate. Hirsch said that if the MPAA would allow him to maintain that pivotal scene showing Alex getting viciously bullied on the school bus, he would agree to remove three uses of the F word from other sections of the film. That compromise ultimately persuaded the MPAA, and on April 5, 2012, it was announced that *Bully* would be given a PG-13 just in time for its expansion into fifty-five markets the following week. The decision was lauded as a huge victory for the parents, educators, lawmakers, and, especially, children everywhere who had been fighting for months to have the film released with the teen-friendly rating.

"I feel completely vindicated with this resolution," Hirsch said. "While I retain my belief that PG-13 has always been the appropriate rating for this film, as reinforced by Canada's rating of a PG, we have today scored a victory from the MPAA." (Also a victory was the exception the MPAA made by allowing the film to be released with the new rating before ninety days, which is the length of time their policy states a film must wait to be in theaters after a rating change to avoid confusion or inconvenience for moviegoers.)

Said Katy Butler: "On behalf of the more than half a million supporters who joined me on Change.org in petitioning the MPAA, I want to express how grateful I am not only to the MPAA for lowering the rating without cutting a vital scene, but to all of the people who used their voices to put a national spotlight on this movie and its mission."

In the end, the new rating, which came about with the great support from MPAA Chairman Dodd, would grant schools and organizations, including the National Education Association, around the country the ability to share the documentary, as an educational tool, with teens. "The changing of the rating for *Bully* from R to PG-13 will enable many more young people to see this film. NEA applauds the Motion Picture Association of America and the producers for the PG-13 rating," said National Education Association President Dennis Van Roekel. "Every teenage student should have the opportunity to see this powerful documentary about a problem that still haunts our schools. NEA also salutes seventeen-year-old Katy Butler and the other young activists whose online petition drive led to having the rating for *Bully* reconsidered."

"Senator Dodd is a hero for championing this cause, and the MPAA showed great courage by not cutting the scene everyone has been fighting to keep," Weinstein added. "Senator Dodd's support gives voice to the millions of children who suffer from bullying, and on behalf of TWC, the filmmakers, the families in the film, and the millions of children and parents who will now see this film, I thank him for recognizing that this very real issue cannot afford to go unnoticed."

REACHING ACROSS THE AISLE: BULLYING GARNERS NONPARTISAN SUPPORT

Bolstered by the ratings victory, *Bully* supporters have been building support for legislation that will take action to ensure that all students are safe and healthy and can learn in environments free from discrimination, bullying, and harassment. Specifically, the Student Non-Discrimination Act (SNDA) and the Safe Schools Improvement Act (SSIA), legislation that has gained both Democratic and Republican support, are critically important to addressing bullying in our schools and safeguarding our most vulnerable students. The Student Non-Discrimination Act, sponsored by Senator Al Franken of Minnesota and Representative Jared Polis of Colorado, would prohibit discrimination in public schools against any student on the basis of actual or perceived sexual orientation and gender identity. And the Safe Schools Improvement Act, sponsored by Senator Bob Casey of Pennsylvania and Representative Linda Sanchez of California, would require school districts to adopt codes of conduct specifically prohibiting bullying and harassment, including on the basis of race, color, national origin, sex, disability, sexual orientation, gender identity, and religion. President Barack Obama supports both of these two important pieces of legislation and said he will work with Congress as they move forward in the process.

Educators Speak Out

"We brought our students to your film today. It was a truly beautiful film and an experience that I know will have a transformative effect on our students' lives."

—Lori Lipkind

For perhaps the first time in our nation's history, a United States president is taking a public stand on bullying. On April 20, 2012, *Bully* was screened at the White House in an event that brought together bully-prevention advocates from a range of communities— LGBT, AAPI, faith, disability, and others—as well as educational partners and key Obama staff, including Arne Duncan, secretary of education, and Valerie Jarrett, senior advisor and assistant to the president for Public Engagement and Intergovernmental Affairs, who work on these issues every day. Before the film, a panel of nationally recognized experts on bullying prevention spoke from their perspectives about challenges and opportunities, and after the film, Lee Hirsch addressed the audience, as did several of the students and families who were directly impacted by bullying and intolerance and whose stories were featured in the film.

In the last few years, President Obama and his administration have demonstrated a strong commitment to alleviate and tackle bullying through legislative efforts and by reaching out to America's youth directly. In March of 2010, the first-ever White House Conference on Bullying Prevention, attended by both the President and First Lady, was held, bringing together students, teachers, advocates, the private sector, and policy makers to discuss ways to make our schools safer. President Obama explained it this way: "If there's one goal of this conference, it's to dispel the myth that bullying is just a harmless rite of passage or an inevitable part of growing up. It's not."

Additionally, the president recorded a video for the It Gets Better Project, as did the vice president, cabinet secretaries, and members of the White House staff, and the Department of Education has issued guidance to schools, colleges, and universities, making it clear that existing civil rights laws apply to bullying and that schools have not just a moral responsibility but a legal one to protect our young people from harassment. The Department of Education has also worked with states to help them in their own antibullying efforts and recently released a report that documents key components of antibullying laws across all fifty states. The department has issued guidance to governors and state school officials in order to help them incorporate the best practices for protecting students.

The Obama administration also relaunched StopBullying.gov, a website that contains detailed descriptions of the work being done on bullying, along with resources for young people, parents, and educators. The president has partnered with businesses, foundations, nonprofits, and universities that are coming up with new, creative ways to make our nation's schools safe. These administrative actions have been critically important—and effective—and the president has said he will continue to work across the entire federal government to address and prevent bullying.

Nonpartisan support for *Bully* and for antibullying legislation continues to be shown at the local, state, and federal level nationwide:

- Washington, DC, Mayor Vincent C. Gray announced the District's first citywide Anti-Bullying Action Plan, led by the DC Office of Human Rights, which will bring together government agencies, nonprofit organizations, community partners, and educators across the city to find solutions to confront and eradicate bullying across DC.
- Acting on his commitment to ensure schools provide safe learning environments for children, free from harassment, intimidation, and bullying, New Jersey governor Chris Christie named his four members to the state's Anti-Bullying Task Force called for in the Anti-Bullying Bill of Rights, originally signed into law in January 2011.
- Former Arkansas governor Mike Huckabee wrote an article in http://thedailybeast.com urging "all parents" to take their kids to see the film.
- On their TV shows, both Sean Hannity and Rush Limbaugh publicly supported the film.
- In March 2011, Representative Danny K. Davis of Illinois introduced the Anti-Bullying and Harassment Act of 2011, which amends the Safe and Drug-Free Schools and Communities Act (SDFSCA) to include bullying and harassment prevention programs. Under this legislation, states would be required to submit data on the incidence and prevalence of reported incidents of bullying and harassment and on the perception of students regarding their

school environment and school responsiveness to incidents of bullying and harassment. States would also need to provide an assurance that they would provide assistance to districts and schools in their efforts to prevent and respond to incidents of bullying and harassment.

In June 2012, at the annual meeting of the U.S. Conference of Mayors, the official nonpartisan organization of cities with populations of 30,000 or more, the following resolution was submitted and passed, co-sponsored by eight mayors—Frank Ortis of Pembroke Pines, Florida; Christopher Cabaldon of West Sacramento, California; Angel Taveras of Providence, Rhode Island; Pedro Segarra of Hartford, Connecticut; Sly James of Kansas City, Missouri; Mike Rawlings of Dallas; Anthony Spitaleri of Sunnyvale, California; and Robert Sabonjion of Waukegan, Illinois—in order to eradicate bullying from America's schools:

1 WHEREAS, more than 18 million American kids a year are affected by bullying, with some driven to suicide; and
2 WHEREAS, teens in grades 6 through 10 are the most likely to be involved in activities related to bullying
3 WHEREAS, approximately 30 percent of students in the U.S. are involved in bullying on a regular basis, either as a victim, bully or both; and
4 WHEREAS, mayors are the civic leaders of the nation's cities and can be tremendously impactful to effect positive change in their communities; and
5 NOW, THEREFORE, BE IT RESOLVED, that The U.S. Conference of Mayors fully supports antibullying activities such as The Bully Project and 1 Million Kids; and
6 BE IT FURTHER RESOLVED, that the nation's mayors will do all they can to call attention to the issue of bullying in schools, and work to develop city-wide programs to combat the problem of bullying to ensure that all students have access to a safe and secure educational environment.

It is through these kinds of cohesive efforts—across all levels of government, political activism, and party affiliations—that we can help spread the message of *Bully* and lead the way for our nation's future leaders to learn and grow without fear and with pride. As President Obama said in a June 2012 news conference, "Americans may be able to serve openly in the military, but many are still growing up alone, afraid, picked on, pushed around for being different, and that's why my administration has worked to raise awareness about bullying . . . I just had a chance to see Lee Hirsch, the director of *Bully* . . . and we thank him for his work on this issue."

1 MILLION KIDS: CREATING COMMUNITIES OF EMPATHY AND RESPECT

Step by step, this growing national movement will change not just our laws and policies, but our behavior, so that every young person is able to thrive in our schools and communities, without worrying about being bullied. "The goal of The Bully Project Social Action Campaign is to turn the tide—community by community—on bullying, increase empathy, and create a national tipping point," Hirsch said. "We aim to foster a movement that will continue to coalesce and use that momentum to create systemic change at the local and federal level."

Just as *Bully* tells the stories of five brave families and challenges viewers to move from shock and resignation about bullying to action, The Bully Project aims to transform schools and communities into places where empathy and respect are valued and bullying is unacceptable. The Project's goal: to have one million young people see the film in theaters and participate in facilitated discussions that will help them process their experience.

So far, the Project is well on its way: More than one hundred thousand students have seen *Bully* and have taken part in meaningful follow-up dialogues and events. In April 2012, some seven thousand kids filled the Nokia Center in Los Angeles for a screening of the film, while in Cincinnati more than ten thousand teens participated in screenings. In Cedar Falls, Iowa, local fundraising paid for one thousand students to see the film. And in Rockville Centre, New York, Lee Hirsch's own middle school, Southside Middle School—the place that inspired him to make this film—screened *Bully* for their nine hundred students, who walked the track three times in silence after watching the film in order to honor those who feel voiceless.

The Bully Project has received more than a hundred videos from young people telling their stories and showing how they are attempting to find solutions. On a daily basis, there is an outpouring of testimonials and photographs showing solidarity and support. The *Bully* Facebook page, with more than one hundred thousand *likes* and counting, has become a space where bullied kids and upstanders have found community and a voice.

Partnering organizations have been instrumental in empowering the success of the campaign. More than thirty thousand students have taken part in a Facebook quiz on DoSomething.org, The Bully Project's Youth Activation Partner, regarding bullying in their schools, offering a glimpse into what impact bullying has on an individual basis and providing further information on how we can better attempt to eradicate it. First Student, which is North America's largest provider of student transportation, is working with The Bully Project to transport one million students to weekday film screenings across the country. And free or discounted tickets are being made available by DonorsChoose.org, whose mission is to engage the public by offering a simple, accountable, and personal way to address educational inequity.

BBYO, a Jewish youth leadership group, took more than four thousand kids to see the film, getting more than 350,000 signatures in their pledge to end bullying. And working with its Special Needs coalition, led by the National Center for Learning Disabilities, The Bully Project hosted an online "day of action," reaching hundreds of thousands in just one day—more than twenty-five thousand people have accessed the Special Needs Toolkit, and 1.9 million individuals have been reached through their social media efforts. Also, in collaboration with Ashoka, a working community of three thousand leading social entrepreneurs in more than eighty countries, thirteen student-run movements have been launched to end bullying in their cities. These are just a few examples of the amazing 1 Million Kids events going on across the country.

Additionally, Facing History and Ourselves, The Bully Project's leading educational partner, has developed a comprehensive curriculum for educators. Facing History and Ourselves is an international educational- and professional-development organization whose mission is to engage students of diverse backgrounds in an examination of racism, prejudice, and anti-Semitism in order to promote the development of a more humane and informed citizenry. The goal of 1 Million Kids is ultimately to foster empathy, action, and a cultural shift in school climate, and the educational component is critical to this mission. Facing History and Ourselves has developed a customized screening guide and teacher training tools to be deployed in thousands of schools across the nation. Educators participate in the online Facing History and Ourselves facilitators' training and are then prepared to lead a robust discussion and training with students following the film screening. To date, nearly ten thousand educators have participated in Facing History and Ourselves' *Bully* training and thousands of guides have been downloaded.

In fall 2012, The Bully Project unveils the next phase of its social action campaign when "Back to School 1 Million Kids" gets under

A 1 Million Kids screening of Bully *at The Nokia Theatre in Los Angeles*

way, which includes the launch of an educational DVD and delivering the film, educational tools, and resources to a wider breadth of schools. It is the hope of the filmmakers and all who support anti-bullying initiatives everywhere that *Bully* and its evolving curriculum will become an evergreen tool used year after year in schools across the United States and beyond.

PART 8

What We Can Do

It's 10 p.m.: Do You Know Who Is Bullying Your Child?

Once upon a time, bullying was something you had to worry about *out there*—when children were out of sight, on their own, unsupervised. Homes were a safe haven, a place to escape the abuse with the bolt of a door, at least for an evening. However, the advancement of technology and its prevalent use among the nation's youth has let bullying infiltrate our homes and private lives like a virus—undetected until the damage, sometimes irrevocably, has been done.

Cyberbullying—when the Internet, cell phones, or other devices are used to send or post text or images that are intended to hurt or embarrass another—comes in many forms. Cyberbullying can be as simple as continuing to send an e-mail to someone who has said they want no further contact with the sender. It includes threats, making victims the subject of ridicule, posting false statements aimed at humiliation, and disclosing victims' personal data.

Many young people are not aware that they are participating in bullying or cyberbullying or of the consequences of doing so. Therefore, it is the job of the caring adults around our children, particularly parents and educators, to offer guidance and support with regard to technology, and to teach them how to stand up to bullying—as an upstander, rather than a bystander—and how they can protect themselves, both online and off-line, before things go too far. Or before it's too late.

Technology Use versus Misuse/Cyberbullying

Technology	Use	Misuse/Cyberbullying
Cell Phones	Mobile devices that allow users to place phone calls, take photos, send text messages and photos, and access the Internet and personal e-mail.	Making hateful, harassing, or intimidating calls or leaving such messages on voice mail; taking humiliating photos of others (sometimes without their knowledge) and distributing them to others; staging acts of bullying and video-recording them.
E-mail	Written messages mailed over the Internet that enable people to communicate online with others from home, school, or at work.	Repeatedly sending harassing messages; masking identity by creating new screen names and using anonymity to send offensive photos, images, or threats; forwarding a person's personal e-mail to someone else without his or her knowledge; sending computer viruses.
Instant Messaging (IM)	Online technology that enables user to communicate in real time with other people via typed messages.	Breaking into someone else's account and, while masquerading as the person, sending inappropriate or embarrassing messages to others; tricking people into revealing personal or embarrassing information and then forwarding that information to others; sending hateful, harassing, or threatening messages or content through either a known or anonymous screen name.
Chat Rooms or Message Boards	Online forums that enable groups of participants with shared interests to have online conversations in real time or to post written messages for others.	Making nasty or threatening comments (often anonymously); excluding people by intentionally ignoring them; encouraging people to disclose private information for the purpose of exploiting them in some way.

Social-Networking Sites (Facebook, Twitter, etc.)	Websites where members create personal profiles that can include personal information, photos, images, and blogs as a means to communicate and share with others.	Posting anonymous comments on other people's home pages (e.g., "Honesty Box" on Facebook); creating a phony profile for a person that includes demeaning, humiliating images and/or content; excluding people by deleting them from lists of linked "friends" or by refusing to respond to messages or comments.
Webcams	A small digital camera on a computer that can be used to record photos or videos or to converse with someone "face-to-face" online.	Producing inappropriate content for the purpose of embarrassing someone and making it available to others.
Video-Hosting Sites (Yahoo! Video, YouTube, Flickr, etc.)	A website that allows people to widely share video clips on any topic.	Recording an embarrassing or humiliating video without a person's knowledge and posting it online.

PARENTS: THE HOME FRONT

Many times, children do not go to their parents when they are bullied because they're embarrassed, or perhaps they don't have the confidence that their parents will understand what they're going through or will do what's right. Parents need to familiarize themselves with and learn to engage in their children's world, a big part of which involves digital communication. The above chart demonstrates the ways in which technology can be used and misused to bully others.

In order to effectively fight cyberbullying on the home front, parents need a multipronged approach that includes discussion, education, and trust. Here are some tips for getting started.

1 **Bring the topic out in the open.** Initiate discussions about your teen's online experiences. Establish a consistent, helpful

presence when monitoring technology use that discourages the perception that adults are violating the child's privacy. If you choose to use filtering and monitoring software, don't rely on it as a substitute for direct participation in your child's online life.

2 **Educate youth about responsible online behavior.** Discuss with your child the dangers of sharing personal information with others online, and continually reinforce the importance of this guideline. Clarify the kinds of things that should never be shared, including names, addresses, phone numbers, school names, age, and grade levels. In addition, provide your child with the necessary skills, tools, and resources to assess the accuracy of website content. Spend time visiting Internet sites with him, and provide supervised opportunities to practice these analytical skills online.

3 **Discuss response strategies.** Instruct your teen to immediately notify trusted adults and/or the appropriate authorities (parent or other adult family member, teacher or other school personnel, technology coordinator, librarian, etc.) when she encounters cyberbullying or hate-related behaviors online. Discuss and provide opportunities for your child to practice strategies for responding to cyberbullying and online intolerance and hate. Even if your child is not being bullied, talk about what it means to be an ally to peers who may be the targets of cyberbullying. Distinguish between immediate strategies (logging out of chat room) and long-term strategies (notifying the local school district, Anti-Defamation League office, or police department about information on a website).

4 **Provide structure.** Restrict time your teen spends online, and provide guidance for structuring online time. Limit unstructured random surfing, and consistently supervise your teen's online activities.

5 **Set an example.** Model safe use of the Internet, avoiding potentially dangerous situations, including online romance

and gambling. Your child is a keen observer of adult behavior and will do likewise, despite warnings to the contrary.

6 **Encourage personal responsibility.** Stress personal responsibility in your child. He should understand his important role in creating respectful online communities. Knowledge and education are key weapons against cyberbullying and other forms of hate and intolerance.

EDUCATORS: THE FRONT LINES

Parents, however, can only do so much. While it's true that cyberbullying has invaded our homes and private lives, it is on school grounds that the vast majority of bullying takes place, and there is mounting pressure on school districts to crack down on bullying with clearly stated policies. In the summer of 2009, around the same time the makers of *Bully* were presenting their idea for the film to the Sioux City Community School Board in Iowa, a federal lawsuit was filed in New York that challenged a Herkimer County school district's failure to protect a gay student from harassment.

J.L., a fourteen-year-old attending Gregory B. Jarvis Junior/Senior High School, had been the victim of bullying during the seventh and eighth grades based on sex and because he did not conform to gender stereotypes. He displayed "feminine mannerisms"—he dyed his hair, wore makeup and nail polish, and maintained predominantly female friendships. The relentless bullying against him had escalated from name-calling to physical threats and violence. His personal property had been damaged, and he had been regularly pushed and had things thrown at him. A fellow student even knocked J.L. down the stairs, causing him to sprain his ankle; another brought a knife to school and threatened to kill him.

The New York Civil Liberties Union filed the lawsuit against the Mohawk Central School District for failing to protect J.L., a violation of the Equal Protection Clause of the Fourteenth Amendment to the United States Constitution and Title IX of the Education

Cyberbullying Checklist for Schools

	We do this well.	We need to give this more attention.
We address acts of name-calling or bullying, including cyberbullying, when they occur anyplace in our school.	☐	☐
As part of our bullying and harassment policies, we include policies on cyberbullying that are clear and well communicated.	☐	☐
We educate all students about cyberbullying policies as well as how to recognize and respond to cyberbullying and cyberthreats.	☐	☐
We educate all faculty and staff about how to recognize and respond to cyberbullying and cyberthreats, and provide information about relevant legal guidelines.	☐	☐
We provide education on how to use the Internet safely and responsibly, including topics such as etiquette, privacy, and other aspects unique to the online environment.	☐	☐
We have established a code of conduct, including provision for cyberbullying and other technology use protocols that includes appropriate sanctions for violating this code.	☐	☐
We have instituted effective and age-appropriate supervision and monitoring of technology and have established an expectation among students that misuse is likely to be detected and will result in disciplinary action.	☐	☐
We include students in the planning and implementation of school-wide programs to counter cyberbullying.	☐	☐
We have informed the families of our students about the dangers of cyberbullying and cyberthreats, and have provided information and resources about how to address these issues in the home.	☐	☐
We have a mechanism for students to report incidents of cyberbullying they have experienced or observed.	☐	☐

We have a mechanism for teachers to report incidents of cyberbullying when they become aware of them.	☐	☐
Administration has a clear review procedure for all reported incidents of cyberbullying, which includes provisions for legal options in cases of off-campus cyberbullying.	☐	☐
We have developed a relationship with local law-enforcement officials to help educate the school community about the legal ramifications of cyberbullying and who can assist with threats and hate incidents that arise online.	☐	☐

Amendments of 1972, as well as state human-rights and civil-rights laws. It was said that the school district had been repeatedly made aware of the abuse and that district officials—including the superintendent and school principal—failed to investigate the harassment, discipline the bullies, or inform J.L. and his parents of their rights to file complaints under the school's grievance procedures. (The district denied the allegations in the complaint.)

In an unprecedented move, the United States Department of Justice filed a motion to intervene in the case on J.L.'s behalf the following January, shining a national spotlight on a matter that for many years had been viewed as a nonissue, a local issue concerning just one family. By March 2010, an out-of-court settlement was reached in *J.L. v. Mohawk Central School District*, in which the Mohawk Central School District agreed to a series of reforms and was now *required by law* to, among other things,

- retain an expert consultant in the area of harassment and discrimination;
- develop and implement a comprehensive plan for disseminating the district's harassment and discrimination policies;
- retain an expert consultant to conduct annual training for faculty and staff; and

■ maintain records of investigations and responses to allegations of harassment for five years.

"All students have the right to go to school without fearing harassment based on sex, including stereotypes about appropriate gender behavior," Thomas E. Perez, assistant attorney general for the Civil Rights Division, said in a statement upon conclusion of the case. "Such conduct has no place in our schools, and the Justice Department looks forward to working with the district and the NYCLU to ensure that all students enjoy educational opportunities without discrimination or harassment."

It's time for schools to take bullying seriously. Like the Sioux City School District featured in *Bully*, schools need to be willing to look at their own climate in order to tackle the complexities of bullying, be it physical, emotional, or cyber. "Far too many parents are marginalized and ignored when they try to advocate on behalf of a bullied child," Lee Hirsch said. "What should be a simple intervention often escalates to a combative situation where the student continues to suffer." What follows are prevention and intervention strategies with regard to cyberbullying, although many can be used for all types of bullying as well.

Prevention

1 **Establish policies.** Set clear guidelines for technology use at your institution, and update policies accordingly. Publicize guidelines by hanging posters or distributing fliers and making youth aware of the consequences for online cruelty.

2 **Educate youth.** Engage youth in activities and discussions about ethical standards for online activities, teach them that all forms of bullying are unacceptable, and help them identify strategies for responding to cyberbullying and online hate. The mentoring of younger students by their older peers is a great way to put such education into practice.

3 **Promote online safety.** Increase awareness of Internet safety strategies among youth and their families by sending home

informational materials and sponsoring community programs that provide practical information about how to respond to cyberbullying.

4 **Monitor technology use.** Institute supervision and monitoring practices that keep relevant staff at your institution informed about how technology is being used at your site and that help them to enforce rules and policies. Include blocking/filtering software as part of a comprehensive monitoring strategy, but do not rely solely on these tools.

5 **Encourage reporting.** Establish safe and confidential reporting mechanisms for cyberbullying incidents, and make youth aware of them. Encourage youth to tell a trusted adult about threatening or harassing messages that they or others receive. Reinforce the difference between "tattling" and responsible reporting, and impress upon youth the destructive consequences of keeping silent about bullying and bias.

6 **Select a point person.** Designate a cyberbullying "expert" at your institution, someone who is responsible for keeping up with laws, policies, best practices, and current trends regarding cyberbullying and Internet safety, and who builds relationships with relevant community members, including local law-enforcement officials that deal with cybercrimes. Make sure youth at your institution know who to go to with concerns about cyberbullying or online safety.

7 **Set an example.** Model appropriate technology use by refraining from sending or forwarding offensive jokes and mean comments and by reporting hate and harassment when it occurs. Avoid texting or talking on a mobile phone in inappropriate places, and demonstrate to youth that you "walk the talk" when it comes to safe and responsible technology use.

8 **Be vigilant.** Look for warning signs that a young person in your care might be the target or perpetrator of cyberbullying. If you observe obsessive technology use, fear or

avoidance of technology, social withdrawal, or other behaviors that concern you, talk with your supervisor or a mental-health expert at your institution about how to intervene.

Intervention

1 **Save evidence.** Advise youth to keep all proof of bullying and harassment, including e-mails, texts, phone numbers, and screen names. Tell them to take screen shots or print the evidence and keep a file to substantiate claims of inappropriate or illegal behavior.

2 **Investigate and respond.** Interview the individuals involved in the incident, and work with Internet and cell-phone service providers to gather as much information as possible about what took place. Determine appropriate consequences for the perpetrators in accordance with your institution's policies and the seriousness of the infraction.

3 **Involve law enforcement.** Report extremely harmful online speech such as harassment, stalking, threats of violence, and pornography to the police.

4 **Consult an attorney.** Before carrying out consequences, check with your institution's legal counsel to make sure that all disciplinary measures are in line with your institution's policies and the law and that you are not inadvertently violating the First Amendment rights of individuals. If appropriate, counsel may also advise the target's family about their options for taking legal action against the perpetrator or the perpetrator's family.

5 **Follow up with the perpetrator's family.** Discuss the incident with the perpetrator's parents or guardians to establish ongoing communication and consistent expectations between home and your institution. Provide information and education as appropriate so that the perpetrator's family understands how best to address the negative behavior, monitor their child's online behavior, and ensure responsible use of technology in the future.

6 **Provide support.** Assist the target and the target's family in coping with the impact of the online cruelty and to build skills for dealing with such problems in the future. Make sure not to blame the target for being bullied or to unintentionally punish the target by limiting access to technology.

7 **Block harassers.** Protect targets from further victimization by helping them to block offending e-mail addresses, screen names, "friends" on social-networking sites, and cell-phone numbers. If necessary, help families to change phone numbers and e-mail addresses.

8 **Report incidents.** Help targets to file complaints with Internet and cell-phone service providers. Most social-networking and media sites (e.g., Facebook, YouTube) have "report abuse" functions and will respond to reports of harassment promptly.

9 **Reach out.** Work with local schools, youth groups, and community organizations to share information about ongoing problems with cyberbullying (making sure to maintain confidentiality where necessary). Since the cyberworld has no boundaries, communicating with the different institutions that youth are a part of can help to establish consistency with regard to the messages and consequences that youth receive.

10 **Educate.** Discuss strategies for responding to cyberbullying and ways to be an ally with all youth. Online harassment and cruelty affect the entire community, not just those who are directly involved in an incident. Broad-based education about responsible technology use can contribute to a climate that is welcoming and inclusive for all members of your institution.

Technology provides today's youth with exciting opportunities to connect, communicate, create, and learn like never before. The wide array of online resources and social-networking sites provides the possibility of exciting, positive educational opportunities as well as healthy social interactions. When technology is used irresponsibly, however, it can cause great harm and pain. It is only by working together that parents and educators can make sure our children use the powers of technology for good and for the benefit of everyone.

Bully-Proofing Kids

What parents can do to help kids be less likely to be bullied and how to respond if they are

Dr. Michele Borba

Dr. Michele Borba is an educational psychologist, bullying advocate, Today *show contributor, speaker, and author of twenty-two books. For more about her work on bullying prevention see: http://micheleborba.com or follow her on twitter @MicheleBorba. These strategies are adapted from her books,* The Big Book of Parenting Solutions: 101 Answers to Your Everyday Challenges and Wildest Worries *and* Building Moral Intelligence.

I know you've heard the dismal statistics or the heartbreaking stories in the news about children who were bullied. Studies find that 160,000 children skip school *every* day because they fear being attacked or intimidated. While you can't guarantee that your child will not be bullied, you can provide the necessary tools to help reduce his chances of being targeted. What follows is a crash course for parents about bullying—everything you need to know and do to help your child be less likely to be victimized, as well as tips to help your child navigate an all-too vicious social jungle. I've included warning signs of bullying, bully-proofing strategies to reduce the odds of bullying, ways to develop a safety plan for your child, how to work with your child's school if your child is bullied, factors that research finds buffer our children's chances for peer abuse, steps to take if victimization continues or escalates, and when to seek help. Every bullying situation is different, so your job is to figure out which strategies may help *your* child. It's time to end the cruelty. So roll up your sleeves, and let's get started.

WHAT CLUES TO LOOK FOR: SIGNS A CHILD MAY BE BULLIED

Many kids are embarrassed or feel uncomfortable telling adults about being bullied. They may worry that they'll be blamed as the cause, or they may fear retaliation from the bully. That's why it's crucial for you know the signs of bullying and tune in to your child's behavior and watch for clues. Every kid can have an "off" day, so *look for sudden unhealthy behavior not typical for your child and see if the pattern continues*. Here are possible signs that a child may be bullied. The clues might mean other problems, but any warrant looking into more closely.

1 A lack of interest in school or refuses to go to school
2 Fears riding the school bus or takes a new and unusual route to school

3 Has physical marks, cuts, bruises, and scrapes not consistent with explanation

4 Unexplained damaged or missing toys, school supplies, electronic items, clothes, lunches, money, etc., or reports mysteriously "losing" possessions

5 Afraid to be left alone; wants you there at dismissal, to take him to school, or is suddenly clingy with you or other adults when around peers

6 Marked change in typical behavior or personality, for instance: sullen and evasive; remarks about being lonely or sad; moody, angry, anxious, or depressed with no known cause

7 Has headaches, stomachaches, or panic attacks, trouble sleeping, or starts bed wetting; frequently visits the school nurse's office

8 Begins bullying siblings or younger kids

9 Runs to use the bathroom the minute he gets home; won't use school restroom

10 Stops talking about peers, withdraws from the social scene, or avoids or doesn't want to be around peers; uses derogatory or demeaning language when describing them

11 Ravenous when he comes home; complains his money or lunch is missing

12 Starts taking your money or makes unconvincing excuses of where it went

13 Sudden drop in grades, trouble focusing or concentrating

14 Blames self for problems; feels "not good enough"

15 Talks about feeling helpless or about suicide; runs away

Get savvy about the signs of cyberbullying.

Bullying has always been one of the tougher problems about growing up; technology just makes inflicting brutality far easier. With just a quick keystroke cyberbullies can send harmful, vicious, and often anonymous e-mails, blog posts, instant messages, or text messages to unsuspecting victims. Cyberbullying is a growing problem. In addition to the clues of being bullied, learn the signs of possible electronic bullying.

1 Hesitant to be online; nervous when an instant message, text message, or e-mail appears
2 Visibly upset after using the computer or cell phone or suddenly avoids it
3 Starts hiding or clearing the computer screen or closing a cell phone when you enter
4 Spends unusual and longer hours online in a more tense, pensive manner
5 Suspicious phone calls, e-mails, and packages arrive at your home

WHAT TO DO IF YOU SUSPECT BULLYING BUT AREN'T SURE

Kids don't always tell us they are bullied, and so they can suffer in silence. If you suspect bullying, here are ways to find out what's really going on, so you can help your child.

Dig deeper.

If you suspect bullying, probe further: "You're always hungry. Have you been eating your lunch?" "Your CDs are missing. Did someone take them?" "Your jacket is ripped. Did someone do that to you?" Then watch your child's reactions. What kids don't say can be telling, so tune into your child's body language. You may have to ask outright: "I hear a lot about bullying. Are there bullies in your school? Do they bully certain kids? Do they ever bully you or your friends?"

Determine if it's really bullying.

All kids will be teased, but bullying is different. Bullying is always intentional cruelty, which is usually repeated, and there is an unequal imbalance (in size, status, power, ability) so the victim cannot hold his own against his tormentor. You might ask: "Was it an accident, or did he hurt you on purpose?" "Did you do or say anything first to upset him?" "Did she mean to be so mean?" "Did he do it more than once?" "Did he know that he was hurting you?" "Did she care that you were sad or angry?" "Did you tell her to stop?" "Did he listen?" Do not ask your child: "What did you do to start this?" or say "It'll get better tomorrow." Children who are bullied rarely do anything to cause their pain and usually need an adult's support because the bullying generally continues.

Ask a peer.

You might be able to gain more information from your child's pal than your own child. Also, if your child is unsure if this is really bullying, encourage her to talk with witnesses to get their take.

Talk to the adult in charge.

If you still suspect bullying and your child won't talk to you, arrange a conference with a trusted adult who is in charge of the situation where the bullying occurs—the coach, teacher, scout leader, play-group parent. Keep in mind that bullying does not happen in *all* school settings, in *all* classrooms, or in *all* play arenas, so go to the adult who oversees the place where the bullying is happening and get his or her take on the situation. If your child has more than one teacher you may need to meet with each educator or coach.

WHAT TO DO IF YOU KNOW YOUR CHILD IS BULLIED

Chances are if your child is bullied she will need advice as to how to handle her tormentor. Here are ways to boost your child's safety and reduce victimization.

- *Believe your child.* One of the biggest parenting mistakes is not taking our kids seriously when they report bullying episodes. Forty-nine percent of kids say they've been bullied at least once or twice during the school term, but only 32 percent of their parents believed them. So reassure your child that you believe him, thank him for coming to you, and stress that you will find a way to keep him safe.

- ***Don't make promises.*** You may have to protect your child, so make no promises to keep things confidential. "I want to make sure you don't get hurt, so I can't guarantee I won't tell. Let's see what we can do so this doesn't happen again."

- ***Gather facts.*** Get specific information so you can help your child create a plan to stop the bullying. Ask: "What happened?" "Who did this?" "Where were you?" "What time did this happen?" "Who was there?" "Were you alone?" "Has it happened before?" "How often?" "How does it start?" "What did you do? "Do you think he'll do it again?" "Did anyone help you?" "Did an adult see this?" "Did anyone try to help?"

- ***Identify allies.*** Brainstorm who are adults your child can feel safe to go to in case of bullying like the nurse, the second-period teacher, or the coach. Kids who have even one friend to confide in can deal with bullying better than those on their own, so help your child find a supportive pal.

- ***Tell the school.*** Arrange for a school conference and let the teacher, counselor, school nurse, or principal know about the bullying. Don't assume they are aware of what is going on—most bullying happens when adults are not present. Share the facts you gathered, and ask what can be done to support your child. The adults must take this seriously, protect your kid, and if necessary, keep this confidential.

- ***Help your child avoid the bully.*** Sometimes the best way to spare your child distress is to avoid the bully altogether— especially if your child's behavior or emotional health is in jeopardy. So identify the place and time bullying usually happens, and then brainstorm ways to reduce contact. Explain that bullying often happens in unsupervised areas,

so tell your child to be near others at lunch, recess, in hallways, near lockers, parks, or other spots. Here are common
places bullying occurs and solutions:

- *On the bus:* "Sit across from the bus driver on right side
  of the bus. Don't sit near the back where the driver can't
  see you." You could also ask an older kid to "watch out"
  for your child, or could offer to pick your child up from
  school.
- *At a locker:* "Let's get a backpack so you can carry your
  books with you and don't have to go to your locker."
- *In the school restroom:* "Avoid using the bathroom during recess or before or after school. Get a hall pass during class time or use the nurse's restroom. She can help
  you." (You may need teacher support.)
- *On the playground:* "Play closer to the yard teachers.
  Avoid the fringe corners or near the equipment. Teachers can't see you there. If you have a problem, walk to an
  adult."

- ***Don't retaliate except when unavoidable.*** Most bullies target children who are weaker or more vulnerable, so telling
  your child to "defend himself" or "fight back" may be an
  impossible feat and also set him up for injury. In addition,
  your child may be suspended or expelled for fighting, and
  the bully could very well get away with the cruelty.
- ***Teach your child the four safety tips for bullying:*** Teach
  your child the acronym PLAN and its four parts to keep
  him safer from bullies or injury.

  P—**Pal up:** "Hang out with a large group; stay with one com-
      panion or find someone who is older or bigger who can
      help look out for you. There is safety in numbers."
  L—**Let adults know.** "Talk to someone you trust and seek
      them out if you don't feel safe."
  A—*Avoid bullying "hot spots":* "Stay away from areas where
      bullying is more likely to happen like bathrooms, the

> back of the bus, far corners of a playground, under
> stairwells."
>
> N—*Notice your surroundings.* "If you think there could be
> trouble, leave that spot. Take a different route, but don't
> go off alone."

■ *Monitor closely.* Bullying is rarely a one-time incident.
Warn your child that the bullying may continue but to
keep coming to you with updates of how things are going.
Stress that you will do whatever it takes to help your child
stay safe.

WHAT YOU CAN DO TO BULLY-PROOF YOUR KID

Kids usually don't know what to say or do if they are bullied, but
using the right comment or "look" can reduce and even stop bullying. In fact, how the child responds the *first* time makes a big
difference as to whether bullying continues, which is why early
intervention is so crucial. While there is no guaranteed bully-
proofing strategy, there are three steps that do help reduce victimization: 1. Stay cool, 2. Be assertive, 3. Use a comeback. I've culled
these techniques from research as well as from kids who told me
what worked to stop bullies: *From victims:* "This is what finally
helped me." *From witnesses:* "These are what kids less likely to be
bullied use." *And even from bullies:* "I stopped picking on her when
she started doing that." Your job is to figure out which steps and
strategies best fit your child's needs and situation, and then help
her practice again and again until she feels comfortable using it in
the real kid world.

Step 1: Stay Cool

The first bully-proofing tip is teaching your child to stay cool and
not react. I know, easier said then done, but when victims look
upset, cry, or flare up, bullying often escalates. Staying calm is
tough—especially for sensitive or impulsive kids—so here are strategies that might help.

■ *Empower your child.* Stress to your child that he has control on how he chooses to react to a bully and can't always rely on you. "You can't control what another person says or does, but you can control how you respond." "You may not be able to stop that kid from being so mean, but if you practice you can learn not to cry when he calls you names. I'll help you learn new responses."

■ *Identify a bully's motivation.* If your child understands that the bully wants a reaction, he may be more likely to stay cooler and halt the insults, sobs, or pleads. Say: "Bullies love power and knowing they can push other kids' buttons, so try to not let a bully know he upset you. If you beg or cry it gives the bully the power he craves."

■ *"Turn down" strong feelings.* If your child doesn't learn to "turn down" or "switch off" her upset facial gestures, she'll never convince a bully that she's not headed for a meltdown. So help your kid learn ways to turn down a heated look and switch to a more neutral expression. Marshall Duke and Stephen Nowicki suggest taking a photograph of your child using a facial expression that conveys little emotion (like when he's watching television or reading a book), then another photo using heightened emotions. Help him study the two expressions, then ask: "Which face would make your classmates less likely to pick on you?" "Which one will make them more apt to pick on you?" Once your child identifies the "right" expression that looks less sensitive, you can help him practice achieving a more neutral look. (See the next tips).

■ *Suggest replacers.* If your child tears-up easily, she'll need to learn what to do instead of crying, such as: "Think of a really fun place inside your head, and make your mind go there. Walk away really quickly. Clear your throat and bite your tongue. Count to ten inside your head. Hum a song (only inside your head). Take a long, slow breath." In order for the "crying replacement" to become a habit, a child must practice repeatedly.

- *Use a stone-faced glare.* Help your child use a mean stare that goes straight through the bully so he seems in control and not bothered (the response a bully seeks). It helps if you can point out someone using the right "stone-face" glare or "unfazed shoulder shrug." A movie clip (*Mean Girls* or *Clueless* are great) with young actors using the technique can be far more instructional than you trying to describe the look.

- *Ignore it.* If your child has a tougher time delivering verbal comebacks in the next section, sometimes a "walk off" is the best approach. It works best in places where your child *can* escape his tormentor such as on a park or playground. It *doesn't* work in closed quarters such on a school bus or at a cafeteria table. Tell your child to walk away without even a look at the bully, pretend the tormentor is invisible, glance at something else, look completely uninterested, or pretend to not hear the abuse.

Step 2. Be Assertive

A kid using unassertive body language and a wimpy, whiny voice is picked up on a bully's radar as an "easier target." So a key to bully-proofing is helping kids learn to "appear assertive and confident" and not "passive or aggressive." How a child looks can be more important in reducing bullying than what they say. Also if you want your child to stick up for herself, don't be so quick to step in and speak for her. Kids need practice being assertive and learning to be confident in their own skin so when they do need to stand up to a bully, they can. Here are tips:

- *Use strong body posture.* Using eye contact helps kids hold their head higher, and once they do their whole body language looks stronger and more assertive. Help your child learn to stand tall and appear more confident using this simple trick: "Always look at the color of the talker's eyes." A less-threatening variation for shyer kids is this tip: "Always look at the bridge of the talker's nose."

- *Use a strong, steady voice.* Bullies seek power or control so whimpering, crying, whining, whispering, or quivering voice tones lets them feel they've won. To help your child distinguish between "firm and whiney" voices, role-play voice variations, and then have her practice until she can speak with a stronger, more confident tone. Then tell your child before speaking to a bully to clear his throat, and think "firm and strong" (more Rambo less Tinkerbell).
- *Say a firm No.* If your child needs to respond to a bully, short, direct commands work best: *"No!" "Cut it out." "Stop."* or *"Back off."* The response must be delivered with a strong, determined voice.
- *Walk away.* Once the response is delivered, teach your kid to walk off with shoulders held back so as not to look like a victim.

Step 3. Use a Comeback

Most bullying begins with verbal harassment, so if a victim can defuse the verbal grenade the first time, the bullying is less likely to advance to the next level. The right comeback line—or a one-line assertive response—delivered using a firm voice and strong body language has that potential. And a pre-rehearsed response to a bully's anticipated barb can also boost confidence and reduce stress because the victim knows what to do. The delivery is crucial: The comeback must be practiced so it is said with as minimum of emotional heat as possible. Annoying, agitating, insulting, threatening, or making fun of a bully can only make things worse. Better for the child just to say the one line and exit with dignity still intact. Tell your child:

- *Refuse to take it.* "Wow, I'm not buying into this." "I'm out of here." "I don't need to hear this. I'm history—bye!"
- *Express plain displeasure.* "Stop it, would ya?" or "Cut it out" are simple ways to express what a child wants to happen. Bullies enjoy it when victims are upset so better for

your child to not voice his distress such as: "That makes me mad." or "I really get upset when you do that."

- **Question it.** "Why would you say that?" "Why would you want to tell me I'm dumb [or fat or whatever]?"
- **Leave.** If a child feels unsafe or his gut says that something might happen, tell your child to exit the scene. "Walk toward other kids or an adult or get help if you need to, and don't look back, so you seem unbothered."

These next comebacks sometimes work for defusing name-calling or a lower level of bullying. The optimum delivery is to sound sincere—never sarcastic—accompanied by an unfazed kind of look. Kids say that using humor—not sarcasm—is one of the best types of comebacks to defuse teasing or taunting.

- **Use manners.** "Hey, thanks. I appreciate that!" "That was really nice of you to notice." "Thanks." "Thank you for that comment."
- **Agree.** "You've got that right." "That's 100 percent correct!" "Right on!" "Yep, people say that a lot about me."
- **Say "So?"** "So?" "Whatever." "Okay." If your child likes this strategy, be sure to read *The Meanest Thing To Say,* by Bill Cosby, Jr., which nails the correct usage.
- **Act amazed.** "Really? I didn't know that." "Thanks for telling me."

WHAT ELSE YOU CAN DO TO HELP YOUR CHILD

Of course, it is all far easier to prevent victimization than to intervene, but it's never too late—or too early—to help your child bounce back from peer abuse. Here are factors that can reduce a child's chances of being bullied.

Strong and Positive Sense of Selfhood

Kids who appear more capable, confident, and resourceful are generally more successful in warding off a bully. That's why arming your child with confidence is one of the best defenses against bullying. A few self-confidence boosters include finding an avenue—such as a hobby, interest, sport, or talent, like weight-lifting or learning martial arts—that your child enjoys and can excel at, giving her opportunities to solve her problems and speak up for herself. While I am not an advocate of telling kids to "fight back," I am a believer in boosting kids' confidence through practicing defensive martial arts and learning assertiveness and to stay focused in the heat of the moment. Find a way to boost your child's inner strength.

Bullying can damage a child's view of self, so I teach victims to say a line under their breath to combat the pain of victimization: "I am a worthwhile, good person, and I don't deserve nor will I accept this treatment. The bully doesn't know another way to get his needs met so he's picking on me." Find a statement your child can learn to preserve her dignity. Surround her also with people who encourage, support, and convey that core message: "I love you, believe in you, and see you as a caring, worthwhile, glorious human being."

Bullies tend to target children who are isolated from their peers. A quick way to find out how your child is faring on the social scene is to ask him to try a map of two places bullies frequent: the playground or cafeteria. Then ask him to point out where he plays or eats—and where the other kids play or eat in relation to where he is. Does he have a peer support network or at least one buddy? Kids don't need a lot of friends, but one loyal buddy sure helps buffer the pain of peer rejection and abuse.

Studies show that kids who know how to join into a peer group, have a sense of humor, are friendlier, more cooperative, agreeable, and willing to share, and can control their anger are less likely to be victimized in school. Social skills do matter when it comes to buffering, bullying, and social skills are teachable. Take an honest look at your child's friendship-making abilities. Could he profit by learning how to start a conversation, join a group, encourage others, or other friendship-making skills? If so, talk to the school counselor to see if child-centric social-skill groups are available. Find parenting resources such as *Good Friends Are Hard to Find,* by Fred Frankel or *Nobody Likes Me, Everybody Hates Me: The Top 25 Friendship Skills and How to Teach Them* by Michele Borba (by yours truly) to teach kids social skills.

Take a good look at how the other kids dress and act. Clothes, haircuts, shoe styles, and accessories really do matter in helping kids gain peer approval. This is not about making your child conform or squelching his identity. It's more about how right now your child needs to fit in, and the truth is, kids' appearance, behavior, and hygiene does influence peer acceptance, and bullying *is* a relationship problem.

Look for opportunities for your child to meet kids anywhere or elsewhere—for example, scouting, park and recreation programs, sports teams, after-school programs, or youth groups. The experience might provide him with the opportunity to practice those new social skills he'll need to navigate that social jungle, and he may even find a pal.

Problem-Solving and Conflict-Resolution Skills

Research published by the American Psychological Association found that teaching kids how to solve problems helps prevent bullying and even reduces children's chances of being victimized. Their analysis of 153 bullying studies over the past thirty years found that children—especially boys—who demonstrate trouble solving problems are more at risk of becoming bullies, victims, or both. So use the following steps I developed to help kids learn to solve problems peacefully. Each letter in the acronym STAND represents a crucial step in conflict resolution.

S = ***Stop and calm down.*** Begin by helping kids calm down by taking a slow, deep breath or walking away until they can tune into their feelings. Once in control, kids can begin to figure out why they're upset and look for an answer.

T = ***Take turns telling the problem.*** After each kid shares what happened, summarize each view, and then end with, "What can you do now to solve this problem?" Enforce no put-downs or interruptions: Each person gets a chance to be heard.

A = *List alternatives.* The rules for generating solutions are the same regardless of age: "Say the first thing that comes into your mind. Don't put down anyone else's ideas. Change or add onto anyone's idea. Try to come up with ideas that work mutually for both sides." Warning: do not offer help unless kids are really stuck!

N = *Narrow your choices.* Kids need repeated, guided practice to learn good decision-making. Two rules move kids closer to resolution: *Get rid of solutions that are unacceptable to either kid. Eliminate solutions that aren't safe, wise, or respectful.*

D = *Decide on your best choice!* Finally kids need to learn how to make the best decision by thinking through possible consequences. Ask: *"What might happen if you tried that?"* Or: *"What is the one change that would make this work for both of you?"* Once kids decide, they shake on the agreement, and then put their plan into action.

Coping Strategies

All kids benefit from learning ways to handle those inevitable bumps of life, but bullied kids also need to learn ways to cope with the horrific injustice of peer abuse. Help your child discover strategies to reduce the fear and anxiety that bullying can cause. Yoga can be effective in curbing stress. Exercise, shooting baskets, listening to soothing music, writing about worries or the pain of a bullying in a journal are other options. Or allocate a cozy place in your home where your kid can chill out when he needs to ease the tension. Your child will need support. Be there!

WHAT TO DO WHEN BULLYING ESCALATES

Despite your best efforts, bullying can escalate. If there's the possibility your child could be injured, step in and be ready to advocate.

Meanwhile, here are things to do if the bullying continues or intensifies.

1 *Check your school's antibullying policy.* As of this writing, forty-three state legislatures have passed antibullying policies. The bullying that your child is enduring may be against the state law and/or school rules. Harassment can be a federal offense. Get a copy of the school's antibullying policy as well as your state's regulations. (Search online under your state's department of education listing.)

2 *Keep records.* Keep evidence of bullying such as torn clothing, threatening e-mails, witnesses' names, phone numbers, and details. Make copies of the records, and show them to the school or in the case of cyberbullying to your service provider. Also, tell your child to never delete a vicious e-mail. A copy should be printed for evidence.

3 *Notify authorities and gather support.* Tell those directly responsible for your child (his teacher, coach, pediatrician, day-care worker) about the continued bullying, and ask for a conference with the teacher and administrator. A multidisciplinary approach in which all adults in your child's life are involved to find a solution is best. The goal of the meeting should be to assure your child protection, support, and a plan for safety. Ask: "What will you do to ensure my child's safety?"

4 *Demand confidentiality.* You don't want retaliation. So limit the number of people you tell wherever possible.

5 *Go up the ladder.* Ask for a conference with the teacher and administrator. If you do not get support go up a level: Call the principal, superintendent, school board or the police.

6 *Insist on, "No face-to-face contact with the bully."* If physical safety is an issue, ask that the bully be distanced (in the class, at lunch, on the bus, etc.) by a certain number of feet. And do *not* allow your child be to placed in "conflict

resolution" with the bully to "resolve" the issue unless your child requests or agrees to the strategy. Bullying is *not* a conflict but an aggressive act. This is the bully's problem—not your child's issue.

7 *Be vigilant.* Don't be surprised if you are told to "toughen your kid up." You may need to change classes, teams, or even schools to protect your kid. Above all, keep the lines of communication open with your child. Let your child know in no uncertain terms, "You know you can always come to me." "I'm so glad you told me." "Let's keep talking about what to do so you're safe." Then continually monitor the situation to ensure that your child *is* receiving protection.

8 *Contact the police for safety issues.* Call the police and notify school officials anytime your child's safety is at stake. In particular, call or go to the police if bullying includes such things as threats of physical harm to a child, stalking or harassment, pornographic images, or extortion. Take such threats seriously. If your child receives a threat that may endanger another child, call the authorities as well. *Do not wait when it comes to threats of violence and extortion—pick up the phone.*

9 *Consider if an attorney is required.* If you have contacted the parents (or you don't feel comfortable doing so), and the bullying continues, you may need to hire an attorney to speak for you. Another option is to have an attorney send a certified letter describing possible legal options if the bullying does not stop. In rare cases you may want to press criminal charges. If so, contact a personal injury attorney if your child has been harassed or threatened in such a way as to cause severe emotional or physical damage or her reputation has been severely damaged. In some counties and states bullying or harassment may be considered a criminal act, and the parents can be held financially responsible if their child engages in wrongdoing that is due to lack of parental supervision.

WHAT TO DO IF YOUR CHILD IS
DEPRESSED OR APPEARS SUICIDAL

Bullying can become a life-and-death issue that we cannot ignore. Here are a just a few heart-wrenching comments I've heard from children tormented from peer abuse:

> *"I'm so scared he's going to come after me again—I just can't think,"* Tyrell, age 8.
> *"I can't get rid of the bad images—all the mean things the bully does keep flashing in my head,"* Kara, age 15.
> *"I go to sleep and pray I won't wake up,"* Sue, age 11.
> *"I hurt so bad I want to die,"* Joaquin, age 14.

The pain from bullying can seem unbearable to a child: Anxiety can build, self-esteem can plummet, depression can set in, post-traumatic stress disorder symptoms can emerge, and suicidal thoughts are possible. If your child has been victimized repeatedly, chances are he will need professional help and you to be his advocate and ensure that he receives the support and unconditional love he so deserves.

- *Find support services.* Enlist the perspectives of the school counselor, psychologist, and teacher. Ask what services the school provides for victims (and whether your child could qualify); for instance, individual counseling, assertiveness training, peer support, social-skill classes, or anger management classes.

- *Watch for depression.* Bullying can cause feelings of immense sadness, loneliness, and rage, and even lead to depression. Some kids hold their pain deep inside while others may release it in bouts of anger or rage. To help you recognize the difference between normal sadness and anger and depression apply the word "too" to these questions: *Is your child's sadness or anger* too *deep? Does the sadness or anger last* too *long or* happen *too* often? *Is it interfering with* too *many other areas of her life such as her home, school, friends?* If you spot that your child clearly is a "different kid," there are no physical problems that can explain the symptoms, and those signs continue over several weeks with no improvement, seek the guidance of a licensed mental health professional.

- ■ *Know when to intervene, ASAP.* If your child is saying scary things, is preoccupied with death or feelings of hopelessness, is drawing, writing, or asking about death, giving away personal belongings, is saying "What's the use?" or your instinct says something is not right, trust your instinct. If you have any thought that your child is suicidal, DO NOT WAIT. Call the USA National Suicide hotline at 800-784-2433 or 800-273-8255 and take him to the nearest emergency room immediately. Please.

FINAL THOUGHTS

> *"Never doubt that a small group of thoughtful,*
> *committed citizens can change the world.*
> *Indeed, it is the only thing that ever has."*
> —Margaret Mead

Bullying must never be tolerated. *No child should ever witness peer cruelty. No child should ever suffer harm inflicted by a peer. No child should ever intentionally cause another child pain.* Our goal must be to break the cycle of violence, stop peer cruelty, and provide our children with caring, safe, and respectful environments they so deserve. And we haven't a moment to lose.

Bullying: What Is a Parent to Do?

Peter Sheras, Ph.D.

Peter L. Sheras, Ph.D., ABPP, is a clinical psychologist and professor of education at the University of Virginia Curry School of Education. He works in his practice with bullies, victims, parents, and couples. He has authored many books and articles on violence, parenting, relationships, and adolescent behavior including, Your Child: Bully or Victim? Understanding and Ending School Yard Tyranny *and* I Can't Believe You Went Through My Stuff: How to Give Your Teen the Privacy They Crave and the Guidance They Need. *Both books are published by Fireside. With his wife, psychologist Phyllis Koch-Sheras, Ph.D., he has recently released* Lifelong Love: 4 Steps to Creating and Maintaining an Extraordinary Relationship, *published by Harlequin. He has worked with schools, institutions, and families for more than thirty-five years.*

The movie *Bully* evoked intense feelings and images of pain, anxiety, frustration, and outright desperation. As a parent of any child who is bullied there are many questions that are difficult to imagine. The fact that some children and teens who are victims might also be involved in bullying behaviors as well is even more confusing. If my child is a victim, my experience and intuition leads me to intervene or ask questions, but how would I even begin to approach the subject of my child as a bully?

As a parent and a clinical psychologist, I have spent decades working with parents, schools, victims, and bullies. I have raised two children of my own and watched them attempt to navigate the troubled waters of peer relationships, friends, bullies, and victims in a variety of settings. The questions below are the ones I have been working to answer and those that came up for me again, over and over, as I watched *Bully*.

For some of us, this world of violence, threats, exclusions, and conflict is only something we remember from our past, maybe as a bystander or with mild anxiety. For others, our recollections are vivid, painful, and traumatic and changed the world for us. Once victimized, how we see life is different. I learned early on as a parent that the most difficult thing to experience in life may very well be watching your child feel pain—physical or emotional. The feeling of helplessness that engenders is like no other.

So, how is it that we are to deal with bullying? Maybe it is so upsetting that we avoid seeing it right away, or at all. Perhaps we attempt to talk our children out of their feelings about what is happening to them. Then, something brings us up short. We realize that something painful, frightening, and even horrible is occurring. Once we know, we can choose the actions we might take; but how do we even access what they are experiencing if we have had no suspicions before or maybe minimized or overlooked them?

The first question is, **how do I know if my child may be being bullied?**

What can we observe to even know if we should ask our child

about it? There are signs, if we look for them. Some of them may be obvious and get our attention, but others might be more subtle. It is important to notice if there are circumstances or conditions that might make your child more vulnerable to being victimized. In most cases, victims are singled out because they are different or unique in some way. There is no universal characteristic of victims or bullies. However, if your child is different in some way from his peer group, it is worth taking note. As a parent, I remember thinking there were attributes my child had that were special, like intelligence, sense of humor, tone of voice, a dimple or birthmark, a way of walking or mannerisms that were endearing. In a school setting or peer group, these are the very differences that may make them targets. Conditions such as obesity, acne, stuttering, shyness, and social awkwardness often lead to separation from the "typical" group in the mind of classmates, playmates, or even in your child's mind. It may be very difficult to ask your son or daughter if they feel different from others. Typically there will be clues if they are trying to cover up their uniqueness.

Some of the most common characteristics that correlate with victimization are physical, emotional, and behavioral. Physical characteristics are most often smallness of stature, physical weakness, or a noticeable physical difference such as weight, extremes in height, or a physical disability of some type.

Emotional characteristics include sensitivity to shame or criticism, anxiety, depression, or feelings of loneliness and isolation. Behavioral characteristics might include autism or autism spectrum disorders (ASD), attention deficit hyperactivity disorder (ADHD), learning disability (LD), poor impulse control, low self-esteem, or social-skills deficits. Other factors to be considered are whether or not the child feels family or community support and secure social or socioeconomic status. A very poor or even a very affluent child may be singled out for attention from bullies.

Increasingly, other lifestyle or identity issues may play a role in victimizations. There is growing evidence that gender identity and lesbian, gay, bisexual, transgendered, questioning, and intersex (LGBTQI) individuals are frequent targets of bullies or peer-bullying activity.

The first step is trying to be aware of the traits and circumstances that might make it more likely that your child will be victimized. Next, parents need to find out if any bullying is actually going on.

HOW WILL I KNOW IF THERE IS SOMETHING WRONG?

Depending upon your child's age and grade in school and the type of school they attend, small or large, elementary, middle, junior high, or high school, there are some basic warning signs to look for. Is your child reluctant to go to school or refusing to ride the school bus? Do they complain about feeling sick in the morning, or often wind up in the school nurse's office needing to come home early? Does your child come home very hungry from school? (Maybe someone stole her or her lunch, or he or she was afraid to go into the school cafeteria.) Do they rush to the bathroom immediately upon returning home? (School restrooms can be havens for bullies.) Do they arrive home with torn clothing, bruises, or marks on their clothes or bodies? (Look especially for new bruises on top of old bruises in the same spots.) Sometimes these wounds may actually be self-induced in gestures of frustration or self-hate. Do they have increasing difficulty making friends or asking people over?

For younger children, signs may also include refusal to leave the house, nightmares, difficulty waking up, or trouble falling asleep. A young girl or boy may demonstrate anger toward parents (especially mothers) or siblings and pets upon return from school. Often this is an expression of the anger that has built up for them during the day as they are teased, humiliated, beaten, or robbed. Home is the first place safe enough to strike back without much fear of retaliation.

Physical bullying of girls, especially in high school and even in middle and elementary school, may involve sexual abuse. In addition to other signs of bullying, parents need to be on the lookout for signs such as general social withdrawal, excessive bathing or poor hygiene, retreating to more childlike or infantile behaviors in social interactions, eating problems such as anorexia or bulimia, binging and purging, or obsession with exercise or body image.

Knowing when to become concerned or even alarmed can be tricky. As our children reach developmental milestones, especially puberty, many of the signs above may be present. A hungry teenager, an angry middle schooler, or a daughter who spends way too much time in the bathtub may not be signs of anything other than normal growing up. So, a real thorny question becomes, how do we find out if our suspicions are warranted? The larger question is, **how can I talk to my child about bullying?**

One of the first mysteries for me as a parent and as a therapist is why children and teenagers who are victims of bullying don't tell their parents about what is happening to them. It must be painful. They must be thinking about getting some help or relief. Is it that they don't trust their parents, or is it just a sign of adolescent development? In figuring out how to talk with them about bullying and victimization, it is important to understand what they might be afraid of.

Consider the following. Your child may not be sharing with you because they are afraid—but not simply because they worry that you may somehow blame them for the situation and be angry with them. The fear is actually more complex. Many of my patients over the years have said they are worried that you will see them as incapable of handling their own lives at a time when they are trying to demonstrate their maturity and assert their independence. They worry that you might take things into your own hands ("I am going right over to talk to that bully's parents right now.") or make matters worse for them by letting the bully know they are talking to an adult. The fear is that the bully will take revenge and escalate the violence or intimidation the next time.

Another reason children don't complain or ask for help is that they may not want to upset you or be a "disappointment" to you. So they avoid sharing their difficulties so you won't have the imagined negative response. Bully victims also are concerned that you might give them advice that they cannot follow or does not turn out to be effective (such as, "Beat up the bully!"). If they take your advice and it fails, now they have to tell you that, and they will feel inadequate all over again. It is just easier to be quiet and hope that the bully moves away or that they can somehow avoid a confrontation.

Starting a conversation about the bullying and violence is quite challenging, even when we are motivated to do so. The key to doing this, I have found, is to not "interrogate" your child. Don't ask, "Are you being bullied?" See if the topic can be approached in a less threatening and less blaming way. Part of the idea here is to share your own experiences first and ask questions about other people in school, not just your child.

With a younger child consider starting the conversation with questions like these:

- Have you been eating your lunch?
- Looks like your shirt got torn today. How did that happen?
- It seems like you haven't wanted to go to school the past week. When I was your age, sometimes other kids would tease or push me. Does that ever happen to you at school or to any of your friends?
- How is the school bus ride these days? Are you ever bored or scared on the bus? Would you prefer that I drive you sometimes?
- Is there a lot of fighting at your school? Does it affect you or your friends much?
- Sometimes I used to get angry while at school and felt like hitting or hitting back at someone even though I knew it was wrong. Do you ever feel that way?

For teens or preteens think about these sorts of questions:

- Are there a lot of cliques in your school? What do you think about them?

- Is there something going on at school recently that you don't like? I notice you seem to be down on going these days.
- Do you feel like your clothes fit in at school? Do lots of other kids wear what you do? Who?
- Are there doors on the stalls in the restrooms? Do you worry about privacy or going in there?
- I developed early when I was your age. Guys always used to tease me about my body. Does any of that kind of stuff go on now?

Some of these questions may seem a bit specific or silly. Use the ones that your child might answer without feeling challenged or defensive. With some children you can just express your concerns straight out, but sometimes it is better to be more subtle or indirect.

If you suspect that your child is a victim of violence or bullying, there are two other things to keep in mind. The first is that the best actions to take against the victimizer are the actions of groups, not individuals. If your child has close friends, it might be that they are bullied as well. When you find out that your child has been negatively affected by other peers or older preteens or teens, consider talking with other parents who might be dealing with the same thing you are. As the movie clearly indicated, collective action can be the most powerful.

The second possibility to keep in mind is forming a partnership with the school. Although many students and some parents feel that the school may have let them down, as *Bully* portrays, and while some teachers and administrators can be rigid or insensitive, many are not. They also want your child to be safe, but they may need information or help from you. Do not be afraid to go to the school and express your concern, but also consider what it is you would like the school to do. If other parents also share your concerns, go together. Many schools have antibullying programs that you may not know about. Likewise, the schools may not be aware that the programs and interventions they have may not be working. An alliance between the school and the parents can be very powerful. Students I see in treatment often don't know that their complaints have been heard because the teachers or administrators may not have shared what has been done. More openness can go a long way to have students and parents feel more effective.

In watching the movie *Bully*, parents are likely to be mortified at the experiences of the victims and wonder if their child might be among the targeted. But you might also wonder **could my child be a bully?** How could you find out if he or she is? It is difficult to imagine the many complex emotions you would feel if you received a call from school reporting that your child has hurt or intimidated another. *How could my child possibly do that? It can't be true. What have I done to foster that sort of behavior?*

First of all, why is it that a child might hurt someone else, using superior strength, status, or intelligence to dominate another? It is important to remember that bullying is not a biological pre-disposition. A person is not destined to be a bully because of their genes or their character. Bullying, like most violent behavior, is learned. The bad news is that they learned it somewhere. The good news is that whatever is learned can be unlearned.

Children learn to bully, sometimes at a very young age, for a number of reasons. The easiest explanation is that they are rewarded for these behaviors. Early attempts to gain attention, possessions, or respect can lead to aggressive behaviors. If there are no adults or peer role models to discourage them and these strategies are successful, they will persist. Lack of parental attention and guidance or lack of supervision at school or in the community, such as at the bus stop, can reinforce negative bullying behaviors.

Students may bully to seek control over situations that are confusing or chaotic for them. Stress or disorganization in their families or in the immediate environment may cause them to seek control. If your parents just informed you that they are separating or your foster home placement is about to be changed, you might tend to assert control where you can to balance the loss of control in areas where you feel powerless. When anxiety about the future is increased, more extreme behaviors may ensue.

Your parenting style may appear to be rigid or threatening to your child. This may model controlling behaviors among those who feel they are overcontrolled or unfairly controlled at home. They may not understand the complexity of social situations and simply emulate your behaviors without question. If your child is aggressive and impulsive by nature, they may be more likely to express these behaviors through physical or even social violence. How they choose to express themselves is learned in the environment in which they live.

Social acceptance can also be a motive for bullying. The fear of being unpopular can cause the desire to gain control by fostering fear in others. Being popular and staying in the "in-group" can be a powerful motivator. Sometimes bullies are not odd or overbearing people. They may be the most popular and high-achieving students. They may bully to stay on top and to gain followers to ensure they will remain popular. Some students participate in group bullying behaviors or imitate bullies to avoid being singled out as targets.

Finally, bullying may be a response to earlier victimization or even current victimization in another context. High levels of anger at being victimized can be converted into aggressive and intimidating behavior toward others. It is estimated that between 15 and 30 percent of bullies have been victims either currently in other contexts or in the past. One of the ways of managing the frustration of being a helpless victim is to make another feel helpless. What seems to be characteristic of all bullies is that they have an inability to manage their anger and frustration in an appropriate and socially acceptable way.

HOW MIGHT A PARENT FIGURE OUT IF THEIR CHILD IS A BULLY?

What kind of questions should you ask or what sorts of behaviors should you look for? Some behaviors to look out for are: unhappiness or anger most of the time, poor or declining grades, reports of behavior or social problems at school, destruction or disregard for property or others' possessions, acting out physically rather than using words, rudeness and swearing, shortened attention span, and alcohol and substance abuse. While many non-bullies exhibit these behaviors, taken all together these characteristics describe many bullies.

Sometimes talking to your child directly is an effective way to find out if the term *bully* would fit them. Here are some possible questions:

- What do you do when you feel angry at someone?
- Do you think other people respect you at school?
- Do you know people who don't stand up for themselves?
- Do kids like to be teased at school?
- Do you need to protect yourself against other kids at school or after school?
- Are there a lot of weird or strange kids in your school?
- Are there lots of fights at school or after school?
- Do you feel stronger than most of the other kids in your school?

Also, keep your ear to the ground. Observe them in social interactions. Listen to what other kids say about them if you can. Speak with teachers, and notice how others act around them. Do they have friends? Do others call them, message them, text them, or otherwise seek them out? If not, you might ask your child what they make of that fact.

The film *Bully* powerfully shows the raw emotions and fears that victims feel. The question that can only briefly be addressed here is, **what to do about it?**

There are a number of steps to take in the face of bullying—when your child is the victim. The first action is to empower your child. Strengthen his or her self-esteem, build pride, and help them feel less guilty or inadequate about how they have acted. Learning martial arts can help many children, not so they can beat up the bully, but to feel better about themselves. Help your child build courage to act in the face of fear, not just when fear goes away. Teach them to get help from adults and rescue others.

The second action is to teach them to name the crime, tell the bully to stop, walk away (if you can), make a joke out of it, or tell friends. Get them to work with you to think of alternatives to submitting. They can actually understand and help the bully with the help of one of their other victimized friends.

A third action is to form partnerships with other parents, your child's friends, and the school. Listen to your child so they can tell you what is working and what is not. Support them in doing what they need to do. Of course, help them if they are in real danger, but let them assert their own skills first to think through a strategy and then to act on it.

A fourth action is to recognize that there may be a bully in all of us, angry, scared, and frustrated. What does the bully want? Sometimes it is friendship or acceptance. Don't go it alone. Work with friends or groups at school to reach out or have adults reach out. If it is your child who is the bully or is just starting some bullying behaviors, teach them to manage their anger. Don't be angry at them, show them how they can channel their anger into positive action. Remember that in the film parents and friends were able to turn their anger and grief into community demonstrations that brought more support and understanding to the problem.

Finally, be sure to follow up. Be persistent. Ask your child regularly how it is going. Check with the school often, and offer to volunteer at school or help in the office or talk to parent groups. Be involved and stay involved. It is collective actions that will stop the bullies. As the film so clearly documents, we must do it together.

No Kidding, I Was Bullied Too!

Joe Pantoliano

Born on September 12, 1951, and raised in Hoboken, New Jersey, the actor spent most of his childhood on the mean streets of Hoboken. After his father's life was threatened by a heart attack, his family was put on welfare and moved into the rough-and-tumble Jackson Street Projects. Joey's family was uprooted many times due to their financial struggles. Their gambling addictions often led to evictions, and Joey found himself "the new kid" sometimes only three blocks away. Joey was the only son of Dominic (Monk) Pantoliano, a World War II veteran, factory foreman, and hearse driver. Monk had street cred because he had skills, and they netted him two suits and a $100 bill for bowling 300. Monk's wife, Mary Centrella-Pantoliano, was a hardworking part-time seamstress/bookie. Joey and his younger sister, Maryann, spent their formative years with their mother's cousin, Florio. When Pantoliano was twelve years old, his parents separated; after Florio was released from federal prison, having served more than twenty-one years for his crimes, he came to live with Mary and the kids. Eventually, the kids had two fathers.
  Pantoliano suffered from severe dyslexia and ADHD (diagnoses were confirmed many years later); at seventeen, he was still reading at a third-grade level. After seeing his son perform in the senior play, Up the Down Staircase,

Florio encouraged him to pursue acting professionally. Joey hired a teacher to teach him how to read so that he could realize his dream of becoming an actor. He cut class to sign up at HB Studios. For the next seven years he learned his craft in small basement theatres where the rats sometimes outnumbered the audience. Eventually he made his way to Hollywood, and today Joey Pants is one of show business's most prominent actors, boasting more than 160 film, television, and stage credits. His string of film classics include: killer pimp Guido in Risky Business *(1983), bumbling Francis Fratelli in* The Goonies *(1985), refugee merchant seaman Frank Demerest in Stephen Spielberg's classic* Empire of the Sun *(1987), Bob Kean (who discovered Ritchie Valens) in the 1987 cult classic* La Bamba*, double-crossed bail bondsman Eddie Moscone in* Midnight Run *(1987), and U.S. Marshal Cosmo Renfro in* The Fugitive *(1994) and* U.S. Marshals *(1998).*

Then in 1995 Pantoliano starred opposite Will Smith and Martin Lawrence in the Michael Bay/Jerry Bruckheimer film Bad Boys *(1995). Next, the Wachowskis and Dino De Larentiis put Joey above the title opposite Gina Gershon and Jennifer Tilly in the lesbian cult classic* Bound *(1996), which he followed with the role of Cypher in the billion-dollar hit* The Matrix *(1999). He then played the role of Teddy opposite Guy Pearce and* Matrix *alum Carrie-Anne Moss, in* Memento *(2000). Around that time, David Chase made Joey an offer he could not refuse with the craziest character on TV, Ralph Cifaretto on* The Sopranos *(2000–2004), netting Pantoliano an Emmy.*

Still, despite all this success, Pantoliano struggled with depression for many years—he was diagnosed with clinical depression in 2007. His life often spiraled into alcohol and drug addiction, a downward journey he details in his latest book, Asylum *(Weinstein Books, 2012). (Pantoliano's first book,* Who's Sorry Now: The True Story of a Stand-Up

Guy, *published in 2002, is a memoir about his New Jersey childhood.) Four years ago, Pantoliano founded No Kidding, Me Too!, a nonprofit organization and advocacy group that aims to remove the stigma attached to mental illness through education. He also produced a documentary of the same name.*

I was thin until I was eleven years old, and then food and television became part of my medicine. When I was a young boy growing up in the projects, my parents would use food as a stabilizer and insist I eat everything on the plate. Every time I threw a fit, this was the scene: "What's the matter? C'mon, stop crying, sit down," my father cried. "Watch some TV and I'll make you a sandwich..." Mommy fed me sandwiches and commercials told me the kind of candy and cereal I should eat, how I should dress, and what a cool kid looks like. I used to imagine myself inside that TV—if only I could be like Frank Sinatra or Dean Martin and Richard Conte and Perry Como, I could be happy.

I don't know about happy, but I became fat, and kids started picking on me. I had a whole slew of bullies who had me in their bull's-eye. In the first grade, I got the honor of cleaning the erasers. You had to go into the boys' room in the basement and bounce them against the wall to get all the dust out. While I was doing that, two fifth graders, black kids, came in. They saw me and started dragging me around. They hit me, got me onto the ground. As one kid held me down, the other kid urinated in my face, and then the other kid took his turn, so they both urinated all over my upper body, my face, my clothes. I think I was more in shock than I was emotionally affected. I wasn't crying. I was in a daze. And I remember going back to my classroom and putting the erasers away and sitting down and kids starting to giggle, like *What's that smell? It's Joe, it's him!*

The teacher realized what was going on and whisked me off to the vice principal, asking me what happened, and I said, "Nuthin'."

That was my stock answer. I was taught at an early age that you never rat—we were all in the same boat, but you were accepted based on whether you were stand up or tough or you could handle yourself, and I wanted people to think I could handle myself. But she took me to the principal's office, and then both of these powerful masters of higher learning decided to parade me through each of the upper classrooms to pick out the kids who did this. (They didn't take me home and clean me up or anything like that, even though I lived across the street.) For years, I thought I didn't pick them out. I thought at least that I was stand up. But I did. So not only was I a victim, but I felt like a rat.

Celebs Speak Out

"I got beaten up by a lot of people when I was younger. It was after I first started acting and I liked to behave like an actor, or how I thought an actor was supposed to be, and that apparently provoked a lot of people into hitting me."

—*Robert Pattinson, actor*

Another time, there was this kid named Rabbit. He was a big target in our neighborhood. We started sounding off on each other. I was going into the seventh grade, so I couldn't have been more than twelve, and we got into an argument and started ragging on each other's mothers, which is what you did back then—you went right for the mothers. Finally, this kid who was maybe sixteen was beating on me, to the point where I was so exhausted—when kids fight after a while they can't lift their arms—that he had me on my back with his knees on my shoulders, and he was pounding me in the face. I pretended to get knocked out, which I thought would scare him, and it did, and he backed away. But then I started laughing like *I got him*, you know? And one of the kids said, "Hey, Rabbit, he's laughing, man." So he came back for some more. Somehow they broke it up, and I was with one of my friends—I think his name was Raymond—and we go upstairs, and my mother sees me, and my eye was just about swollen shut. "What happened?" she asked. "Nuthin'," I said. And she grabs Raymond and throws him up against the wall and says, "What happened to my son?" and he says, "Rabbit hit 'em."

So my mother, who had been sweeping the house with a broom, is going down to the playground, and she's going to find this kid, right? And I'm going, "No, mommy, leave him alone." I don't want my mother to fight my battles. And so my mother walks out the front door of the building, and there's this fence on either side, and she takes the broom and slams it over the fence, and the handle breaks off. So now she's got a broom with a jagged edge. She finds the kid and starts smacking him around. She got him on the ground and says, "You ever touch my son again, I'll kill you." Here's a woman in a housedress beatin' this kid, and it made my situation even worse—although, I have to say, a lot of the bullies stopped because they were afraid of her.

I had to go to the hospital and everything, because I almost lost vision in my eye—the white of my eye was beet-red with blood from a vessel that was broken. So now I'm going to junior high school with a swollen eye. I'm already a target, before I even start school, because these kids saw this as a mark of weakness.

There was a black kid who had brothers who were tough. This kid was a little teeny thing, but he would shake you down for money. (There was also a girl who would shake me down every day and say, "Give me your money," you know? A girl bully. And I would try to avoid her and walk different ways to school.) I remember it was Halloween, and I put a plan together with some of my cousins and my friends—there were five or six of us. We would go trick-or-treating together, and I said, "Look, if this kid shows up, we're gonna have to beat him up. United we stand, divided we fall." I was saying this dressed up as a hobo like Emmett Kelly, so I have a broomstick with a hobo bag tied to the end of it, a fake beard, a stocking hat, and makeup all over my face. Not what you would call a tough guy.

So we're at Fourth Street Park, and we hear, "Hey, hey"—it's so funny because I walk my dog over there now when we're at the apartment in Hoboken, and a day doesn't go by that I don't think of this incident, fifty years later—and so as he's running toward us, my friends start running away, and I'm going "Don't run, you dopes, get back!" So sure enough, it's just him and me, and he goes, "Give me your candy," and I said no. He said, "What?" And I said no again, so he pushed me, right? He said, "Give me your candy," and while he said it I remember everything starting to slow down. I'm thinking and looking around to see if there were any adults around, if I could hit him with the broomstick, where I was gonna hit him. Finally I swing the stick, and I remember hitting him across the side of his head by his ear and him going down to one knee and holding his ear with both hands. He looked at me stunned—stunned that this kid could hit him like that. And then he just went, "Mama!" I was so afraid. I started running to my cousin's house on Fifth and Jefferson, and I had this big shopping bag filled with candy, and it was like a breadcrumb trail of candy right to my cousin's house—the candy was popping out of my bag and left a direct route for me. By the time I got there, I had hardly any candy left, and she could see my face through the makeup and said, "What happened to you? You look like you saw a ghost."

Kids Speak Out

"I find it extremely disappointing that some people would purposely hurt others for reasons that shouldn't matter. Some people do it for no reason at all, too. If you're one of these people, I suggest you watch this and really think about the effect you're having on other people. Anybody who is or ever has been bullied, stay strong because there will be something done about this."

—*Skyler Harmon*

Months later, if not years, I was at this candy store playing pinball, and that same kid shows up, and I'm going, *Oh, no*, but he didn't recognize me. He said, "Give me a quarter." And I gave him the quarter, and that was that.

I was ashamed to tell these things to my stepfather, Florio. Florie wouldn't have given that kid a quarter. Florie was a bona fide made guy, he was a member of the mafia, and he was handsome, cool—there was nobody cooler than Florio. I remember when he came home to live with us after he was released from the Atlanta federal penitentiary. We were all at the airport to meet him, and he's looking around going, "Where's my Joey?" and I'm going, "I'm Joey. I'm Joey." And he's ignoring me. "Mary," he asked my mother, "where the hell is Joey?" And I'm going "I'm Joey. I'm Joey." And he goes, "Mary, who is this fat kid? Did he eat Joey?" He's like, "Joey, are you in there?" I was so ashamed that I didn't make him happy to see me, and I blamed it on my frame.

So I started dieting and starving myself, refusing to eat. Even when my body was craving food, I wouldn't do it. I was going to emulate Florie and all the movie stars who were thin. Montgomery Clift became my hero. I decided to create a new me. When I moved from Hoboken to Cliffside Park for the tenth, eleventh, and twelfth grades, I decided I was going to create a character—it was the first character I ever created. I put a little bit of Florie in there, I put more of the *dese*, *dems*, and *dose* in there, because I was really tough, you know, since I was from Hoboken. I would give 'em a smack if they messed with me. I bullied the bully, I became a bully. Because bullies bully, they gotta feel better then! At somebody else's expense. *I didn't know.* I wanted to avoid being beat up, so I smacked them before they had a chance at me.

Now I'm living in Fort Lee, and I'm the new kid again, and there was this kid—I'm telling ya, they just spot you—so one day I'm walking down the hall when he shoulders me into the lockers. This time I see *red* and I *slam* this punk back... Pushing *him* up against the locker with my forearm under his neck, just like that. All of a sudden!... I see *red* and my body would act, and before my brain could even think it, I was off to the races—and this kinda followed me throughout my adult life—dormant like. And then something would go off. So now I've got my forearm on this kid's throat, and they pull me off of him. The bully straightens his rumpled tie, stilled pissed... and he goes "After school," while I'm like...Oh s———!... "Yeah, all right, f———, after school." Later

DID YOU KNOW...?

Homes in which bullies live will most likely be:

- Void of consistent adult supervision
- Hostile
- Supportive of aggression as a way of solving conflicts
- In neighborhoods where violence is commonplace
- Run by adults who model bully behavior (either consciously or not)

Source: catholicdos.org

at cafeteria, my cousins are going, "All right! There's going to be a fight after school!" And after school we fight, and I crack this kid in the nose, and that's all she wrote. There's blood gushing out of his face. It's all over me, and it's all over him. He cries uncle, and my cousin and me walk down the front steps of the high school where Florie would always pick me up. Florie sees blood all over me, and he jumps out of the car. "What happened?" he said. I said, "Nuthin'." He said, "Don't give me 'nuthin'. What happened?" My cousin told him there was a fight. Florie used to keep a golf club in the back of his car as a weapon, and he said, "You go back there and bash this kid's head in with this club." I had to beg him and tell him it was over, that I won, that the blood on me was the other kid's, because you don't run away from a fight. Florie didn't run away from a fight, and that's why he spent twenty-one years of his life inside a federal penitentiary.

We are programmed to believe what we see on television, that there's always a first act, a second act, and in the third act we find out who the bad guy is. That's not the way it is in real life. It's too complicated. Back then, I didn't want to tell anyone that I was scared or that I had trouble learning in school, because I didn't want to look like I couldn't handle myself. But I didn't feel good inside. Ever. So for a long time, I took on a physical life, as a result of alcoholism and drug addiction. I married several times. My first wife was beautifully exotic. She was Eurasian, half Chinese and half American, and my wife Nancy the Irish Spring girl. Literally. Nancy was a beautiful model—five-foot-ten, blue eyes, red hair, peaches and cream skin. And she loved me? What was that all about? That still wasn't enough to make me feel better. I thought, *What's it gonna take? How much more do you need, Joey?* I kept medicating my depression, which I didn't even know I had until many years later, by doing all the things that I thought would make me whole. I call them the "Seven Deadly Symptoms"—alcohol, sex, food, shopping, prescription drugs, vanity, and an overwhelming drive for success. I was trying to fill that emptiness inside of me with all the things they say are supposed to make us happy. And I couldn't understand why I was always feeling bad because at face value I had nothing to be depressed about. I was successful.

When I was in the second grade, we began to realize I had difficulty keeping up with the rest of my class, but I didn't know why. Years later, I was carrying all this shame from being left back twice. I didn't realize I had dyslexia or ADHD until two of my four kids were diagnosed thirty years later. Back then, they thought I was stupid, lazy, or crazy. I remember in fourth grade, me and two other kids were behind, and the teacher threw a fit, permanently taking our reading book away and declaring in front of the whole class, "if you three won't do the work with the rest of your class, you don't deserve to read." Finally I remember thinking, *Forget it, I'm busting my butt and getting it kicked in too, trying to get this stuff right, but I can't.* So by the tenth grade I stopped trying. I was gonna show them—the teachers passed you through as long as you didn't disrupt the class.

Much later I was diagnosed with ADHD and dyslexia, and it was like, *Eureka!* I felt like I hit a home run. You mean, it's not me? I'm not alone?

I had a mental illness, what I like to call a "brain dis-ease." Nobody talks about it. You've got tons of ads for erectile dysfunction. How did erectile dysfunction become cooler than mental dis-ease? They've got Bob Dole. Who do we have?

That's why I began NKMTOO.

DID YOU KNOW...?

Over 50 percent of students with undiagnosed mental "dis-ease" age fourteen and older drop out of high school—the highest dropout rate of any disability group.

Source: nami.org

Four years ago, I started my nonprofit organization, No Kidding, Me Too!, in part because I wanted to teach kids to have emotional intimacy. I think the answer is education. Educating ourselves. Educating other people. Don't keep it in, let it out, talk about it. Or else it really does affect you—in ways you might not even know. We have to make kids understand that talking about what's happening to you, talking about your feelings—as embarrassing as you might think it is—is cool. Because when you talk about it, you realize that you're not alone.

ABOUT US

Mission

No Kidding, Me Too! is a 501(c)(3) public charity, whose purpose is to remove the stigma attached to brain dis-ease (BD) through education and the breaking down of societal barriers. Our goal is to empower those with BD to admit their illness, seek treatment, and become even greater members of society. For more information please visit http://nkm2.org

PART 9

Where Are
They Now?

ALEX LIBBY

After the Libbys and the Sioux City School District were made aware of the terrible bullying that Alex had been enduring at school, Jackie Libby, Alex's mom, successfully petitioned to have Alex moved to a different school within the district.

Although Alex was content there and told his mother "he wasn't getting bullied as much," he was failing almost all of his classes. "My husband and I weren't happy with the situation," Jackie said. "I mean, it was great that they were pick-ing Alex up for Friday night football games and before school started they introduced Alex to the most popular kids in school so they would friend him, but my husband and I struggled a lot with that at night. We would talk about it and say, 'But that's *just* Alex. What are they doing for other bullied kids?' We couldn't let go of the families we had left behind at East Middle, and also we have four other children—they weren't going to do that for all of them."

Ultimately, the Libbys decided to move, but were unsure of where to go until they attended the premiere of *Bully* in New York City in April 2011. "We met the Smalleys and the Johnsons, and they were the most ostracized out of all of us by their communities," Jackie said. "My husband and I went home after that trip thinking we really wanted to do something for them, because as alone as we felt, we hadn't felt anything near what they were feeling, and it broke our hearts."

The Libbys decided to move to Edmond, Oklahoma, because they had an award-winning school district—plus, the town just

> "I thought [the film] was going to be on TV, and since people watch TV all the time, I thought if the bullies see this, they'll realize what they're doing and try to change it. So I was doing it because I wanted to make a change, not just for me, but I just hoped that we could all come together and be friends."
>
> —*Alex*

happened to be smack dab, about forty-five minutes, from both the Johnsons, who live in Tuttle, and the Smalleys in Perkins. "It occurred to us that that's where we should go," Jackie said. "That's what we can do for them. We can be in Oklahoma. We can stand up together."

She added that Edmond Memorial High School, which Alex has been attending since November 2011, has a mentorship program for kids with disabilities. "Everyone who is a grade higher than all the children with disabilities is considered responsible for them," Jackie said. "And they're taught not to allow anything to happen to them, verbally or physically, and if it does they are to report it. Alex hasn't had a single incident of abuse there since we moved here."

"It's much better," said Alex, now fifteen. "The first day I came, nobody knew nothing about how I was in the movie, and some kids just asked me to sit at their table. I just made friends from then on."

If in Sioux City Alex had become sad and disconnected from his family because of bullying, over the course of his first school year in Edmond he was reborn. "We watched our son come back to us," Jackie said.

KELBY JOHNSON

"You start life out thinking everything will go as planned, but sometimes it doesn't," said Kelby Johnson, nineteen. "Sometimes life starts spiraling out of control at a very early age, and sometimes, just sometimes, it makes you stronger."

By the end of *Bully*, although Kelby (who is now transgender

and identifies as a man) had been determined to stick it out in Tuttle, Oklahoma, and take a stand against the physical and emotional violence against him, he decided that perhaps his message would be more effective elsewhere and will be working with the Gay, Lesbian and Straight Education Network (GLSEN) and other organizations to learn how to make laws and lobby Congress on behalf of the Safe Schools Improvement Act (SSIA) and Student Non-Discrimination Act (SNDA) legislation. "I will do everything I can to ensure that every child feels safe and protected at school, and I won't stop fighting until that happens," Kelby said. "We have an obligation to the next generation to do something about this. We can be the ones to make a change and stop the hate. This movie and this opportunity gave me the strength to pick myself up and to try to motivate other kids to help make a change. These kids need to know that they are not alone and that they have a hand to pick them back up. I want to be that hand."

Kelby hadn't realized the pervasiveness of bullying in schools until he met Lee Hirsch. "I am so proud to have been a part of this film," he said. "The look of inspiration on the kids' faces after they have watched it still humbles me. They immediately want to help, to stand up with us, because most of them have been hurt, too."

Although his family remains in Tuttle, Kelby received his GED and now lives in Oklahoma City. His family plans to join him there

"This whole experience has been more than I could have ever imagined. The people in and involved with the movie have not only become my friends, but they are allies. My *family*. And it has helped me and my family find our spirit, our calling. We have become closer and stronger than ever, and I would do this all over again."

—Kelby

once his brother graduates from high school. "I hate to be called a victim," Kelby said, "because that is the past. I am no longer that person. My future is what is important now. I am an informed, strong, compassionate fighter who is ready for this battle. My dad always says, 'You get what you tolerate.' So once the schools say they won't tolerate bullying anymore, then the standard will be set, and most of the hell these kids are going through will stop. It's as simple as that."

JA'MEYA

In the final moments of *Bully*, Ja'Meya Jackson—who had been incarcerated for brandishing her mother's handgun on the school bus—has had the charges against her dropped. And after a brief judge-ordered hospitalization, she finally returns home to Yazoo County, Mississippi. In a heartwarming scene of the film, Ja'Meya walks through her front door after so much time away and travels room after room, telling her mother, Barbara, "It's so pretty here!"

These days, Ja'Meya, now seventeen, is blossoming, too. Although when she first went back to school after her arrest, there was a difficult adjustment period, as time went along she found her footing and again maintains high academic achievement. "They just love her now," Barbara said of Ja'Meya's teachers. "Everything's great."

Ja'Meya currently attends the school she left originally because of bullying, and her school bus commute is back to fifteen minutes rather than the hour-long ride she endured before.

"I feel great," Ja'Meya said. "I'm getting along with everyone, going to the mall, to the movies. Everyone's coming up to me and talking to me and stuff. They're saying they heard about the movie.

> "I thank God for all of the people in the movie. I love Lee dearly. He has been a blessing for me and my daughter."
>
> —Barbara, Ja'Meya's mom

I watched it, too. It brought tears to my eyes."

When Ja'Meya graduates from high school, she plans to enlist in the Armed Forces. "Either the Air Force or the Army," she said. "My grand-daddy, he passed away, he was in the military."

Barbara said she is happy to have been a part of the *Bully* experience.

"The film's given everyone attention of what's really going on out there," Barbara said. "When it first happened, it had me just worried. I thought that there wasn't gonna be no good end in this. I thought what was happening to Ja'Meya was something bad, but everything that looks bad isn't always bad. Now things are looking up for her. It's like a blessing."

DAVID AND TINA LONG

Since the death of their son Tyler in 2009, David and Tina Long struggled to have their school district, the Murray County School District in Georgia, take more of a stand on bullying. After numerous public engagements, including town-hall meetings and appearances on *The Ellen Show* and in *Bully*, they wished they had better news.

"The school district has ignored the film, has ignored the issue," Tina said. "As a matter of fact, we feel that they went backward. It's been very hard on Troy and Teryn. They started pre-K in this school and have many friends. Teryn is at the top of her class and may possibly be valedictorian. She would hate to lose something that she has worked so hard on." Tina added that while she and David continue to look for options for their children, they do not feel supported by the school administration. "David and I just want to get them graduated as safely as possible. It's so sad that this school system has placed them in such an awful position."

"It's very disheartening to see," David agreed. "They couldn't care less, and until that whole administration and school board is replaced in that county, it's going to continue to be the same way. There needs to be a federal definition of what bullying is, because state by state it differs, and educators—or local school systems such as ours—can take that and twist it to however it works best for them."

In 2010, the Longs sued the Murray County schools, accusing the district, and the high school principal, of "deliberate indif-

ference" with regard to the ongoing bullying of Tyler, which resulted in his suicide. While in May 2012 a federal judge ruled in favor of the school district— stating the district did not have to protect Tyler from harm by private individuals—he acknowledged that Tyler had endured "nearly constant bullying." "There is little question that Tyler was the victim of severe disability harassment, and that Defendants should have done more to stop the harassment and prevent future incidents," the judge ruled.

The Longs are appealing the ruling and vow to continue their fight. "Our kids are crying out for help," Tina said. "We must all come together to make a change. Parents need to realize that when they drop their child off at school, the school isn't required by law to protect the child. As parents, we must demand that laws be put in place to keep our kids safe. We owe it to our children."

"At some point in time, school districts are going to have to be held accountable, and I'm going to continue to be an advocate for those families going through those issues and try to help them get through their struggles as well," David said. "It's a long hard road that's going to take a lot more people than me, but I was glad to see the American Federation of Teachers and the National Education Association have endorsed the film and say that it needs to be a requirement throughout the nation. That's a start."

The Longs are working with organizations such as the National Center for Learning Disabilities (NCLD) in New York as well as the BBYO, a leading Jewish youth leadership group in Atlanta, to elevate their antibullying campaign to a national level. "We're going to continue speaking out any way we can to keep this message going, that kids don't have to die, that there are solutions to this," Tina said. "My fear is that the message will die along with our son and then where will we be? We'll be in the same place we were when all of this started."

But despite all the suffering the Longs have endured, Tina said being a part of *Bully* has helped her family heal in the wake of her son's death. "I think that is a big thing that this movie has done for us," she said. "And we were able to get the word out that this did happen and it is happening and it needs to stop. I think Lee and Cynthia being present in our lives and understanding what our family was going through, meeting the other families from the movie and forming a bond with them has helped us tremendously. I can never repay the bond that we have with some of those other families. We call them our *Bully* family."

KIRK AND LAURA SMALLEY

Since their son Ty's suicide on May, 13, 2010, Kirk and Laura Smalley have traveled tirelessly across the nation as ambassadors of their organization, Stand for the Silent (SFTS), to spread their antibullying message.

The SFTS program addresses the issue of school bullying with an engaging, factual, and emotional methodology. With the help of student leaders, Kirk presents his inspirational story, and students are shown firsthand the life and death consequences of bullying. It is through this unique approach he believes that lives can

be changed for the better, because students—some for the first time—can develop an empathetic awareness through education and understanding.

The Smalleys have already been to hundreds of schools and spoken to hundreds of thousands of children. Their mission even reached the White House, where in March 2010 they met privately with President Obama and First Lady Michelle Obama prior to attending the first-ever White House conference on bullying. Kirk and Laura Smalley also met with Lady Gaga, a strong antibullying proponent, at the February 2012 launch of the Born this Way Foundation to empower kids to end bullying.

The Smalleys hope to start an SFTS chapter at each participating site along the way. Chapters consist of a group of students committed to change. At the end of each event, pledge cards are given to those who agree to stand for the silent. The pledge speaks of respect and love, hope and aspiration.

Next Steps

Dr. Edward F. Dragan

The following section is adapted from "The Bully Action Guide: How to Help Your Child and Get Your School to Listen," by Dr. Edward F. Dragan, http://www.thebullyactionguide.com

Dr. Dragan provides consultation and expert witness services to attorneys, parents, and schools across the country and internationally on matters dealing with school bullying, school accidents, student supervision, sexual harassment, and various other school liability issues. For more information regarding his practice please visit Education Management Consulting, LLC, at http://www.edmgt.com

---

School should be a place where children feel safe and secure—a place where they can count on being treated with respect. The unfortunate reality is that many students are the targets of bullying, resulting in long-term academic, physical, and emotional consequences. Kids don't often go to adults when they are being bullied because they feel that most adults won't help. And when parents do realize that their child is the victim of bullying they don't know how to respond to it. They don't know how to effectively communicate with their child about bullying, and they don't know how to effectively communicate with the school to end bullying. Parents often need tools to help. It is my hope that the information shared in my book and in this companion to *Bully* will help parents recognize bullying, effectively communicate with children about bullying, and effectively communicate with the school to hold it accountable to end bullying.

If you followed the school's procedures for bringing your concerns to the board of education but have yet to receive a satisfactory resolution, is there more you can do? Yes.

Additionally, some states have criminal laws against harassment and stalking. Prosecutors can rely on both when filing criminal charges against school bullies. As a parent, you can't bring criminal charges against individuals for harassment, stalking, or other persecution against your child. Only a prosecutor can do this if the law provides for it. You can, however, invoke civil laws when you believe your child has been physically or emotionally harmed because the school ignored the bullying and allowed it to fester.

FEDERAL OFFICE FOR CIVIL RIGHTS

If by now you are thinking, "The teacher, principal, and superintendent didn't address my child's situation—why would the board of education be any different?" then consider this: Federal funding may be at stake, especially if your child's civic rights are being violated. That's why public school systems have an interest in listening to you.

The U.S. Office for Civil Rights (OCR) enforces federal civil-rights laws that prohibit discrimination on the basis of race, color, national origin, sex, disability, and age in programs or activities that receive funding from the Department of Education. These civil-rights laws extend to all state education agencies, elementary and secondary school systems, colleges and universities, vocational schools, proprietary schools, vocational rehabilitation agencies, libraries, and museums that receive federal financial assistance from the Department of Education.

Keep in mind that if your child is in a private school, you do not have the option to rely upon these laws because private schools do not receive federal financial assistance.

Anyone who believes that an educational institution that receives federal financial assistance has discriminated against someone on the basis of race, color, national origin, sex, disability, or age may file a complaint with OCR. The person who files the complaint does not need to be a victim of the discrimination and may file a complaint on behalf of another person or group.

HOW TO FILE A COMPLAINT

If you file a complaint with OCR, you must file within sixty days after the last act of the school district's grievance process. In other words, you have sixty days after you have (a) sent a letter to the board of education complaining about your child's harassment and (b) received an unsatisfactory solution from the board to file a complaint with the OCR.

The website for the Office of Civil Rights is located at http://www2.ed.gov/about/offices/list/ocr/index.html. At this site, you can read an informative section entitled "Know Your Rights." The "How to File a Complaint" section escorts you through the process of filing a complaint and submitting it over the Internet. Be sure to include enough detail so that the OCR understands what occurred and when, as well as the basis for your complaint (e.g., was the alleged discrimination based on race, color, national origin, sex, or disability?).

The U.S. Department of Education's Office for Civil Rights will determine whether it has jurisdiction over the issue stated in your complaint. You will receive a response indicating whether it will investigate, and if so, when you should receive a report. One thing to remember is that the complaints are filed in anonymity. The school is not informed of who files a complaint. Realistically, however, the issue behind the complaint most frequently identifies the complainant. You should know that you and your child are protected from retaliation for filing a complaint, though you might need to keep an eye on how your child is treated once a complaint is filed.

TALKING TO A LAWYER

When is it time to talk to a lawyer about a lawsuit? When you have done all that you can with the school to prevent your child from harm and yet harm is done, you should talk with a lawyer who has expertise in education law. This may not always be easy to find; most lawyers do not have training in education law and have little experience in the realm of schools and education matters.

The first place to search for an education-law attorney is your state's bar association. The American Bar Association website has a function to help you find state and local bar associations; to find one, visit http://www.americanbar.org/groups/bar_services/ resources/state_local_bar_associations.html. Each state bar association's website should have a section listing lawyer specialties. Many state bar associations have education-law sections with a list of member attorneys who specialize in education law.

When you locate several choices in your state, carefully read each lawyer's profile and experience; many lawyers who list themselves as "education lawyers" specialize in personal injury and may have had one or two education-related personal injury cases. Make a list.

Before you call anyone, put your story together in very clear, concise terms. When you do call, ask to speak with a person who can tell you about the attorney's experience litigating school cases.

Social and Emotional Learning and Bullying Prevention

EDC, CASEL, American Institute for Research

Overview: *While bullying is a pervasive problem in many schools, schools can take specific steps to improve the school climate and encourage positive interactions designed to reduce or prevent bullying. Schools using a social and emotional learning (SEL) framework can foster an overall climate of inclusion, warmth, and respect, and promote the development of core social and emotional skills among both students and staff. Because bullying prevention is entirely congruent with SEL, it can be embedded in a school's SEL framework. The aims of this brief are to (a) provide a basic description of a school-wide SEL framework, (b) illustrate the relationship between social and emotional factors and bullying, and (c) explain how an SEL framework can be extended to include bullying prevention.*

RESEARCH, PRACTICES, GUIDELINES, AND RESOURCES

Bullying may be the most frequent form of school violence (Nansel et al., 2001). Surveys consistently indicate that almost one-quarter of all students experience hurtful interactions with peers on a monthly or daily basis (Dinkes, Cataldi & Lin-Kelly, 2007).

State legislatures are increasingly requiring schools to develop and implement bullying prevention policies and approaches (National Council of State Legislatures, n.d.).[1] But even without these legislative mandates, many schools are addressing bullying as part of their efforts to create physically and emotionally safe learning environments.

Because much remains to be learned about best practices in bullying prevention, when schools seek to identify a bullying prevention program to implement, they face a confusing array of interventions, many of which have not been evaluated or have produced only marginal gains in reducing bullying behaviors (Merrell, Gueldner, Ross & Isava, 2008).

Research does indicate, however, that multifaceted approaches to reducing bullying in schools are more likely to succeed than single-component programs. Such programs may include a *school-wide component* centered on training, awareness, monitoring, and assessment of bullying; a *classroom component* focused on reinforcing school-wide rules and building social and emotional skills, such as social problem solving and empathy; and an *intervention component* for students who are frequent targets or perpetrators of bullying. Programs directed at only one of these levels, or interventions designed only for the targets and perpetrators of bullying, are less likely to be effective (Birdthistle et al., 1999; Ttofi & Farrington, 2009; Vreeman & Carroll, 2007).

When schools are able to scaffold bullying prevention onto a larger, more comprehensive framework for prevention and positive youth development, they strengthen their prevention efforts while also addressing some of the underlying contributing social, emotional, and environmental factors that can lead to bullying. A social and emotional learning (SEL) framework can serve just this purpose.

---

1 See http://www.bullypolice.org for a list of state-by-state laws and related information.

WHAT IS SEL?

SEL is an educational movement gaining ground throughout the world. It focuses on the systematic development of a core set of social and emotional skills that help children more effectively handle life challenges and thrive in both their learning and their social environments. The Collaborative for Academic, Social, and Emotional Learning (CASEL) defines SEL as the processes through which children and adults acquire the knowledge, attitudes, and skills they need to recognize and manage their emotions, demonstrate caring and concern for others, establish positive relationships, make responsible decisions, and handle challenging social situations constructively.

CASEL has identified five core categories of social and emotional skills:

- *Self-awareness*—accurately assessing one's feelings, interests, values, and strengths/abilities, and maintaining a well-grounded sense of self-confidence
- *Self-management*—regulating one's emotions to handle stress, control impulses, and persevere in overcoming obstacles; setting personal and academic goals and then monitoring one's progress toward achieving them; and expressing emotions constructively
- *Social awareness*—taking the perspective of and empathizing with others; recognizing and appreciating individual and group similarities and differences; identifying and following societal standards of conduct; and recognizing and using family, school, and community resources
- *Relationship skills*—establishing and maintaining healthy and rewarding relationships based on cooperation; resisting inappropriate social pressure; preventing, managing, and resolving interpersonal conflict; and seeking help when needed
- *Responsible decision making*—making decisions based on consideration of ethical standards, safety concerns,

appropriate standards of conduct, respect for others, and likely consequences of various actions; applying decision-making skills to academic and social situations; and contributing to the well-being of one's school and community

These skills allow children to calm themselves when angry, initiate friendships, resolve relationship conflicts respectfully, and make ethical and safe choices. To develop these capacities, children need to experience safe, nurturing, and well-managed environments where they feel valued and respected; to have meaningful interactions with others who are socially and emotionally competent; and to receive positive and specific guidance.

Many excellent SEL curricula and programs are available that provide sequential and developmentally appropriate instruction in SEL skills, and structured opportunities for children to practice, apply, and be recognized for using these skills throughout the day. SEL programs are ideally implemented in a coordinated manner throughout the school district, from preschool through high school. Lessons are reinforced in both classroom and non-classroom settings (such as the hallways, cafeteria, and playground), as well as during out-of-school activities and at home. Educators receive ongoing professional development in SEL, and families and schools work together to promote children's social, emotional, and academic success.

WHAT IS BULLYING?

In its *Safe Communities ~ Safe Schools* Fact Sheet, the Center for the Study and Prevention of School Violence (2008) uses three criteria to distinguish bullying from other occurrences of misbehavior or isolated cases of aggression:

1 It is aggressive behavior or intentional harm doing.
2 It is carried out repeatedly and over time.
3 It occurs within an interpersonal relationship characterized by an imbalance of power.

Thus, a student is bullied or victimized when he or she is the repeated target of deliberate negative actions by one or more students who possess greater verbal, physical, social, or psychological power.

Direct bullying is a relatively open attack on a victim that is physical (hitting, kicking, pushing, choking) and/or verbal (name-calling, threatening, taunting, malicious teasing) in nature. *Indirect bullying* is more subtle and difficult to detect. It involves one or more forms of relational aggression, including social isolation, intentional exclusion, rumor spreading, damaging someone's reputation, making faces or obscene gestures behind someone's back, and manipulating friendships and other relationships.

Students increasingly bully others using electronic communication devices and the Internet. *Cyberbullying* involves sending hurtful or threatening text messages and images with these devices in order to damage the target's reputation and relationships.

This form of bullying can be very difficult for adults to detect or track, and almost half of those victimized do not know the identity of the perpetrator. Electronic bullying most commonly involves the use of instant messaging, chat rooms, and e-mail (Kowalski & Limber, 2007).

BULLYING PREVALENCE AND CONSEQUENCES

According to the 2008 *Indicators of School Crime and Safety* report from the Institute of Education Sciences, 24 percent of elementary and secondary schools report daily or weekly bullying incidents (Dinkes et al., 2009). The frequency of actual bullying incidents is probably much greater, since adults are often unaware of, or fail to adequately respond to, bullying (Pepler & Craig, 2000). In 2007, 32 percent of students ages twelve to eighteen reported being bullied within the past year, with 63 percent of these students bullied once or twice over the year, 21 percent bullied once or twice a month, 10 percent bullied once or twice a week, and 7 percent bullied almost every day.

Most forms of bullying begin to decline by the end of the elementary grades and continue to decrease through the middle and high school grades. This decline is temporarily reversed, however, if students transition from an elementary school to a middle school or junior high school during the middle grades. In these cases, there is frequently a spike in bullying during that transition year, perhaps reflecting a desire for students to reestablish dominance or achieve a position of leadership (Pelligrini, 2002).

The damage to victimized children is compounded by the relatively stable nature of victimization, such that the same children often remain victims from one school year to the next (Nansel, Haynie & Simons-Morton, 2007). Consequences for such children include emotional distress, such as loneliness, anxiety, and depression, as well as poor school performance and attendance, low self-confidence and self-concept, and social marginalization. These effects can be very long-lasting. For example, being a target of bullying during adolescence is linked to higher levels of depression and anxiety in early adulthood (Dempsey & Storch, 2008).

As for children who bully, while some socially "high status" bullies often appear well-adjusted, other children who bully frequently experience a range of negative outcomes, including poorer school adjustment, more peer rejection, and more externalizing and internalizing behaviors, such as conduct problems, delinquency, criminal activity, and depression (Paul & Cillessen, 2007; Vreeman & Carroll, 2007; Whitted & Dupper, 2005).

Witnessing bullying incidents can produce feelings of anger, fear, guilt, and sadness in observers (Batsche & Porter, 2006). Bystanders who witness repeated victimization of peers can experience negative effects similar to the victimized children themselves (Pepler & Craig, 2000).

SOCIAL-ECOLOGICAL PERSPECTIVES ON BULLYING

Although the definition of bullying focuses on the aggressive behavior of individual students, bullying is actually a *group* phenomenon, playing out in a social context (Salmivalli, 1999). It is important to remember that many students engage in some form of bullying behavior on a periodic basis, and that most students are teased or experience some form of peer harassment during the school year (Espelage & Swearer, 2003). Peers are also present as bystanders during most bullying episodes and play a pivotal role in either the prevention or the promotion of bullying (Storey & Slaby, 2008). For these reasons, some researchers stress that bullying should be viewed along a continuum, rather than a categorical labeling of some children as bullies, others as victims, and the remainder of students (and adults) as uninvolved (Espelage & Swearer, 2003). Others caution that labeling children further contributes to a negative climate, overemphasizes the role of individual children while minimizing contextual factors, and fails to accentuate the positive capacities of children to contribute and interact in positive ways (Brown, 2008).

There are numerous individual, peer-level, school-level, familial, and community factors that influence bullying. At the level of the peer group, social theories describing why bullying increases during late childhood and early adolescence include homophily theory, dominance theory, and attraction theory, and there is some research evidence supporting each (Espelage & Swearer, 2003). *Homophily theory* states that people tend to form friendships and spend time with those who are similar to them in certain key ways. Students tend to hang out with others who bully at the same frequency, and among these bully-prone groups, bullying frequency increases over time. According to *dominance theory*, students use bullying as a strategy for moving higher in the social pecking order, particularly during the transition from elementary school to the middle grades, when patterns of social hierarchy are being established. *Attraction theory* posits that as children enter middle school, their attraction to aggressive peers increases.

Family interaction patterns may also influence peer interaction patterns. Children who are both victims and perpetrators of bullying at school are much more likely to also bully and/or be victimized by siblings (Duncan, 1999). Parents of children who bully others are more likely to lack emotional warmth and be overly permissive (Rigby, 1994). Parents of victimized children, in contrast, are more likely to be highly restrictive, controlling, and over-involved (Bowers, Smith & Binney, 1994).

THE CONNECTION BETWEEN SEL AND BULLYING PREVENTION

Given these contributing social factors, preventing and reducing bullying requires a focus on the social, emotional, and moral climate of the school, as well as on the social and emotional competence of the entire school body (Bosaki, Marini & Dane, 2006; Knoff, 2007; San Antonio & Salzfass, 2007; Vreeman & Carroll, 2007; Whitted & Dupper, 2005). Although much remains to be learned about best practices for bullying prevention and intervention, the existing research suggests that universal school-based prevention programs (i.e., those designed for all children) can be effective. A recent report by the Task Force on Community Preventive Services (Hahn et al., 2007) concluded that universal school-based programs designed to prevent or reduce violent behavior, including bullying, significantly reduced rates of violent behavior and aggression for all grade levels.

Vreeman and Carroll (2007), in their systematic review of school-based interventions designed to prevent bullying, concluded that the most effective interventions typically use a whole-school approach consisting of some combination of school-wide rules and sanctions, teacher training, classroom curricula, conflict-resolution training, and individual counseling. Antibullying programs exclusively directed at the bully, the victim, or both, without involving other students or addressing larger school climate issues, are less likely to be effective.

In order to successfully address bullying problems, the entire school must comprise a culture of respect. Expectations for how staff and students treat one another should be clearly reflected in school policies, and the rules for classroom interaction should be consistently modeled by adults and enforced and reinforced in all school settings.

At the student level, schools using an SEL framework teach students skills in the areas of self-awareness, self-management, social awareness, relationships, and responsible decision making. These core SEL skills are the foundational competencies that students need in order to deal with bullying. The six skills often overlap and complement one another, as illustrated below.

Self-Awareness and Self-Management Skills

Recognize and manage emotions in order to respond to conflict in calm and assertive ways. In order to handle conflicts effectively, children need to be able to recognize when they are getting angry and learn to calm themselves before reacting. Children who frequently bully others tend to have trouble managing anger and to strike out aggressively. Bosworth, Espelage, and Simon (1999) found that children who are the angriest are the most likely to bully others. Children report that the need to relieve stress and having a bad day are the primary reasons they bully others (Swearer & Cary, 2007).

A recent study found that students expressing higher levels of sadness and emotional instability are more likely to be bullied (Analitis et al., 2009). Hyperactivity and emotional outbursts are the two factors most likely to annoy and provoke peers. Such provocation increases the likelihood of being victimized and not supported by peers over time (Rodkin & Hodges, 2003).

Research suggests that many victims (43 percent) respond to being bullied in an aggressive, retaliatory, or emotionally reactive manner that both prolongs and escalates the bullying episode (Wilton, Craig & Pepler, 2000). These victims lack effective emotional regulation skills and may yell, scream, or cry in response (the least effective ways to stop bullying), thereby rewarding the aggressor (Goldbaum et al., 2006; Salmivalli, 1999) and making themselves more vulnerable to further victimization.

Social Awareness

Be tolerant and appreciative of differences, and interact empathetically with peers. Research suggests that children often lack empathy for the victims of bullying and that they view being different from the social ideal, or social norm, as the cause of bullying (Swearer & Cary, 2007). When active bystanders were asked why they chose to intervene, they were likely to attribute feelings of empathy for the victim and a general concern for the well-being of others as motivating factors. Bystanders are also more likely to intervene when they have positive feelings and attitudes toward the victim (Rigby & Johnson, 2006).

Relationship Skills

Initiate and sustain friendships and other relationships. Victimized children tend to have fewer friends, to only have friends who are also victimized, and to have more enemies than nonvictimized children (Rodkin & Hodges, 2003). Many are socially withdrawn and lack confidence and skills in effectively interacting with peers (Pelligrini, 2002; Salmivalli, 1999). Because of their lack of peer support, victimized children are less likely to have other children come to their defense when they are bullied (Rodkin & Hodges, 2003; Slaby, 2005).

Research suggests that having high-quality friendships, or at least one best friend, can help prevent children from being victims (Boulton, Trueman, Chau, Whitehand & Amatya, 1999; Goldbaum, Craig, Pepler & Connolly, 2006). Interventions that help peer-rejected children learn how to positively communicate with peers (e.g., ask questions, show support, make suggestions) can help them be more accepted by peers, less likely to be bullied, and more likely to be assisted by peers if targeted by a bully (Pelligrini, 2002).

Resist social pressure to enable, encourage, or directly participate in bullying, and actively defend victims. Studies have revealed that when bystanders observe bullying, they spend most of their time either actively participating in the act or passively encouraging the aggressor by serving as an audience; less than one-quarter of the time do they try to assist the victim (O'Connell, Pepler & Craig, 1999; Slaby, 2005).

There are a variety of reasons that bystanders don't come to the assistance of victims:

- They are intimidated by the social or physical power of those doing the bullying
- They fear retaliation
- They are reluctant to challenge group norms supporting bullying
- They don't recognize the act as bullying
- They lack a sense of personal responsibility or self-confidence
- They don't know what to do to help

It's worth noting that when bystanders do assert their disapproval of a bullying act, the episode usually ends quickly—in fewer than ten seconds in about half the cases (Craig & Pepler, 1997; Salmivalli, 1999).

Be able to seek help from peers or other adults when needed. Research suggests that victims and bystanders typically do not seek help from peers or adults when they are unable to solve the problem on their own (O'Connell et al., 1999). Self-identified victims are particularly likely to blame themselves for their victimization and to "suffer in silence" (Graham, Bellmore & Juvonen, 2006).

Responsible Decision Making

Think through and resolve social problems effectively and ethically. Effective social problem solving requires an accurate assessment of the situation. Research indicates that children who frequently bully tend to misinterpret social interactions as being more hostile, adversarial, or provocative than their peers do (Dodge, 1993). These children also tend to hold more supportive beliefs about using violence and are less confident about using nonviolent strategies to resolve conflict (Bosworth et al., 1999).

Not surprisingly, these students' relationships with friends and family members tend to be fraught with conflict (Society for Research in Child Development, 2008).

Problem solving also requires an evaluation of possible and likely consequences. Youngsters who are both bullies and victims tend to be emotionally volatile and to react aggressively before thinking through the consequences (Pelligrini, 2002).

Bullies may narrowly consider the positive short-term consequences of bullying for themselves but are less likely to consider the negative consequences of their actions on others or on their own relationships over time (Arsenio & Lemerise, 2001).

Because of the potentially anonymous nature of cyberbullying, students may be even less likely to recognize and consider the effects that these actions will have on the victims.

Victims also often lack effective social problem-solving skills (Biggam & Power, 1999). Problem-solving strategies are thirteen times more effective at de-escalating conflicts than are the aggressive, retaliatory, or emotionally reactive responses most frequently used by targeted children (Wilton et al., 2000). Even among victims who use a problem-solving strategy in response to bullying, the vast majority employ a passive strategy, such as avoiding, acquiescing to, or ignoring the bully, instead of a more effective assertive strategy, such as talking with others to find a solution or asking others for help (Wilton et al., 2000).

APPLYING AN SEL FRAMEWORK TO BULLYING

To effectively reduce bullying behavior, schools need to provide students with instruction and practice in applying their SEL skills to a variety of bullying situations. An SEL framework provides a supportive foundation for these prevention efforts. Ttofi and Farrington (2009) conducted a meta-analysis of fifty-nine well-designed evaluations of bullying interventions to identify the specific features that had the greatest impact on decreasing bullying behavior and rates of victimization. They found that the most important components were parent training, improved playground supervision, disciplinary methods, school conferences or assemblies that raised awareness of the problem, classroom rules against bullying, classroom management techniques for detecting and dealing with bullying, and the work of peers to help combat bullying.[2]

Building on these findings and other SEL research, the following strategies can help schools apply an SEL framework to bullying prevention.

School-Wide Approaches

Assessment

Schools need to conduct an assessment in order to determine how often bullying occurs, the forms it takes (e.g., sexual harassment, relational aggression, cyberbullying), where the incidents occur, and how students and adults respond to such incidents.

Experts recommend conducting bullying assessments annually in the spring, after peer groups have formed in schools (Swearer, Espelage, Love & Kingsbury, 2008). See "Selected Resources" at the end of this brief for sample assessments.

Awareness and Training

All adults who oversee groups of children (staff and volunteers) need to be trained to respond to bullying incidents. School staff, students, and parents need to be aware of what bullying is, the various forms that it can take, the factors that put children at risk for victimization, the warning signs that a child has been victimized, and what they should do when bullying occurs. Adults and students need to examine their own beliefs about bullying and its causes and consequences.

Numerous helpful resources exist for developing this awareness. *Eyes on Bullying: What Can You Do?* (Storey & Slaby, 2008), for example, is a downloadable toolkit designed to help children and

---

2 While a bullying prevention curriculum is also generally believed to be an effective school-wide strategy, there were not sufficient studies to evaluate the effectiveness of specific classroom curricula.

adults examine their beliefs about bullying, learn how to recognize and effectively respond to bullying both at the time of the incident and after it has ended, and take strategic steps to help prevent bullying from occurring. Additional resources can be found under "Selected Resources."

Rules and Reporting Procedures

When staff reach a consensus on what bullying is and agree to intervene to prevent and reduce it, rates of bullying can drop significantly (Wright, 2004). To help establish the moral climate of the school, school-wide rules prohibiting bullying need to be developed, with students as part of the process. The rules then need to be clearly communicated and distributed in writing (Whitted & Dupper, 2005). Examples of rules a school might establish are as follows:

- *We will not bully others.*
- *We will try to help students who are bullied.*
- *We will include students who are easily left out.*
- *When we know somebody is being bullied, we will tell an adult at school and at home* (West Regional Equity Network, 2008).

There is some evidence that children who frequently bully others are more morally disengaged and view bullying behavior as much more acceptable or justified (Hymel, Rocke-Henderson & Bonanno, 2005). Clear standards of conduct that do not allow bullying can help to decrease this disengagement among both students who bully others and bystanders who witness the acts.

Anonymous reporting procedures should also be established and communicated.

Discipline Policy

The discipline policy should clearly indicate that bullying is not acceptable, specify the consequences for policy violations, and be consistently enforced.

However, according to Swearer et al. (2008), the traditional punitive and reactive responses to bullying, such as zero-tolerance policies and security equipment and personnel, often cause problem behaviors to *increase* rather than diminish.

Such responses are also not effective ways to improve school climate or academic engagement.

The consequences for policy violations around bullying should instead include some form of remediation that helps students understand the incident and practice prosocial behaviors.

Adult Supervision

As determined by the assessment, all areas where bullying tends to occur (e.g., hallways, cafeteria, playground) should be adequately monitored by adults.

Adult Models of Behavior

Adults in the school need to model respectful and caring behavior toward students and one another and demonstrate social problem-solving skills. For example, a principal who has lunch with a small group of students once a week demonstrates caring for the students on the part of the administration (and also promotes cohesiveness among the students by helping them learn more about one another).

Adults also need to model active bystander behavior by intervening quickly when bullying incidents occur and by not dismissing or minimizing bullying (Slaby, 2005).

Promoting Positive Peer Interactions

Creating opportunities for students to interact with one another in cooperative, positive, and inclusive ways can help generate cohesion and compassion among students and encourage them to apply the SEL skills they have been taught. At times when adult supervision is less available, such as during recess, problem behaviors among students can be reduced by giving them access to a variety of games and sporting equipment, such as Frisbees, hula-hoops, and Bingo (Swearer et al., 2008).

During the transition from elementary to middle school, promoting ongoing and cooperative interactions among groups of students is especially important. Some schools have students remain in intact cohorts throughout the year to encourage and increase cohesion among the group (Pelligrini, 2002).

Classroom Approaches

Classroom Climate

Teachers play an enormously important role in setting the classroom climate. If aggressive norms become established and are not corrected, the students in these classrooms display more aggressive acts in future years (Rodkin & Hodges, 2003). As Rodkin and Hodges (2003) state:

> Teachers lie just outside of the peer ecology and help shape, intentionally or unintentionally, the critical microsystems in which children at school interact. Successful teachers guide children toward higher levels of moral reasoning, show warmth, and anticipate interpersonal problems by knowing their students' social status, peer groups, friends and enemies (p. 391).

Teachers need to establish respectful standards of conduct for interactions and take action when student norms support aggression. Teachers need to work with students to develop classroom rules for respectful interactions and to hold periodic classroom meetings to discuss bullying.

Classroom activities and discussions that help change students' views about the "coolness" of bullying may represent an important strategy for reducing bullying (Rodkin & Hodges, 2003). Because of their social power among peers, "high status" bullies can have a particularly negative impact on the overall classroom climate (Rodkin & Hodges, 2003)—and when the peer group norms favor bullying, aggressive acts among both boys and girls increase, particularly at the middle-school level.

However, if other students and adults disapprove of bullying, and this disapproval is reflected not only in the school rules but also in the established classroom climate, students may suffer a "social cost" when they bully and may be less likely to do so (Arsenio & Lemerise, 2001).

Teachers should model inclusive behaviors, making a special effort to reach out to peer-rejected and withdrawn students and to encourage students to be inclusive of their peers. There is evidence that when teachers are warm and caring to everyone, including aggressive and peer-rejected children, all students in the classroom are less rejecting of their peers (Rodkin & Hodges, 2003). Peer-rejected children should have a valued and respected place in the classroom, for example, as an "expert" in some content or skill area or as a classroom assistant.

Teachers should work to promote caring learning communities through such strategies as class meetings, group celebrations, and cooperative group work (San Antonio & Salzfass, 2007).

SEL Curricula and Activities

Helping children think about the harmful consequences of their bullying behaviors on others and on their own relationships may reduce these behaviors. Students need opportunities to practice their SEL skills by role-playing how to respond appropriately in bullying situations. For example, when learning about empathy, students can discuss what it feels like to be bullied and to watch an incident of bullying. They can practice effective responses to bullying situations and help-seeking behaviors for both victims and bystanders. Teachers can brainstorm with students how bystanders should behave, and then practice these actions in role-play situations. Teachers should then encourage students to apply what they are learning outside the classroom.

Giving children opportunities to practice effective helping behaviors can help them develop the confidence to intervene in bullying situations, as they are more likely to do so once they have done it successfully, even in a role play (Rigby & Johnson, 2004).

Children who actively defend victims of bullying tend to feel more confident than their peers about how to help victims and how to do it effectively (Gini, Albiero, Benelli & Altoè, 2008).

Likewise, prevention curricula are much more likely to significantly reduce rates of bullying and victimization when students have opportunities to apply what they learn in the classroom to real-life situations (Hirschstein, Edstrom, Frey, Snell & MacKenzie, 2007). See "Selected Resources" for suggested classroom curricula and activities.

Interventions

Beyond classroom curricula, students who are victimized, who witness bullying, or who regularly bully others need extended opportunities to practice relevant SEL skills, such as anger management, assertive communication, and social problem-solving. Pairing at-risk children with more well-adjusted and socially competent peers through a buddy system may help less socially and emotionally competent children develop these skills and may also help protect at-risk children from further victimization (Rodkin & Hodges, 2003).

Schools also need to establish a support system for victims of bullying, as some may need therapeutic interventions to address their resulting psychological issues, such as depression and anxiety. Victimized children who are in pernicious bully-victim dyads with another child may benefit from the intervention of a school psychologist or social worker (Rodkin & Hodges, 2003).

Parental Involvement

Since family interaction patterns can contribute to both bullying behavior and victimization, it's important to help parents reflect on their own parenting styles and behavior and to provide them with specific guidance on handling conflicts at home. Parents also need guidance on how to best encourage the adoption of prosocial values and promote social and emotional skill development.

In addition, since many victims are more likely to confide in their parents before other adults, parents need to be aware of what bullying is and what they should do at home and in concert with the school if their child is either a victim or a perpetrator of bullying. Schools can use awareness- and skills-building resources as a starting point for school-family dialogues about bullying.

SUMMARY

Bullying is a pervasive problem in many schools. Unfortunately, many attempts to reduce the problem—such as engaging bullies and victims in peer mediation, punishing bullies, telling victimized children to ignore the bullying or to work things out on their own (Merrell et al., 2008), inserting a few bullying prevention lessons in the curriculum, or adopting an antibullying policy without any of the needed supports—are not effective and are unlikely to have a lasting impact.

However, schools *can* take specific steps to improve the school climate and create more positive interactions among students. When schools embed bullying prevention efforts within an SEL framework, these efforts become a natural extension of the underlying SEL practices in the school and are more likely to succeed. By fostering an overall climate of inclusion, warmth, and respect, such schools can promote the development of core social and emotional skills in students and staff alike. Students with greater social and emotional competency are less likely to be aggressors, targets of bullying, or passive bystanders.

Just as bullying involves the entire school community, bullying prevention likewise requires the school community as a whole to get involved and take appropriate action. Schools that create a positive school-wide learning environment simply are not conducive to bullying, and these behaviors are much less likely to occur or continue.

ACKNOWLEDGMENTS

Our thanks to Dorothy Espalage for her careful review and valuable suggestions, and to Ron Slaby for similarly thoughtful reading and feedback. We remain responsible for any limitations of this report.

Prepared for the National Center for Mental Health Promotion and Youth Violence Prevention by the Collaborative for Academic, Social, and Emotional Learning (CASEL) and the Social and Emotional Learning Research Group at the University of Illinois at Chicago. November 2009. Authors: Katharine Ragozzino and Mary Utne O'Brien.

SELECTED RESOURCES

American Association of University Women

This organization's free guide *Harassment-Free Hallways: How to Stop Sexual Harassment in Schools* provides background information on the problem; surveys for students to help them understand what sexual harassment is, if they've been victimized, and what they should do if they are harassed; and recommended actions for schools and parents to help prevent sexual harassment. http://www.aauw.org/research/upload/completeguide.pdf

Bullying in Schools and What to Do About It

This website by Dr. Ken Rigby provides background information on bullying, recommended approaches for schools to use, bullying assessment questionnaires, and articles about ways to help children become more active bystanders. http://www.education.unisa.edu.au/bullying/

CDC Violence Compendium

This website offers a variety of downloadable assessment measures, many of which relate to bullying. http://www.cdc.gov/ncipc/pub-res/measure.htm

Collaborative for Academic, Social, and Emotional Learning (CASEL)

CASEL's *Safe and Sound* guide (available at http://www.casel.org/ pub/safeandsound.php) provides information on numerous outstanding SEL programs that can be expanded on and directly applied to bullying. Below are some programs that have specifically extended their SEL instruction to include bullying:

- *Steps to Respect*: Using this Committee for Children program, the school establishes a school-wide framework of antibullying policies and procedures and determines consequences for bullying. Parents also receive materials about bullying. All school staff members are trained to work directly with children involved in bullying incidents. Classroom teachers deliver the lessons in the upper elementary grades (third through fifth or fourth through sixth). Children learn and practice bullying prevention skills, including how to recognize, refuse, and report bullying, and how to make friends. The website includes a sample lesson on bystander involvement that may be downloaded. http://www.cfchildren.org/media/files/ str%5Fms%5Flesson.pdf
- **Lions Quest**: This organization has prepared a bullying prevention document that summarizes how its programs address key elements of bullying prevention. It also offers an in-service workshop on bullying prevention for schools using its programs. http://www.lions-quest.org/
- *Responsive Classroom* (http://responsiveclassroom.org) and **Developmental Studies Center** (http://www.devstu. org): These websites offer books, activity guides, and curricula that promote positive and inclusive student interactions between students within the classroom and school-wide. The Developmental Studies Center Caring School Community program has been found to significantly reduce bullying in a large-scale evaluation.

■ **Committee for Children**: This organization has developed a bullying report for teachers using the *Steps to Respect* program, which can also serve as a helpful checklist for teachers to evaluate their classroom bullying prevention practices. http://www.cfchildren.org/media/files/str_sel_checklist.pdf. The accompanying *Staff Preparedness Survey* is designed for teachers to assess how prepared they feel to deal with bullying. http://www.cfchildren.org/media/files/STRStaffPrepSurvey.pdf

Eyes on Bullying

This website offers information and activities on many bullying topics. Its downloadable toolkit, *Eyes on Bullying: What Can You Do?*, includes activities to help children and adults recognize and respond to bullying. http://www.eyesonbullying.org

Jim Wright

School psychologist Jim Wright has prepared a free booklet for educators, titled *Preventing Classroom Bullying: What Teachers Can Do*, which lists concrete steps that schools and classroom teachers can take to educate students about bullying. Included are lesson ideas for having students practice assertive victim and bystander responses, recommended classroom rules, tips on confronting students about bullying, considerations for providing appropriate consequences, activities to determine bullying "hot spots," and recommended strategies for promoting inclusive behaviors among students. http://www.jimwrightonline.com/pdfdocs/bully/bullyBooklet.pdf

MindOH

This website offers numerous resources on bullying, including Bullying Tips and Tools for teachers and parents, several "Thinking It Through" classroom lessons for students on bullying topics (e.g., teasing, bystander roles), tips for preventing cyberbullying, an entire lesson plan series, and parent-child activities on bullying. http://www.mindoh.com/

New Jersey Department of Education Model Policy

This example of an antibullying policy lists factors to consider when determining consequences and appropriate remediation strategies, and suggests a range of individual, classroom, and school-wide responses to consider. http://www.state.nj.us/education/parents/bully.pdf

Stop Bullying Now

This U.S. Department of Health and Human Services website is directed toward children, with twelve bullying "webisodes," surveys to help kids understand if they're bullying others or are themselves a victim of bullying, and various other resources to help children understand what bullying is and the harm it does. http://stopbullyingnow.hrsa.gov/index.asp?area=main

Substance Abuse and Mental Health Services Administration

This website offers a variety of helpful assessment tools, for example:

- *Inventory of Wrongful Activities*
  http://pathwayscourses.samhsa.gov/bully/pdfs_bully/bully_supps_pg3.pdf
- *Handling of Bullying Staff Questionnaire*
  http://pathwayscourses.samhsa.gov/bully/pdfs_bully/bully_supps_pg4.pdf

This SEL Brief was prepared for the National Center for Mental Health Promotion and Youth Violence Prevention by the Collaborative for Academic, Social, and Emotional Learning (CASEL) and the Social and Emotional Learning Research Group at the University of Illinois at Chicago (copyright © 2009 by Education Development Center, Inc.) which was funded by the Substance Abuse and Mental Health Services Administration, U.S. Department of Health and Human Services (Grant No. 2HR1SM54865). Any opinions, findings and conclusions or recommendations expressed in this material are those of the author(s) and do not necessarily reflect the views of the Department of Health and Human Services, Substance Abuse and Mental Health Services Administration.

Use of all original material is by permission.

Creating Just and Caring Communities

Stephanie Jones, Richard Weissbourd, Suzanne Bouffard, and Trisha Ross at the Bullying Prevention Initiative at the Harvard Graduate School of Education

The Harvard Graduate School of Education was founded in 1920 and is located in Cambridge, MA. It offers thirteen master's programs and two doctoral programs, as well as numerous professional education programs.

"At the Harvard Graduate School of Education, we believe that stopping bullying starts with developing respectful people and caring communities. Our work aims to strengthen the abilities of schools, parents, and communities to support children's ethical, emotional, and social capacities, so that children care about and take responsibility for others, think clearly about and pursue justice, and sacrifice for principles larger than themselves. We aim to accomplish these goals by developing and disseminating key messages, materials, strategies, and practices for promoting respect and kindness."

How can we develop just and caring communities for children? How do we create communities where adults take responsibility for children and where children are inspired and taught to care about those who are different from them, to think clearly about and pursue justice, and to stand up for themselves and others?

Parents, school staff, sports coaches, religious leaders, and many other adults have roles to play in creating these communities. What concretely can these adults do?

A ROAD MAP FOR SCHOOLS

Stopping bullying is vital for all young people to thrive. But it isn't enough. We have to create school environments where children develop key social, emotional, and ethical capacities, and we need to stop bullying before it starts. Preventing bullying begins with

HOW DO EXPERTS DEFINE BULLYING?

Bullying isn't always easy to define or recognize. Many young people may not see their own or others' behavior as bullying, using other words like drama, meanness, or teasing. And even adults who care deeply about young people may not see how derogatory language like "you're so gay!" can contribute to a hostile school culture.

Experts define bullying as aggression or harassment that one or more people direct toward another person. The person who is targeted usually has less social or physical power. Bullying can include physical aggression, taunting, threats, and exclusion. Often, these behaviors are targeted toward someone because of his or her sexual orientation, gender, race, or other characteristics that seem "different."

Bullying is a relationship problem. It is affected by social norms and can change across different situations. Over time, the same person can be a bully, a victim, or a bystander. And while the consequences for victims are easiest to see, bullying also hurts those who participate in the bullying, those who stand by, and the whole community.

creating just and caring communities. In just and caring communities, children, teenagers, and adults are expected to be respectful, responsible, and ready to stand up for what is right, and children and adults are given the support and tools they need to act responsibly. Decades of research indicate that just and caring school communities promote stronger academic, social, emotional, and moral outcomes in children.

Schools commonly have mission statements that describe values such as caring, honesty, and respect. But walk in the hallways and cafeterias of many of these schools and one hears homophobic slurs, cruel insults, and students taunting and degrading classmates.

At the heart of creating caring communities in schools is closing this rhetoric-reality gap. This means moving beyond posters in hallways and assembly chants; it means that adults work to assure that values of respect and responsibility live and breathe in every aspect of schools and schooling. Here are some concrete things that can be done to close this gap and to create just and caring school communities that promote respect and prevent bullying.

THE PROJECT

Use Data and Get Serious About Accountability

There is a simple way to test whether your school is truly committed to creating just and caring communities and preventing bullying: Are you willing to collect data and hold yourself accountable? The old adage "what gets assessed gets addressed" doesn't apply to just academics. Collecting data from students and staff is a critical foundation for efforts to build a just and caring school community. Too often schools adopt curricular programs that claim to curb cruelty and bullying, but they have no idea whether these programs work or even if they are implemented with fidelity. That is why good surveys are essential. Ask students and staff questions about how often, when, and where bullying occurs. Ask students whether there are adults and peers they can talk to if they feel threatened and about their feelings about the school climate and culture more broadly. Find out whether students believe that staff and classmates care about them, about whether students are proud of the school, and about whether they have symptoms of depression, anxiety, or loneliness.

Data aren't useful if only some have access to them. Share the results with students, families, and staff to create impetus for change and to establish genuine accountability. Use data to select intervention programs that target the school's biggest needs. And crucially, use data to determine whether strategies are actually working, and be ready to change course if necessary. Finally, be willing to share data with district administrators in an effort to build a broad knowledge base that can support more effective and aligned practices district-wide.

Adopt High-Quality, Evidence-Based Prevention Programs

Many schools use antibullying or social-emotional learning programs that simply don't work. Schools should adopt evidence-based interventions. These interventions should be selected based on how effective they are in addressing the problems identified from data. The most effective programs tend to be comprehensive and seek to improve school climate and school relationships, and they feature targeted lessons on social and emotional skills, diversity and acceptance, and self-regulation skills such as being reflective and intentional about one's actions.

Even the best programs have to be implemented well to be effective. Intervention programs should be an integral part of the school's mission, and adults in the school must be committed to them. A weekly half-hour lesson with no follow-through or application to students' behaviors in the hallways rarely has any impact. School leaders need to build staff buy-in and commitment, which means that teachers and other school staff should be involved in decision-making. Further, minimize the number of prevention programs or new initiatives that your school is participating in at one time, and focus on unifying and connecting efforts so that participation rates are high, implementation is consistent and monitored, and programs and initiatives are used across contexts. Ensure you allocate the necessary resources; successful prevention efforts require time, and the most effective last at least two years and allow for consistency between years.

BIG ACTIONS ARE IMPORTANT, BUT EVERYDAY ACTIONS ARE TOO

When it comes to forming caring communities and preventing bullying, big actions are important, like standing up for someone who is being harassed and speaking up when school policies treat some students unfairly. But smaller actions are important, too. Change begins with establishing expectations and norms for how young people and adults treat each other every day. Students should be expected, for example, to say hello to people who are usually excluded, treat visitors with respect, and to pay attention to whether language contains slurs that could be hurtful to others. A caring school community articulates explicitly these day-to-day forms of decency and models and reinforces these behaviors for young people. Students are encouraged to be reflective and to engage in dialogue. Differences among students are recognized as a strength and opportunities are created to celebrate difference. Programs can help schools establish a positive, caring culture, but they can't do it alone. School staff must be purposeful about creating these communities, and they need to carve out at least some time at several points during the year to reflect, based on data, on whether their school is functioning as a just and caring community and to take up new strategies if necessary.

BULLYING HAS STRONG ROOTS IN ADULT ATTITUDES AND BEHAVIOR

We have a tendency to blame bullying on youth or a small group of "bad kids," but bullying has roots in adult attitudes and behavior.

Too often adults are passive bystanders when they witness either students or other adults act inappropriately or cruelly. Teachers and all school staff need more training and support in how to foster trusting relationships with students, promote just and caring communities, prevent bullying, and intervene effectively when bullying occurs. Few educators receive this training. Without training, too often adults miss opportunities to help or, even worse, turn their backs because they don't know what to do. Training must be provided to all staff in the school community, not just teachers. Administrative staff, bus drivers, cafeteria workers, and coaches play crucial roles, especially because many bullying incidents happen on playgrounds, school buses, and in school hallways and bathrooms. Training should include opportunities for staff to learn about strategies, share best practices, reflect on challenges and lessons learned, and identify areas in need of improvement.

WORK WITH PARENTS

Many schools don't view parents as valuable partners. Some schools even see parents as a disturbance. But parents are the strongest influence on children's social, emotional, and moral development, and schools need to find ways to work with parents, even difficult parents, in developing children's capacity for caring and responsibility. Your school can, for example, support and train teachers so they are more effective in parent-teacher conferences and better able to establish alliances with parents. You can establish systems for two-way school-home communications so that families know what's going on in the school community and so that they are informed and empowered to become involved with prevention and intervention efforts. You can share school culture and climate data with parents, welcome them as members of the community, and provide advice and resources that help families reinforce what students learn at school. You can create contracts with parents that state what you as a school will do to create a just and caring community, but also what parents are expected to do. Parents should be expected, for example, to consider not only the needs of their own child but the needs of other children in the school building, and they should expect their children to treat their school as a community to which they have obligations.

STUDENTS MUST PLAY A CENTRAL ROLE

Although adults play vital roles in creating caring school communities, students play vital roles as well. It is students who have the most wisdom about their social environments, and it is students who have the most leverage with other students. And when students feel ownership of their communities and believe they have a stake in them, they can be powerful agents of change. Adults should share data on school culture and climate with students and provide opportunities for students to serve in leadership positions in school culture and climate initiatives, consult students in understanding problems and pursuing solutions, and help students develop their own social, emotional, and moral capacities.

Too often, the things that adults do to protect young people disempower them. Antibullying efforts that focus solely on reporting incidents to authorities or on punishing the perpetrators don't give young people the opportunities and skills they need to stand up for themselves and others, solve problems, and navigate challenges. This doesn't mean that adults shouldn't step in. It means that they have to work with young people, not around them.

A ROAD MAP FOR PARENTS

Here are some concrete things that parents can do to create just and caring communities that promote respect, responsibility, and readiness.

Make Caring for Others a Primary Goal of Child-Raising

Research suggests that modern American parents are often significantly more focused on their children's self-esteem and happiness than on their concern for others. The intense focus on happiness, as opposed to respect and responsibility for others, appears to be unprecedented in our history.

As parents, we can shift the focus back to caring for others in many ways. As a start, instead of telling children, "The most important thing is that you are happy," we can tell them, "The most important thing is that you are kind, and that you are responsible for others."

More importantly, we can avoid subtly prioritizing our children's happiness day to day over their responsibility for others. That means, for example, not letting our children simply write off friends they find annoying or fail to return phone calls from friends. It means encouraging our children to give other children credit for their achievements, requiring children to be respectful of others even when they're preoccupied, and letting our children know when they're not listening to others or dominating the airwaves in conversations. We can also be mindful of whether we are practicing what we are preaching in our interactions with our own friends.

Make Caring and Taking Responsibility for Others Routine Parts of Life

Too often as parents we reward our child for every act of helpfulness, such as clearing the dinner table or helping out with a younger sibling. But children develop caring habits and dispositions when caring is woven into everyday life. It is important as parents that we expect our child to help around the house and to be helpful to siblings and neighbors and only reward uncommon acts of kindness and helpfulness.

Too often we fail to remind children that they have responsibilities to groups larger than themselves. We let them quit the soccer team or a dance group because they're not having fun, for example, without asking them to consider their responsibilities to the group. How many of us tell our children that their classrooms, their schools, and their neighborhoods are communities to which they have obligations? As parents, we can routinely talk with our children about their responsibility to these communities. We can also offer our children opportunities to give back to others—through community service or youth activism—in ways that help them develop a sense of agency around their contributions to groups larger than themselves.

THE PROJECT

Widen Our Children's Circle of Concern and Promote Moral Awareness

Developing a caring community is not just about caring for our friends. It's about being mindful of everyone in the community. We can help our children appreciate people who may not be on their radar, whether a bus driver or a custodian, and we can insist that our children reach out to a new kid on the playground or in the classroom. Rather than being narrowly focused on how our own children are feeling moment to moment on a playground, we can spend some time tuning in to how other children are feeling and encouraging our children to reflect on other children's experiences. When our children meet someone who is different in terms of culture, religion, economic background or other characteristics, we can ask our children to consider how these children's perspective might differ from their own.

At the same time, we can help our children register kindness and unkindness and justice and injustice in the world around them. We should point out to our child when someone is treated unfairly and ask them how that person should have been treated. Issues of justice and injustice are all around us—including in the media—and we can use these moments as opportunities to talk to our children about their views and to share our own.

Think Carefully About Whether We Are Modeling Responsibility for Others and the Community

Almost all parents think they're good role models for their kids. But often as parents we are very focused on our own children, and we don't model concern for other people's children. Many parents, for example, want children with behavior problems or special needs removed from a classroom because those children are interfering with their children's learning. Our children are not likely to develop respect and concern for others who are struggling if we don't model this concern.

Parenting may be the most important and hardest thing we do, yet often parents feel isolated as they struggle to make complex decisions about how to parent, and all parents have blind spots. As a community, we can support each other; we can have the courage to invite people we are close to and respect to give us feedback about our parenting. We can work to support parents who are stressed and struggling.

Don't Assume Teenagers Are Selfish and Egocentric: Assume the Best

A good deal of literature now suggests that teens are inevitably selfish and egocentric and are a kind of separate species (a popular book on teens is called *A Tribe Apart*). Some media reports of the scientific literature even suggest that teens are selfish because their brains are wired differently. Because of these widely held notions, many parents let teens off the hook when they act selfishly or don't hold teens to high moral standards.

In fact, though teenagers are engaged in a deep process of identify formation and self-exploration, they are also quite conscious of and interested in the feelings of others. Teenagers are developing a stronger conscience and greater abilities to take other perspectives. By showing that we believe in their ability to be empathic and respectful—and by holding them to high standards of moral responsibility—we can support our children to draw on their capacity to care about their friends and communities.

Expect Our Children to Appreciate Us

That doesn't mean making ourselves the focus. It means not allowing our children to treat us as a doormat, expecting them to express some modicum of interest about major events in our lives, and to thank us for our generosity. After all, their relationship with us will be the primary model for their other relationships.

Don't Make High Achievement the Goal of Life

Too much achievement pressure can diminish children's sense of self, make them less able to care for others, and make them more likely to experience others primarily as competitors and threats. Make achievement one theme in the large composition of life while elevating caring and concern for others as a vital goal.

EACH OF US CAN MAKE A DIFFERENCE, BUT TOGETHER WE CAN MAKE A BIGGER DIFFERENCE

Just and Caring communities do more than prevent bullying. They promote academic and social-emotional success and moral children.

For more information on:

- How to evaluate school climate, student outcomes, and program outcomes: http://casel.org/in-schools/assessment/; http://prevnet.ca; http://safesupportiveschools.ed.gov/index.php?id=133
- How to select and implement evidence-based social-emotional and bullying prevention programs and curricula: http://casel.org/in-schools/selecting-programs/
- How to create a positive school climate: http://www.schoolclimate.org/
- How to build strong relationships with families: http://casel.org/publications/school-family-partnership-strategies-to-enhance-childrens-social-emotional-and-academic-growth/
- How to promote and sustain positive relationships: http://prevnet.ca/
- How to support LGBT youth or students with learning differences: http://www.glsen.org; http://www.pacer.org/bullying

Websites

121help.me

A website for children offering free, safe phone numbers for children to call for anonymous counseling. E-mail and chat assistance is also available through the website.

America Learns
http://americalearns.net/cyberbullying

America Learns collaborated with Vanessa Van Petten of Radical Parenting to develop the Cyberbullying Toolkit for Tutors and Mentors. The toolkit provides volunteers who work with youth specific steps they can take to help students address online harassment and arms volunteers with guidance they can provide to school administrators, parents, and guardians if they're unfamiliar with the appropriate steps to follow.

American Psychological Association
http://www.apa.org/helpcenter/bullying.aspx

The APA provides information on bullying and recommends action plans for teachers such as being knowledgeable and observant, involving the students and parents, and setting positive expectations about behavior for students and adults. In the Parents section, APA gives guidelines such as how to observe your child for signs they are being bullied, methods to handle bullying, and setting technological boundaries.

Anti-Defamation League
http://www.adl.org/about.asp

The Anti-Defamation League was founded in 1913 "to stop the defamation of the Jewish people and to secure justice and fair treatment to all." Now, the ADL seeks to be a voice and premier civil rights/human relations agency.

Originally established to fight anti-Semitism, the ADL combats all forms of bigotry, defends democratic ideals, and protects civil rights for all. They offer resources for bullying and cyberbulling. They work to create safe, inclusive schools and communities.

Beat Bullying
http://beatbullying.org

Based in the United Kingdom, Beat Bullying is an organization that works with children and young adults to stop bullying through a peer mentor program. Mentors are carefully trained and communicate with students through online chat on the website. Mentors offer advice and council on all types of bullying.

bNetS@vvy
http://bnetsavvy.com

A monthly e-newsletter, published by the National Education Association, the National Center for Missing & Exploited Children, and Sprint, offering parents, guardians, and teachers tools to help kids ages nine to fourteen stay safer online. They define cyberbullying as nasty text messages, threatening e-mails, the viral spread of nasty and threatening e-mails, as well as spreading rumors on social networking sites. bNetS@vvy hopes to educate parents and teachers on this topic.

Bully Beware
http://www.bullybeware.com/

This site is especially helpful for adults. It offers a comprehensive blog, bullying statistics, and articles.

BullyBust
http://schoolclimate.org/bullybust/

BullyBust is a bully awareness effort started in 2009 by the National School Climate Center (NSCC). It aims to help students and adults stand up against bullying. They offer advice for kids on how to deal with being bullied and how to stop bullying in everyday situations.

Bullying. No Way!
http://www.bullyingnoway.gov.au/

This Australian based site is very interactive. There are sections for parents, students, and teachers to get information on their role in preventing bullying. The parents' section features facts and advice on what to do if your child is being bullied or is the bully. The student section is divided by age, and offers advice on the major issues associated with growing up. The teacher section offers facts about bullying, whole-school prevention strategies, as well as resources for the classroom.

BullyingUK
http://www.bullying.co.uk/

This website is great for kids, parents, and teachers. The site provides advice if you are being bullied on Facebook or via cell phone. They also have a section for parents that includes general tips, practical help with racism, and ways to figure out if your child is the bully. There is also a special section for TeenBoundariesUK that aims to prevent sexual bullying and promotes positive gender relationships by challenging attitudes and promoting tolerance, understanding, and cohesion between young people.

CASEL
http://casel.org

Founded in 1994, CASEL is a not-for-profit organization committed to improving the American educational environment by promoting Social and Emotional Learning. "SEL" teaches students how to develop skills to effectively and constructively manage their emotions in various relationships. Inherent in this mission is a dedication to substantiating all findings with empirical data and scientific research, which is readily available on their website.

Center for Safe and Responsible Internet Use
http://www.csriu.org

Provides effective strategies to assist young people in developing the skills to behave in a safe, responsible, and legal manner when using the Internet.

Common Sense Media
http://www.commonsensemedia.org

Provides tools and resources to help youth become responsible digital citizens. Common Sense Media is dedicated to improving the lives of kids and families by providing trustworthy information, education, and the independent voice they need to thrive in a world of media and technology. Common Sense Media is a non-partisan, not-for-profit organization that gives families a choice and a voice about the media they consume. Their website features movies, books, and websites that educate kids on bullying, giving them the confidence to take a stand.

Cyberbullying.us
http://www.cyberbullying.us

Explores the causes and consequences of online harassment; includes fact sheets and resource lists. This is a good website to gain research and understand the extent of online aggression among adolescents. This website serves as a clearinghouse of information concerning the ways adolescents use and misuse technology. It is intended to be a resource for parents, educators, law-enforcement officers, counselors, and others who work with youth. When you visit this site you will find facts, figures, and detailed stories from those who have been directly impacted by online aggression.

Documatica
http://www.documatica-forms.com/bullying

Offers a free, customizable notice of harassment kit, which can help targets of bullying record incidences of bullying (including cyberbullying) and notify their teachers or the aggressor's parents that the events are occurring.

Dr. Michele Borba
http://www.micheleborba.com

Dr. Michele Borba is a child expert, author, speaker, and educational consultant. Her work aims to strengthen children's character and resilience, reduce peer cruelty, and create compassionate, just learning cultures. Go to her website to read her blog *Reality Check* where she discusses parenting issues and solutions to solve them.

Dr. Robyn Silverman
http://www.drrobynsilverman.com/

Dr. Robyn Silverman is author of the hard-hitting book *Good Girls Don't Get Fat* and is a body-image and parenting expert.

Education World
http://www.educationworld.com/a_lesson/lesson/lesson191.shtml

This site is aimed at teachers and offers tools and templates, worksheets, and many bullying lesson plans. The site offers ten lesson plans that teach students to respect diversity and resolve ideological differences peacefully. There are also ten activities for teaching students empathy, anger management, and effective conflict resolution.

Facing History and Ourselves
http://www.facing.org/

Facing History and Ourselves is a website set out to combat racism, anti-Semitism, and prejudice and nurture democracy through education programs worldwide. The website provides current news, events, books, and videos. They teach educators how to improve their effectiveness in the classroom, as well as their students' academic performance and civic learning.

Girl Talk
http://www.desiretoinspire.org

Girl Talk founder and executive director Haley Kilpatrick dreamed up the idea of creating a program that would help middle-school girls deal with the pressures and anxieties of being a young teen. Girl Talk is a peer-to-peer mentoring program where high-school girls mentor middle-school girls and help them deal with the triumphs and trials of the early teenage years. Currently Girl Talk reaches over 40,000 girls in forty-three U.S. states and in eight countries.

GLSEN
http://glsen.org

The Gay, Lesbian, and Straight Education Network is an organization dedicated to creating safe and healthy school climates. They offer safe space kits, guides to forming gay-straight alliances, tools and tips, and links to similar programs and resources.

Harvard Graduate School of Education
http://www.gse.harvard.edu

Although the Harvard Graduate School of Education conducts research widely, they show a distinct commitment to issues of bullying. Their Bullying Prevention Initiative, for instance, endeavors to address social problems before they occur: by substantiating antibully rhetoric (e.g., posters) with school-wide policies, by implementing prevention programs based on data, and by working closely with the parent population. Their website provides up-to-the-minute articles regarding current inroads of the anti-bullying campaign.

Human Rights Campaign
http://www.hrc.org

The Human Rights Campaign, founded in 1980, is an organization primarily committed to the equality of gay, lesbian, bisexual, and transgender Americans. Their work also extends to issues that plague the LGBT family: on their website, find articles on navigating school politics, avoiding cyberbullying, and exercising personal rights in the American educational system.

i-SAFE
http://www.isafe.org

A nonprofit foundation that incorporates classroom curriculum with community outreach to empower students, teachers, parents, and law enforcement to make the Internet a safer place.

It's My Life
http://pbskids.org/itsmylife/friends/bullies/

This website is great for kids. There are sections for Friends, Family, School, Body, and Emotions. These categories all advise on how to deal with these difficult but very common growing pains among kids. The site has online activities, games, and a section for parents and teachers. It's My Life is also available in Spanish.

KAM Kindness Above Malice
http://www.kindnessabovemalice.org/

The KAM foundation started amidst a great loss, the suicide of Kameron Jacobsen. Kameron, a victim of bullying himself, also defended those without a voice, those left behind by their peers. As a foundation, KAM hopes to acknowledge that compassion in others. The foundation's mission statement is to affirm those individual students that have raised the self-esteem of another person, thereby preventing the injury that results from bullying. Protecting and nurturing a high self-esteem is the key to unlocking the motivating factors behind bullying for both the bully and the victim.

Katy Butler
http://www.change.org

A social-action platform used by Katy Butler, a seventeen-year old Michigan high school student who was the victim of bullying in middle school after revealing her sexual orientation. She started a petition on Change.org to bring more attention to *Bully*'s rating. This was one of Change.org's most popular campaigns in history. You can log on and make a difference!

Kids Health
http://kidshealth.org/parent/emotions/behavior/bullies.html

Kids Health offers a variety of extremely pertinent information for teachers, parents, kids, and teens. The website defines why kids bully, and the different signs of bullying as well. There are also great articles for continued reading on each topic such as "Why Is My Child Anxious About Going To School?" or "Should I Intervene During Teasing?" This website differs from others in that you can access the information in audio form right from your computer.

Kids Help Phone
http://kidshelpphone.ca

An interactive website offering a free, confidential, 24-hour phone line for under-20s in Canada. The website also hosts forums to discuss problems with counselors online, as well as games and places for kids to express themselves.

Kidpower
http://www.kidpower.org/resources/articles/prevent-bullying.html

The mission of Kidpower is to work together to create cultures filled with care, respect, and safety for everyone, everywhere. This website seeks to teach people of all ages and abilities how to use their own power to stay safe, act wisely, and believe in themselves. Kidpower fosters goals to develop a wide range of high-quality, upbeat, and effective personal safety, self-protection, and confidence-building programs, locally and around the world. They also build on values such as honesty, support, and courage.

Make a Difference for Kids
http://www.makeadifferenceforkids.org

An organization dedicated to the awareness and prevention of cyberbullying and suicide, created in memory of Rachael Neblett and Kristin Settles, two Kentucky teens who died as the result of suicide from cyberstalking. The mission statement of this website is to educate the community on the dangers of the Internet, especially cyberbullying, and to teach parents and their children how to be safe online; the warning signs of suicide; how to act vigorously to question, persuade, and refer a suicidal teen for help; and to work with school administrators, law-enforcement officials, and local government leaders to plan strategies and adopt policies dealing with cyberbullying and teen suicide.

NAMI National Alliance on Mental Illness
http://www.nami.com

The National Alliance on Mental Illness is a grassroots organization built around providing information about mental illnesses of kids and adults. Mental illness impacts the lives of at least one in four adults and one in ten children—or sixty million Americans. NAMI's goal is to provide information and support by focusing on education, research, and advocacy to help individuals and families affected by mental illness.

National Center for Learning Disabilities
http://ncld.org

A website offering articles, information, activities, and more for children and teenagers with learning disorders and their parents. See also p. 276, Special Needs for Parents.

National Crime Prevention
http://www.ncpc.org/topics/by-audience/
parents/bullying/cyberbullying

Dedicated to keeping children, families, and communities safe from crime, NCPC offers research, information, tips, and public-service announcements on cyberbullying. On the website you can find specific information about cyberbullying, ways that parents can make a difference, FAQs, tipsheets, and even online banners.

National School Climate Center
http://www.schoolclimate.org

Founded at the Teachers College of Columbia University in 1996, the NSCC is an organization designed to promote social and emotional wellness in the U.S. educational system. Through research, advocacy, and policy the NSCC hopes to create a social environment complimentary to academic achievement. In addition to the bully-prevention information presented on their website, the NSCC also offers on-site development workshops and consultations.

NetSmartz
http://www.netsmartz.org

Run by the National Center for Missing & Exploited Children, this site offers information and resources on Internet Safety for educators, parents/guardians, teens, younger children, and law enforcement.

No Kidding, Me Too!
http://www.nkm2.org/

No Kidding, Me Too! is a nonprofit organization run by founder and president Joe Pantoliano dedicated to removing the stigma associated with brain disorders through education and the breaking down of societal barriers. No Kidding, Me Too! aims to communicate through humor and direct dialogue the message that we must remove the stigma of brain disorders and reap the benefits of a fully integrated society.

Not in Our Town|Not in Our Schools
http://niot.org/nios

NIOS is an organization that aims to bring communities together to stop hate and discrimination in schools. It provides lesson plans and workshops for teachers, as well as videos and advice for students. There is also a downloadable quick start guide for starting a Not in Our Schools campaign in any town.

One Million Kids
http://action.thebullyproject.com/million

This website is part of the movement dedicated to getting one million kids to see the movie *Bully*. The site includes a place for kids to leave their names if they have seen the movie, offers teachers and educators assistance in organizing field trips to see *Bully*, and provides access to an online training session for discussing the movie in the classroom.

PACER's National Bullying Prevention Center
http://www.pacer.org/bullying

Although the PACER organization was developed initially as support for parents of children with disabilities, they have also launched a website dedicated to the antibullying campaign. Because the site includes videos and first-person experiences, it appeals specifically to children and teens. However, the easy-to-access "info and facts" section makes the site perfect for parents, too.

Parents, Families and Friends of Lesbians and Gays
http://community.pflag.org

PFLAG is a national nonprofit organization started in the 1970s by a mother with a gay son. Its goal is to eradicate bullying and discrimination based on sexual orientation or gender identity through education, support, and advocacy. The website offers a wide variety of resources and support for LGBTQ individuals as well as for friends and family members.

Partners Against Hate
http://www.partnersagainsthate.org

Partners Against Hate is a collaborative project of the Anti-Defamation League, The Leadership Conference Education Fund, and the Center for Preventing Hate, which offers promising education and counteraction strategies for young people and the wide range of community-based professionals who work and interact with youth, including parents, law-enforcement officials, educators, and community/business leaders. Partners Against Hate provides downloadable guides for educators and parents on teaching Internet safety skills to students.

Positive Parenting Solutions
http://www.positiveparentingsolutions.com/
parenting-expert-amy-mccready

Created in 2004 by Amy McCready, Positive Parenting Solutions, Inc., the author of the book *If I Have to Tell You One More Time.*

PREVNet
http://www.prevnet.ca

PREVNet is a Canadian coalition of researchers and non-governmental organizations dedicated to eradicating the bullying epidemic by promoting healthy relationships in schools. Their website provides tips—targeted to both child and adult audiences—on how to foster such relationships. The section of the site for educators provides methods for coping with bullying in the classroom in addition to handbooks and sample lesson plans.

Radical Parenting
http://www.onteenstoday.com

Radical Parenting is a website for parenting advice written by kids. Vanessa Van Petten, a self-described youthologist, writes Radical Parenting along with 120 other teen writers. She created the program to give both sides of parenting an equal voice.

Roots of Empathy
http://rootsofempathy.org

A charitable organization that brings a mother and child into a middle school classroom to interact with the students in order to encourage empathetic growth. Students watch the mother and child interact and learn about emotions and the importance of positive social interaction.

Rosalind Wiseman
http://rosalindwiseman.com

An expert in parenting, bullying, and social dynamics, Rosalind Wiseman is also the author of renowned nonfiction title *Queen Bees and Wannabes.* In addition to pioneering the Owning Up Curriculum social justice program, Rosalind is a columnist for *Family Circle* through which she addresses child and teen issues. She has spoken widely at national bullying conferences, the most significant of which was the White House Summit on Bullying in 2011.

Special Needs for Parents
http://specialneeds.thebullyproject.com/parents

This was created by the National Center for Learning Disabilities (NCLD) in partnership with the film. Parents of children with special needs know all too well the daily struggles their children face. Bullying, especially at school, is one challenge that can sometimes be hidden from parents. Check out the resources on the website and talk to your child about whether he or she has been bullied and what you can do to make a difference for your child and all children who are bullied.

Stand for the Silent
http://standforthesilent.org

SFTS is a program designed to bring empathetic bullying awareness to schools around the country through student leaders. After each presentation, students are handed a pledge card and encouraged to vow to help stand for the silent.

Stop Bullying
http://www.Stopbullying.gov

Stopbullying.gov is a website dedicated to defining the different types of bullying and the right way to respond to them. The Stop Bullying on the Spot section of the website directs parents to respond quickly and consistently to bullying behavior, enforcing the message that the behavior is not acceptable. Some steps are to intervene immediately, separate the kids involved, make sure everyone is safe, and to model respectful behavior when you intervene.

Stop Bullying Now
http://www.stopbullyingnow.com

Stan Davis has worked for human rights for many years. Now, with Dr. Charisse Nixon, Stan is coleading the Youth Voice Research Project, which has collected information from more than thirteen thousand young people about what does and does not work in bullying prevention.

Stop Bullying, Start Empathy
http://thebullyproject.startempathy.org/

A website that supports The Bully Project, the Social Action Campaign for the film *Bully*. Across the country students are taking a stand against bullying by putting empathy into practice. The website explains that empathy means putting yourself in someone else's shoes and working to understand a situation from their perspective. It's about standing up rather than standing by.

Stop Cyberbullying
http://www.stopcyberbullying.org

Provides definitions, strategies, and legal considerations relating to cyberbullying. There is also a downloadable game, "Alex Wonder Cyberdetective Agency," to help stop cyberbullying.

Teaching Tolerance
http://tolerance.org

A project of the Southern Poverty Law Center, Teaching Tolerance is dedicated to fostering conversations about diversity, equal opportunity, and respect for differences in schools. The website provides educators with teaching kits, activities, and articles from other teachers as well as articles, curricula, and presentations for dealing with topics and situations around diversity.

The Bully Project
http://TheBullyProject.com

Created in conjunction with the recent documentary, The Bully Project has a two-fold mission: both to address acute issues caused by bullying and to effect persistent change. In addition to posting production information and viewing guides for the film, the website also defines "bullying" as it is today by clarifying its many and varied forms.

United Federation of Teachers
http://www.uft.org/campaigns/be-brave-against-bullying

The UFT is responsible for a campaign to combat bullying in schools: BRAVE stands for Building Respect, Acceptance and Voice through Education. The goal of the campaign is to provide educators with tools, knowledge, and support to be proactive in confronting and stopping bullying. The site also offers the Brave*line*, where you can call, chat, or text if you are being bullied.

Warning Signs Indicating
Possible Bullying Behavior
http://www.search-institute.org/downloadable/
Warning-Signs-Bullying-Behavior.pdf

This downloadable handout is available to help adults accurately decide when a student should be referred to the appropriate adult at school.

Welcoming Schools
http://www.welcomingschools.org

Welcoming Schools is a practical organization designed to provide both parents and educators with the tools necessary to create an accepting and comfortable K–5 educational climate. In pursuit of this goal, Welcoming Schools promotes familial diversity and condemns gender and LGBT stereotyping by providing research articles, interviews, and conversation starters on the their website. Additionally, they offer a database of experts listed by location available for consultation.

Wired Kids, Inc.
http://www.wiredkids.com

Dedicated to protecting all Internet users from cybercrime and abuse, and teaching responsible Internet use. It operates several programs and websites, including http://Cyberlawenforcement.org, http://InternetSuperHeroes.org, http://NetBullies.com, http://Teenangels.org, http://WiredKids.com, http:// WiredKids.org, and http://WiredSafety.org

REFERENCES

PROLOGUE

The 2009 Youth Risk Behavior Surveillance System (Centers for Disease Control and Prevention) indicates that, nationwide, 20 percent of students in grades nine through twelve experienced bullying. (stopbullying. gov)

The 2008–2009 School Crime Supplement (National Center for Education Statistics and Bureau of Justice Statistics) indicates that, nationwide, 28 percent of students in grades six through twelve experienced bullying. (stopbullying.gov)

http://www.xtimeline.com/timeline/The-History-of-Bullying

http://en.wikipedia.org/wiki/Tom_Brown%27s_School_Days

http://www.washingtonpost.com/wp-dyn/content/article/2006/05/15/AR200
6051501103.html

http://journalistsresource.org/studies/society/education/federal-state-anti-
bullying-legislation-laws/

http://www.barackobama.com/news/entry/president-endorses-two-anti-
bullying-measures

http://www.justice.gov/opa/pr/2010/March/10-crt-340.html

http://www.nyclu.org/news/nyclu-doj-and-herkimer-co-school-district-
settle-lawsuit-with-school-agreeing-protect-gay-stude

http://www.nyclu.org/case/jl-v-mohawk-central-school-district-challenging-
school-districts-failure-protect-gay-student-ha

http://www.dwkesq.com/index.cfm/mediabulletins/publication-details/?
dynapsisfuse=showdetails&pkid=533&type=7&tableid=2

http://www.sprc.org/sites/sprc.org/files/library/Suicide_Bullying_Issue_Brief.
pdf

http://pediatrics.aappublications.org/content/early/2011/03/28/peds.2011-
0054.full.pdf+html

http://pewinternet.org/Reports/2007/Cyberbullying/1-Findings/01-
Introduction.aspx

http://pewinternet.org/Reports/2011/Teens-and-social-media/Part-2/
Section-3.aspx

http://mashable.com/2011/03/10/facebook-anti-bullying/

https://www.facebook.com/note.php?note_id=196123070408483

http://en.wikipedia.org/wiki/Anti-bullying_legislation

http://www.stopbullying.gov/at-risk/effects/index.html

http://mayor.dc.gov/release/mayor-vincent-c-gray-announces-district-anti-bullying-action-plan

http://www.ncpc.org/topics/bullying/what-parents-can-do

http://nj.gov/governor/news/news/552012/approved/20120424a.html

http://movies.nytimes.com/2012/03/30/movies/bully-a-documentary-by-lee-hirsch.html?ref=movies

ADL & Haber & Cyberbullying materials

THE MAKING OF BULLY

http://www.imdb.com/name/nm1097276/bio

http://dailycollegian.com/2012/04/24/%E2%80%98bully%E2%80%99-documentary-reveals-painful-reality/

http://www.coloradosprings.com/articles/never-14934-producer-bully.html

http://nerdrepository.com/features/interviews/interview-bully-producer-cynthia-lowen/

http://www.sethwalsh.org/governance.html

http://www.leehirsch.net/1./Biography.html

http://www.violencepreventionworks.org/public/olweus_authors.page

http://www.nytimes.com/2010/10/10/fashion/10Cultural.html?pagewanted=all

http://learning.mchb.hrsa.gov/archivedSeriesWebcasts.asp?id=56

THE TRUTH ABOUT BULLYING AND LD

The statistics cited come from a variety of sources: 55 Facts about Bullying; References and Resources from StopBullying.gov; Walk a Mile in Their Shoes: Bullying and the Child with Special Needs; and Bullying Statistics.

BULLY-PROOFING KIDS

Teach a relaxed look: M.P. Duke, S. Nowicki, E.Q. Martin, *Teaching Your Child the Language of Social Success,* Atlanta: Peachtree, 1996, p. 60.

H. Estroff Marano, "Fending Off Bullies: Quit Picking On Me! Self-Confidence Is the Best Way to Fight Bullies," *Psychology Today,* May/Jun. 1998.

S. Pierce, doctoral dissertation: "The Behavioral Attributes of Victimized Children" as quoted by B. Coloroso, *The Bully, The Bullied and the Bystander.* Toronto, Canada: HarperCollins, 2009, p 138.

S.K. Egan and D.G. Perry, 1998 as quoted by B. Coloroso, *The Bully, The Bullied and the Bystander.* Toronto, Canada: HarperCollins, 2009, p. 143.

E. D. Barker, M. Boivin, M. Brendgen, N. Fontaine, L. Arseneault, F. Vitaro, C. Bissonnette, R. E. Tremblay: "Predictive Validity and Early Predictors of Peer-Victimization and Trajectories in Preschool," *Arch Gen Psychiatry,* Vol. 65 (No. 10), Oct. 2008.

"Predictors of Bullying and Victimization in Childhood and Adolescence: A Meta-analytic Investigation," Clayton R. Cook, Ph.D., Louisiana State University; Kirk R. William, PhD, Nance G. Guerra, Ed.D., Tia E. Kim, Ph.D., and Shelly Sadek, MA, University of California, Riverside; School Psychology Quarterly, Vol. 25, 2010.

A. Weintraub, "Yoga: Not Just An Exercise: Yoga Can Help You Beat Depression. How Hatha Yoga Saved the Life of One Manic Depressive," *Psychology Today,* Nov./Dec. 2000.

Issues to contact police: R.M. Kowalski, S.P. Limber, P.W. Agatston: *Cyber Bullying.* Malden, MA: Blackwell Publishing, 2008, p. 105.

Contact an attorney: Cited by R.M. Kowalski, S.P. Limber, P.W. Agatston: *Cyber Bullying.* Malden, MA: Blackwell Publishing, 2008, p. 105 based on the work of Nancy Willard, "A Parent's Guide to Cyberbullying and Cyberthreats: Addressing Online Social Cruelty," *Center for Responsible Internet Use.* Retrieved Aug. 3, 2006: http://www.cyberbully.org/docs/cbct.parents.pdf

NO KIDDING, I WAS BULLIED TOO!

http://www.joeypants.com/content/biography.asp

http://www.imdb.com/name/nm0001592/

http://www.catholicdos.org/file/WhatCausesBulliesPeggy5-2011.pdf (boxed text item)

http://www.nami.org/Template.cfm?Section=About_Mental_Illness&Template=/ContentManagement/ContentDisplay.cfm&ContentID=53155 (boxed text item)

THE MOVIE THAT BECAME A MOVEMENT

http://blog.mpaa.org/BlogOS/post/2012/02/28/Ratings-System-Enables-Parents-to-Make-Informed-Decisions.aspx

http://www.thewrap.com/movies/article/weinstein-company-considers-leaving-mpaa-over-bully-rating-35681

forbes.com

http://www.commonsensemedia.org/movie-reviews/bully

http://www.hollywoodreporter.com/news/bully-continues-run-pg-ratings-299064

WHERE ARE THEY NOW?

http://lexch.com/news/regional/father-featured-in-bully-film-to-speak-in-g-i/article_df84a29c-a033-11e1-83c1-0019bb2963f4.html
http://journalstar.com/lifestyles/family/parents-share-son-s-story-in-an-effort-to-end/article_5be03ef8-d9a9-5033-9882-6eff469305a3.html
http://townhall.com/photos/2011/03/10/kirk_smalley_and_his_wife_laura_are_pictured_at_the_white_house_in_washington
http://www.standforthesilent.org/
http://www.standforthesilent.org/program.html
http://www.abajournal.com/files/TylerLong.pdf

NEXT STEPS

ADL: Cyberbullying Checklist for Schools (pdf)
ADL: Cyberbullying Statistics and Studies (pdf)
ADL: Prevention and Intervention Tips for Families (pdf)
ADL: Use & Misuse of Technology (pdf)
ADL: Prevention and Intervention Tips (pdf)
http://en.wikipedia.org/wiki/Cyberbullying
http://www.barackobama.com/news/entry/president-endorses-two-anti-bullying-measures
http://www.justice.gov/opa/pr/2010/March/10-crt-340.html
http://www.nyclu.org/news/nyclu-doj-and-herkimer-co-school-district-settle-lawsuit-with-school-agreeing-protect-gay-stude
Teach a relaxed look: M.P. Duke, S. Nowicki, E.Q. Martin, *Teaching Your Child the Language of Social Success,* Atlanta: Peachtree, 1996, p. 60.
H. Estroff Marano, "Fending Off Bullies: Quit Picking On Me! Self-Confidence Is the Best Way to Fight Bullies," *Psychology Today,* May/Jun. 1998.
S. Pierce, doctoral dissertation: "The Behavioral Attributes of Victimized Children" as quoted by B. Coloroso, *The Bully, The Bullied and the Bystander.* Toronto, Canada: HarperCollins, 2009, p 138.
S.K. Egan and D.G. Perry, 1998 as quoted by B. Coloroso, *The Bully, The Bullied and the Bystander.* Toronto, Canada: HarperCollins, 2009, p. 143.
E. D. Barker, M. Boivin, M. Brendgen, N. Fontaine, L. Arseneault, F. Vitaro, C. Bissonnette, R. E. Tremblay: "Predictive Validity and Early Predictors of Peer-Victimization and Trajectories in Preschool," *Arch Gen Psychiatry,* Vol. 65 (No. 10), Oct. 2008.

"Predictors of Bullying and Victimization in Childhood and Adolescence: A Meta-analytic Investigation," Clayton R. Cook, Ph.D., Louisiana State University; Kirk R. William, Ph.D., Nance G. Guerra, Ed.D., Tia E. Kim, Ph.D., and Shelly Sadek, MA, University of California, Riverside; School Psychology Quarterly, Vol. 25, 2010.

A. Weintraub, "Yoga: Not Just An Exercise: Yoga Can Help You Beat Depression. How Hatha Yoga Saved the life of One Manic Depressive," *Psychology Today,* Nov./Dec. 2000.

Issues to contact police: R.M. Kowalski, S.P. Limber, P.W. Agatston: *Cyber Bullying* Malden, MA: Blackwell Publishing, 2008, p. 105.

Contact an attorney: Cited by R.M. Kowalski, S.P. Limber, P.W. Agatston: *Cyber Bullying.* Malden, MA: Blackwell Publishing, 2008, p. 105 based on the work of Nancy Willard, "A Parent's Guide to Cyberbullying and Cyberthreats: Addressing Online Social Cruelty," *Center for Responsible Internet Use.* Retrieved Aug. 3, 2006: http://www.cyberbully.org/docs/cbct.parents.pdf

SOCIAL AND EMOTIONAL LEARNING
AND BULLYING PREVENTION

Analitis, F., Velderman, M. K., Ravens-Sieberer, U., Detmar, S., Erhart, M., Herman, M., Berra, S., Alonso, J., Rajmil, L. & the European Kidscreen Group. (2009). Being bullied: Associated factors in children and adolescents 8 to 18 years old in 11 European countries. *Pediatrics, 123*(2), 569–577.

Arsenio, W. F. & Lemerise, E. A. (2001). Varieties of childhood bullying: Values, emotion processes, and social competence. *Social Development, 10*(1), 59–73.

Batsche, G. M. & Porter, L. J. (2006). Bullying. In G. G. Bear & K. M. Minke (Eds.), *Children's Needs III: Development, Prevention, and Intervention* (pp. 135–148). Bethesda, MD: National Association of School Psychologists.

Biggam, F. H. & Power, K. G. (1999). Social problem-solving skills and psychological distress among incarcerated youth offenders: The issue of bullying and victimization. *Cognitive Therapy and Research, 23*(3), 307–326.

Birdthistle, I., De Vos, E., Lang, C., Northrop, D., Slaby, R. G. & Whitman, C. V. (1999). *Violence prevention: An important element of a health-promoting school.* (World Health Organization Information Series on School Health #3.) Geneva, Switzerland: World Health Organization. Retrieved October 26, 2009, from *www.who.int/school_youth_health/media/en/93.pdf.*

Bosaki, S. L., Marini, Z. A. & Dane, A. V. (2006). Voices from the classroom: Pictorial and narrative representations of children's bullying experiences. *Journal of Moral Education, 35*(2), 231–245.

Bosworth, K., Espelage, D. L. & Simon, T. R. (1999). Factors associated with bullying behavior in middle school students. *Journal of Early Adolescence, 19*(3), 341–362.

Boulton, M. J., Trueman, M., Chau, C., Whitehand, C. & Amatya, K. (1999). Concurrent and longitudinal links between friendship and peer victimization: Implications for befriending interventions. *Journal of Adolescence, 22*(4), 461–466.

Bowers, L., Smith, P. K. & Binney, V. (1994). Perceived family relationships of bullies, victims, and bully/victims in middle childhood. *Journal of Social and Personal Relationships, 11*(2), 215–232.

Brown, L. M. (2008, March 4). Commentary: 10 ways to move beyond bullying prevention (and why we should). *Education Week*. Retrieved March 4, 2008, from http://www.educationweek.org.

Center for the Study and Prevention of School Violence (2008). *Safe schools, safe communities: Fact sheet*. Retrieved October 26, 2009, from http://www.colorado.edu/cspv/publications/factsheets/safeschools/FS-SC07.pdf.

Craig, W. M. & Pepler, D. (1997). Observations of bullying and victimization in the school yard. *Canadian Journal of School Psychology, 13*(2), 41–60.

Dempsey, A. G. & Storch, E. A. (February 2008). Relational victimization: The association between recalled adolescent social experiences and emotional adjustment in early adulthood. *Psychology In Schools, 45*(4), 310–322.

Dinkes, R., Kemp, J. & Baum, K. (2009). *Indicators of School Crime and Safety: 2008* (NCES 2009-022/NCJ 226343). Washington, DC: National Center for Education Statistics, Institute of Education Sciences, U.S. Department of Education, and Bureau of Justice Statistics, Office of Justice Programs, U.S. Department of Justice. Retrieved November, 17, 2009, from http://nces.ed.gov or http://www.ojp.usdoj.gov/bjs.

Dodge, K. A. (1993). Social-cognitive mechanisms in the development of conduct disorder and depression. *Annual Reviews of Psychology, 44*, 559–584.

Duncan, R. D. (1999). Peer and sibling aggression: An investigation of intra- and extra-familial bullying. *Journal of Interpersonal Violence, 14*(8), 871–886.

Espelage, D. L. & Swearer, S. M. (2003). Research on school bullying and victimization: What have we learned and where do we go from here? *School Psychology Review, 32*(3), 365–383.

Gini, G., Albiero, P., Benelli, B. & Altoè, G. (2008). Determinants of adolescents' active defending and passive bystanding behavior in bullying. *Journal of Adolescence, 31*(1), 93–105.

Goldbaum, S., Craig, W. M., Pepler, D. & Connolly, J. (2006). Developmental trajectories of victimization: Identifying risk and protective factors. In J. E. Zins, M. J. Elias & C. A. Maher (Eds.), *Bullying, victimization, and peer harassment* (pp. 143–160). New York: Haworth Press.

Graham, S., Bellmore, A. & Juvonen, J. (2006). Peer victimization in middle school: When self- and peer views diverge. In J. E. Zins, M. J. Elias & C. A. Maher (Eds.), *Bullying, victimization, and peer harassment* (pp. 121–141). New York: Haworth Press.

Hahn, R., Fuqua-Whitley, D., Wethington, H., Lowy, J., Liberman, A., Crosby, A., et al. (2007). The effectiveness of universal school-based programs for the prevention of violent and aggressive behavior: A report of recommendations of the Task Force on Community Preventive Services. *Morbidity and Mortality Weekly Report, 56*(RR07), 1–12.

Hirschstein, M. K., Edstrom, L. V., Frey, K. S., Snell, J. L. & MacKenzie, E. P. (2007). Walking the talk in bullying prevention: Teacher implementation variables related to initial impact of the Steps to Respect program. *School Psychology Review, 36*(1), 3–21.

Hymel, S., Rocke-Henderson, N. & Bonanno, R. A. (2005). Moral disengagement: A framework for understanding bullying among adolescents. *Journal of Social Sciences, 8*(Special issue), 1–11.

Knoff, H. M. (2007). Teasing, taunting, bullying, harassment, and aggression: A schoolwide approach to prevention, strategic intervention, and crisis management. In J. E. Zins, M. J. Elias & C. A. Maher (Eds.), *Bullying, victimization, and peer harassment* (pp. 389–412). New York: Haworth Press.

Kowalski, R. M. & Limber, S. P. (2007). Electronic bullying among middle schools students. *Journal of Adolescent Health, 41*(6, Supplement), S22–S30.

Merrell, K. W., Gueldner, B. A., Ross, S. W. & Isava, D. M. (2008). How effective are school bullying intervention programs? A meta-analysis of intervention research. *School Psychology Quarterly, 23*(1), 26–42.

Nansel, T. R., Haynie, D. L. & Simons-Morton, B. G. (2007). The association of bullying and victimization with middle school adjustment. In J. E. Zins, M. J. Elias & C. A. Maher (Eds.), *Bullying, victimization, and peer harassment* (pp. 49–65). New York: Haworth Press.

Nansel, T. R., Overpeck, M., Pilla, R. S., Ruan, W. J., Simons-Morton, B. & Scheidt, P. (2001). Bullying behaviors among U.S. youth: Prevalence and associations with psychosocial adjustment. *Journal of the American Medical Association, 285*(16), 2094–2100.

National Council of State Legislatures. (n.d.). *Select school safety enactments (1994—2004): Bullying and student harassment.* Retrieved September 5, 2007, from http://www.ncsl.org/programs/cyf/bullyingenac.htm.

O'Connell, P., Pepler, D. J. & Craig, W. M. (1999). Peer involvement in bullying: Insights and challengers for intervention. *Journal of Adolescence, 22*(4), 437–452.

Paul, J. J. & Cillessen, A. H. N. (2007). Dynamics of peer victimization in early adolescence: Results from a four-year longitudinal study. In J. E. Zins, M. J. Elias & C. A. Maher (Eds.), *Bullying, victimization, and peer harassment* (pp. 29–47). New York: Haworth Press.

Pelligrini, A. D. (2002). Bullying, victimization and sexual harassment during the transition to middle school. *Educational Psychologist, 37*(3), 151–163.

Pepler, D. J. & Craig, W. M. (2000). *Making a difference in bullying.* LaMarsh Research Report # 60. Toronto: York University. Retrieved October 26, 2009, from http://psycserver.psyc.queensu.ca/craigw/Craig_Pepler_2000_REPORT_Making_a_Difference_n_Bullying.pdf.

Rigby, K. (1994). Psychosocial functioning of families of Australian adolescent schoolchildren involved in bully/victim problems. *Journal of Family Therapy, 16*(2), 173–187.

Rigby, K. & Johnson, B. (2004, September). Innocent bystanders? *Teacher,* 38–40.

Rigby, K. & Johnson, B. (2006). Expressed readiness of Australian schoolchildren to act as bystanders in support of children who are being bullied. *Educational Psychology, 26*(3), 425–440. Retrieved October 26, 2009, from http://www.education.unisa.edu.au/bullying/Bystander-Educational-Psychology.pdf.

Rodkin, P. & Hodges, E. V. E. (2003). Bullies and victims in the peer ecology: Four questions for psychologists and school professionals. *School Psychology Review, 32*(3), 384–400.

Salmivalli, C. (1999). Participant role approach to school bullying: Implications for interventions. *Journal of Adolescence, 22*(4), 453–459. Retrieved October 26, 2009, from http://www.education.unisa.edu.au/bullying/Bystander-Educational-Psychology.pdf.

San Antonio, D. M. & Salzfass, E. A. (2007). How we treat one another in school. *Educational Leadership, 64*(8), 32–38.

Slaby, R. G. (2005). The role of bystanders in preventing bullying. *Health in Action, 3*(4), 6.

Society for Research in Child Development. (2008, March 26). Children who bully also have problems with other relationships. *ScienceDaily.* Retrieved April 25, 2008, from http://www.sciencedaily.com

Storey, K. & Slaby, R. (2008). *Eyes on bullying: What can you do?* Newton, MA: Education Development Center, Inc. Retrieved October 26, 2009, from http://www.eyesonbullying.org.

Swearer, S. M. & Cary, P. T. (2007). Perceptions and attitudes toward bullying in middle school youth: A developmental examination across the bullying continuum. In J. E. Zins, M. J. Elias & C. A. Maher (Eds.), *Bullying, victimization, and peer harassment* (pp. 67–83). New York: Haworth Press.

Swearer, S. M., Espelage, D. L., Love, K. B. & Kingsbury, W. (2008). School-wide approaches to intervention for school aggression and bullying. In B. Doll & J. A. Cummings (Eds.), *Transforming school mental health services* (pp. 187–212). Thousand Oaks, CA: Corwin Press.

Ttofi, M. M. & Farrington, D. P. (2009). What works in preventing bullying: Effective elements of antibullying programs. *Journal of Aggression, Conflict and Peace Research, 1*(1), 13–24.

Vreeman, R. C. & Carroll, A. E. (2007). A systematic review of school-based interventions to prevent bullying. *Archives of Pediatric Adolescent Medicine, 161*(1), 78–88.

West Regional Equity Network. (March 2008). *Bullying and cyberprevention brochure.* Tucson, AZ: University of Arizona. Retrieved October 26, 2009, from http://uacoe.arizona.edu/wren/publications.html.

Whitted, K. S. & Dupper, D. R. (2005). Best practices for preventing or reducing bullying in schools. *Children and Schools, 27*(3), 167–175.

Wilton, M. M., Craig, W. M. & Pepler, D. J. (2000). Emotional regulation and display in classroom victims of bullying: Characteristic expressions of affect, coping styles and relevant contextual factors. *Social Development, 9*(2), 226–245.

Wright, J. (2004). *Preventing classroom bullying: What teachers can do.* Retrieved October 26, 2009, from http://www.interventioncentral.org.

About the Authors

Lee Hirsch's debut film, AMANDLA! A REVOLUTION IN FOUR PART HARMONY, is a feature documentary chronicling the history of the South African anti-apartheid struggle through a celebration of its musical heroes. This film was released to wide acclaim, winning the Audience and Freedom of Expression Awards at the 2002 Sundance Film Festival. Among the many honors the film received were five Emmy nominations and a win. Lee Hirsch was born and raised on Long Island, New York, and attended the Putney School in Vermont and Hampshire College. He currently lives in Manhattan.

Cynthia Lowen is an award-winning writer and recipient of the Discovery Prize. She is the coauthor of *The Essential Guide to Bullying* forthcoming from Alpha Books, and her work has been published widely in journals including *A Public Space, Best New Poets 2008, Boston Review, Provincetown Arts,* and *Tin House,* among others. She is also the producer of GOING HOME, a two-part documentary about teenage incarceration and recidivism. She lives in New York City.

Dina Santorelli is a freelance writer and editor who has written for a variety of publications, including *Newsday, First for Women,* and CNNMoney.com. She is the coauthor of *Good Girls Don't Get Fat,* a nonfiction book about girls' self-esteem and body image (Harlequin, 2010), and currently serves as Executive Editor of *Salute* and *Family* magazines for which she has conducted numerous celebrity interviews. Her first novel, *Baby Grand,* will be published in fall 2012, and she blogs about the writing life at http://makingbabygrand.com. She lives on Long Island, New York.

About the Project

The Bully Project highlights solutions that both address immediate needs and lead to systemic change. Starting with the film's STOP BULLYING. SPEAK UP! call to action, The Bully Project will catalyze audience awareness to action with a series of tools and programs supported by regional and national partners.

The Bully Project is a collaborative effort that brings together partner organizations that share a commitment to ending bullying and ultimately transforming society.

Help keep The Bully Project alive by donating to the film's social action campaign through our nonprofit partner, Fractured Atlas. Fractured Atlas is a publicly supported 501(c)3, which supports the power of media and the arts to affect positive change in the world. All donations are tax deductible.

To donate visit: http://thebullyproject.com

THE BULLY PROJECT SOCIAL ACTION CAMPAIGN

The goal of The Bully Project Social Action Campaign is to turn the tide—community by community—on bullying, increase empathy, and create a national tipping point. We aim to foster a movement that will continue to coalesce and use that momentum to create systemic change at the local and federal level.

THE BULLY PROJECT FUNDERS AND PARTNERS INCLUDE

121Help.me
AbilityPath.org
Ad Council
American Federation of School Administrators (AFSA)
American Federation of Teachers (AFT)
America's Promise Alliance
Anti-Defamation League
Ashoka/Youth Ventures
Association for Supervision and Curriculum Development (ASCD)
AutismSpeaks
BBYO
BeCause Foundation
Bing
BullyBust/National School Climate Center
Cartoon Network
Causes.com
Cinereach
DonorsChoose.org
DoSomething.org
Education Management Consulting
Education.com
Einhorn Family Charitable Trust
Facing History and Ourselves
First Student
Gay, Lesbian, and Straight Education Network (GLSEN)
Good Pitch
Great Schools
GSA Network
Harvard Graduate School of Education
Human Rights Campaign (HRC)
JP Morgan Chase & Co
Love is Louder
National Association of Elementary School Principals (NAESP)
National Center for Learning Disabilities (NCLD)
National Education Association/ Bully Free It Starts With Me
NoVo Foundation
PACER Center
Parents, Friends, and Families of Lesbians and Gays (PFLAG)
Robert F Kennedy Center for Justice & Human Rights
Sears/Team Up to Stop Bullying
Teaching Tolerance, a Project of the Southern Poverty Law Center
The Fledgling Fund
Townsend Press
United Federation of Teachers (UFT)
Waitt Institute for Violence Prevention
World Pac Paper

CAMPAIGN OUTREACH ADVISORY BOARD

Mary Pat Angelini, MPA
Sheldon Berman, ED D.
Michele Borba, ED D.
Ed Dragan, ED D.
Mark Greenberg, ED D.
Joel Haber, PH D.
Alan Heisterkamp, ED D.
Kevin Jennings
Jackson Katz, PH D.
Molly McCloskey, M ED.
Esta Soler
Rosalind Wiseman

Index

THE WEINSTEIN COMPANY
and WHERE WE LIVE FILMS

Present

"BULLY: PG-13 VERSION"

MUSIC BY
Ion Furjanic, Bishop Allen

EDITED BY
Lindsay Utz, Jenny Golden

CINEMATOGRAPHY BY
Lee Hirsch

EXECUTIVE PRODUCER
Cindy Waitt

PRODUCED BY
Lee Hirsch, Cynthia Lowen

DIRECTED BY
Lee Hirsch